RECONSTRUCTION IN INDIAN TERRITORY

KENNIKAT PRESS

NATIONAL UNIVERSITY PUBLICATIONS

SERIES IN AMERICAN STUDIES

General Editor

JAMES P. SHENTON

Professor of History, Columbia University

M. Thomas Bailey

RECONSTRUCTION IN INDIAN TERRITORY

A Story of Avarice, Discrimination, And Opportunism

National University Publications
KENNIKAT PRESS
Port Washington, N.Y./London/1972

Library of Congress Catalog Card No: 77-189551
ISBN: 0-8046-9022-7

Manufactured in the United States of America

Published by
Kennikat Press, Inc.
Port Washington, N.Y./London

To Bob, Barbara and Travis

ACKNOWLEDGMENT

Appreciation is sincerely extended to many for making possible the research and writing of this volume. I am pleased to offer my sincere gratitude to library staffs of the second, fourth and fifth floors of the Oklahoma State University for locating material and for their general assistance. I am grateful for unlimited help given me by Mrs. Elizabeth Wassom and Mrs. Josephine Monk. Especially do I thank Mrs. Marguerite Howland and Mr. Guy W. Logsdon for arranging the purchase of microfilm that was necessary for the completion of this study.

I am indebted also to Mr. Jack Haley of the Manuscripts Division of the University of Oklahoma, Norman, Oklahoma, for the use of microfilm. Gratitude for courtesy and assistance rendered to me is due to Mrs. Rella Lonney of the Indian Archives Division of the Oklahoma Historical Society, Oklahoma City, Oklahoma; Mrs. Manon B. Atkins and Mrs. Arlene Simpson of the Library of the Oklahoma Historical Society; Mrs. O. J. Cook of the Newspaper Room of the Oklahoma Historical Society; Mrs. Obera Cude of the Cherokee Collection located in the Library of Northeastern State College, Tanlequah, Oklahoma; Mrs. Eugenia Maddox of the Robertson Collection located in the Library of the University of Tulsa, Tulsa, Oklahoma; Mrs. Marie Keene of the Library of the Thomas Gilcrease Institute of American History and Art, Tulsa, Oklahoma; Mrs. Amelia Taylor of Langston, Oklahoma; and Mrs. J. Mozee Williams of Stillwater, Oklahoma.

My deepest appreciation is extended to Dr. Homer Knight, Head of the History Department, Dr. LeRoy H. Fischer, Dr. Norbert R. Mahnken, Dr. Daniel Selakovich, and Dr. Norman G. Wilson, and others of the Oklahoma State University faculty for their contribution toward this effort.

An immeasurable debt of gratitude is due Professor Fischer under whose direction the original research was initiated. His assistance throughout the basic writing and editorial process was of inestimable value in making this book an accomplished fact.

ACKNOWLEDGMENT

Many of my colleagues of the Grambling College faculty and administration have rendered invaluable assistance to me in preparation of this volume. Dr. Robert Hunter, Dean of the Division of Education, Miss Elizabeth Robinson, Director of Student Teaching, Dr. Eva Harvey, Coordinator of Teaching High School Subjects and Acting Chairman of Secondary Education, cooperated with Dean William McIntosh of the Division of Liberal Arts and Dr. Arlandus Johnson, Chairman of the History Department, in allowing a reduction of my scheduled responsibilities in the Department of Secondary Education in order to facilitate the completion of my research and the rewriting of this manuscript. President R. W. E. Jones and Vice-President Earl Lester Cole gave their approval during a period of faculty shortage. Mr. Grant Moss of the English Department helped in additional editing; Mrs. Hazel Jones, Director of Reader Services, obtained much of the material needed for necessary revisions; Mrs. O. W. Hobdy provided secretarial assistance; Mrs. Daisye Johnson, Mrs. Hattie Perkins and Miss Bessie Dickerson offered constructive suggestions and moral support throughout this endeavor.

Contents

INTRODUCTION 1

1. BEFORE RECONSTRUCTION 5

    Education and Religion
    Slavery and Abolitionist Activity
    Removal and Adjustment
    Civil War

2. EARLY PROBLEMS OF RECONSTRUCTION 32

    The Exiles
    Cattle Thieving
    Other Difficulties Within the Nations
    The Freedmen in Indian Territory

3. UNITED STATES REQUIREMENTS FOR RECONSTRUCTION   55

    Efforts Toward Tribal Unity
    The Fort Smith Council Convenes
    Beginning the Reconstruction Process
    The United States and the "Indian Problem"
    Completing the Washington Formulae for
        Reconstruction

4. RECONSTRUCTION IN THE SEMINOLE NATION 83

    Agricultural and Boundary Adjustment
    Negotiations for Financial Restitution
    Tribal Relations
    Intertribal Relations
    Reestablishment of Social Agencies

5. RECONSTRUCTION IN THE CREEK NATION 99
   Agricultural and Boundary Adjustments
   Negotiation for Funds Due
   Railroad Development in the Creek Nation
   Reorganization of Government and Politics
   Social Agencies Reestablished

6. RECONSTRUCTION IN THE CHOCTAW AND CHICKASAW
   NATIONS 126
   Agricultural and Natural Resources
   The Question of Sectionizing
   Financial Negotiations
   The Development of the Railroad
   Political Readjustment
   Education and Religion
   Freedmen in the Two Nations

7. RECONSTRUCTION IN THE CHEROKEE NATION 159
   Agricultural Adjustment
   New Uses for Cherokee Land
   Old Settlers Seek Funds
   Other Financial Negotiations
   Railroad Development in the Nation
   Other Economic Aspects of the Nation
   Internal Political Problems
   Freedmen Seek Citizenship
   Social Agencies Reestablished

8. RECONSTRUCTION IN RETROSPECT 192

   BIBLIOGRAPHY 204

   INDEX 213

MAPS

Indian Territory on the Eve of the Civil War 31
Indian Territory During Reconstruction 82
The Seminole Nation 98
The Creek Nation 125
The Choctaw Nation 157
The Chickasaw Nation 158
The Cherokee Nation 191

RECONSTRUCTION IN INDIAN TERRITORY

INTRODUCTION

This one-volume history is a narrative and critical account of the significant political, economic and educational efforts toward reconstruction by the Five Civilized Tribes in Indian Territory from 1865 to 1877. The historical background and certain aspects of reconstruction not completed by 1877 are also included. This book is designed for use as a reference or for collateral reading for high school and college students concerned with the Civil War and Reconstruction Era, American history courses, and Oklahoma history and for any individual interested in United States history. It is also designed to fill a need in historical research. Though there are individual volumes that depict certain aspects of reconstruction within the Five Civilized Tribes singly, there is not at present a one-volume comprehensive scholarly synthesis of reconstruction in Indian Territory.

It is not the purpose of this work to trace the history of the Five Civilized Tribes through the Civil War, although a background chapter utilizing outstanding secondary sources covering this topic is included. This research delineates the adjustments necessary to initiate compliance with the 1866 treaty stipulations imposed upon the Five Civilized Tribes by the United States government. Although the treaties were similar, they were not identical, despite the fact that a few articles were common to all.

The Five Civilized Tribes operated as sovereign republics within a definite administrative system provided by the United States for Indian Territory. Hence they considered themselves to be independent nations. This area was administered through the Bureau of Indian Affairs, which was transferred from the control of the Department of War to the Department of the Interior in 1849. Indians were grouped according to regions into an administrative unit called a superintendency, with the individual in charge being known as the superintendent. The Five Civilized Tribes belonged to the Southern Superintendency. An agent was placed in charge of each individual tribe or nation and he reported to the Southern Superintendent, who reported to the Commissioner of Indian Affairs, who was in turn responsible to the Secretary of the Interior.

This administrative system was altered in 1869, when the office of the superintendent was abolished. The agents thereafter reported directly to the Commissioner of Indian Affairs. The system was further altered on July 1, 1874, when the government consolidated the work of the different agencies by an act of Congress. The agency established for the Five Civilized Nations was known as the Union Agency, and was located at Muskogee, Oklahoma. This agency served the Indians until 1914, when it was abolished by an act of Congress. During the early seventies, the United States changed the method of conducting political relations with the Five Civilized Nations that had been in practice since the British controlled the area. After 1871 the United States did not deal with the Indian republics as sovereign nations, negotiating through the treaty system, but viewed them as territories subject to Congressional control and ultimate statehood. An act of Congress of 1898, sponsored by Charles Curtis, a representative from Kansas, abolished tribal courts and prepared the way for final tribal dissolution; and an act of Congress in 1901 declared all Indians in Indian Territory citizens of the United States.

Although the political relations of the Five Civilized Nations with the United States after the Civil War cannot be described as typical of political reconstruction in the seceded states of the South, there were many common problems including the problem of determining the status, citizenship and civil rights of freedmen. This story of reconstruction on the eastern side of the Mississippi River has been repeatedly told in history, legend, poetry, fiction and song. The same story for the western side of the Mississippi River has been neglected, and only a few Americans other than those of Oklahoma even know in outline of the great tragic drama that developed in Indian Territory during reconstruction. It is hoped that this volume will reliably portray this phase of American history.

Chapter One

BEFORE RECONSTRUCTION

Immediately following the Civil War the Five Civilized Tribes or Nations of Indian Territory—the Cherokee, Creek, Seminole, Choctaw and Chickasaw—were forced by unavoidable circumstances to deal with a variety of difficult problems. Many were tribal and intertribal in nature, but there were also problems involving relations with the United States government. Reconstruction was by no means a new process to these Indians, for they were just completing a period of adjustment when the Civil War began. The first reconstruction era experienced by these Indians followed their removal from their ancestral homeland east of the Mississippi River.

Removal and Adjustment

The idea of Indian removal seems to have originated with President Thomas Jefferson. In a special message to Congress on January 18, 1803, he suggested the removal of Indian tribes to the country beyond the Mississippi. An act of Congress a year later provided for the division of the recently purchased Louisiana into two territories and appropriated $15,000 annually for the negotiation of the Indian removals. There were no immediate results at this time, and the anticipated large-scale removal was postponed until the election of Andrew Jackson as President of the United States. The seventh president favored ownership of Indian lands by Southern planters and settlers who had for many years coveted the fertile tracts occupied by the various tribes. In his message to Congress of December 8, 1829,

5

Jackson reviewed the condition of the various Indian tribes east of the Mississippi and pointed out the necessity of adopting a new policy regarding them. He recommended that Congress enact legislation setting apart an ample district west of the Mississippi to be granted to the Indian tribes as long as they should occupy it. In that setting they could have the privilege of organizing their own governments, Jackson emphasized, without control from the United States other than that might be required to keep the peace on the frontier and between the several tribes.

Between the year 1817 and the 1840s the major migration of the Five Civilized Tribes from east of the Mississippi to west of the Mississippi took place. These Indians were removed chiefly to further the interests of the Caucasian race. All of the tribes suffered varying degrees of injustice and hardship during removal. Even the Chickasaws, while suffering least, had to endure hardships and tragedy. In all of the removal treaties with the Five Civilized Tribes the United States government expressly agreed and pledged that the Indian land granted by these treaties should never be included within the limits of a state or organized territory. The Treaty of New Echota, often referred to as the Treaty of 1835, was the most significant treaty in the series begun by President Jackson's Indian Removal Bill of 1830. These treaties, supplemented by others for clarification of details, were recognized by the United States government as transferring to it the lands of the Five Civilized Tribes east of the Mississippi and providing for their removal to new homes within the present state of Oklahoma. The removal was substantially completed by 1846 though numerous small groups of Indians continued to come from the eastern states for years.

From the time of the removal of the Five Civilized Tribes to Indian Territory until the outbreak of the Civil War, conditions for them were often chaotic and disturbed. In the Cherokee country hatred, suspicion and hostility engendered during the removal period between those who had favored the signing of the treaty and those who had opposed still smouldered and threatened on the eve of the Civil War, and often caused problems. Similar conditions prevailed among the Creeks and Seminoles. Only among the Choctaws and Chickasaws were conditions fairly peaceful and quiet, but even here political issues were sharply drawn and elections bitterly contested. Thus the decades before the Civil War were times of readjustment and pioneer hardship for all of the Five Civilized Tribes.

Leaders of the western or Arkansas Cherokees, who in 1794 had migrated from around Chattanooga, Tennessee, signed a treaty with the United States government in 1828 providing for an exchange of their Arkansas lands for an adjacent western tract of seven million acres, soon to be known as a part of Indian Territory, but also including the Cherokee Outlet. The year after the treaty the western Cherokees left their homes in Arkansas and moved to the new location in which all the Cherokees, both west and east, were to settle. By 1831 they had reestablished their written laws and their government, which they continued until the coming of their eastern tribesmen under the leadership of Chief John Ross in 1839. Before the emigrating parties had left the East, the General Council on August 1, 1838, adopted a resolution declaring the inherent sovereignty of the Cherokee Nation, together with its constitution, laws, and customs and leaders to be in full force and effect and to continue in perpetuity.

The immigrants were received at first as friends by the Old Settlers and were soon at work making improvements for homes. But during June and July of 1839 feeling ran high between the western leaders and chiefs and the eastern leaders and chiefs over participation in and control of the government. The assassination of Major Ridge, John Ridge, and Elias Boudinot, signers of the Treaty of New Echota, also threatened a civil war between the treaty faction and antitreaty faction.

On July 1, 1839, a convention called by Chief Ross assembled at Illinois Camp Ground not far from Chief Ross's home. Though western Chiefs John Brown and John Rogers refused to attend the Ross Conference and joined the members of the Treaty party, a formal Act of Union was adopted on July 12 by which the eastern and western Cherokees were declared one body politically under the title of Cherokee Nation. By the time the Illinois Camp Ground Convention was adjourned, the Treaty party Council was in session at Tahlonteskee. When Chief Ross visited this council to make known the results of his convention, he and his supporters were driven away. This turn of events did not prevent a national convention from being held September 6 of the same year at Tahlequah, at which time John Ross was unanimously elected Principal Chief of the Cherokee Nation and David Vann, a western Cherokee, was elected Assistant Chief. At this time a constitution was drafted and adopted; it was finally accepted and approved by a convention of Old Settlers[1] meeting at Fort Gibson on June 26, 1840.

The constitution of 1839 was based upon the one of 1827 written in Georgia. The new constitution and laws of the Cherokee Nation required that all officers of the legislative, executive and judicial departments be Cherokee by blood. The land was held in common and the individual had the right to establish improvements anywhere under certain limitations. All the country, exclusive of the Cherokee Outlet, was organized into eight districts for governmental purposes, with Tahlequah designated as the capital. Before adjourning, the council decided to send a delegation to Washington to request that the New Echota Treaty be superseded by a better one; to explain as well as possible the unfortunate deaths of the three leaders of the Treaty party; and to ask for $800,000 spoliation claims. The western Cherokees also sent delegates. Since Washington officials seemed to sympathize with the western Cherokees nothing tangible was gained or settled.

Although the Cherokees were united de jure by June 1840, de facto they were far from united. Relations between these Indians and the men at the United States Army posts, and with the administration in Washington, were frequently strained. Since nothing was settled as a result of the negotiations that took place in Washington by the two factions in 1840, the Nation was kept in a state of apprehension and excitement until the end of 1846. It was almost impossible to determine the exact causes of the constant strife existing between 1841 and 1846. *The Cherokee Advocate* attributed most of the trouble to the removal and to whiskey. Other suggested causes were general unrest, excitement caused by the Starr boys,[2] charges of corruption in office, annuity contests, the Ridge-Boudinot mur-

---

[1] Those Cherokees who removed prior to 1835 were known as Old Settlers or Cherokees West.

[2] Harry F. and Edward S. O'Beirne, *The Indian Territory: Its Chiefs, Legislators, and Leading Men* (St. Louis: C. B. Woodward Company, 1892), pp. 92–96. The Starr family, headed by the father, James Starr, moved to the West in 1833. The Starr boys, as they were known, were joined by relatives and friends during the troublesome years of the forties. This organized band of desperadoes numbered about a dozen men, of whom the most notorious was Tom Starr, son of James. Tom was a mere youth of nineteen when the Ridges and Boudinot were killed and his father's death was attempted. Anticipating that his father would sooner or later suffer the same fate, he assumed the offensive and dealt death to many Cherokees.

ders of 1839, and the failure of the special United States commission appointed in December 1844 to bring about a settlement in the Cherokee Nation. In an attempt to alleviate existing conditions delegations from each Cherokee faction again met in Washington in 1846 and this time signed a new treaty on the sixth of August. It provided for a patent to be issued by the United States to secure all lands in the Nation for the common use and benefit of all Cherokees, a general amnesty for all past offenses in the Nation, and the adjustment of other matters that had long waited settlement.

Many Cherokees slowly improved their material conditions from year to year. Property was accumulated, better homes were built, farms were enlarged and improved, and trade increased. However, some Cherokees were wealthy, some were in moderate circumstances, and many were poor. Economic conditions were severe for the poor from 1840 until per capita payment was made under the treaty of 1846, but even then it was not long until this money was spent. The Cherokee National Council in 1842 alleviated the severe circumstances for many by enacting a law which prohibited the forced sale of property. This law was renewed each year until 1847.

The only source of income for meeting the Cherokee government expenses was interest from investments in state bonds. As a result the general indebtedness of the Nation spiralled and this became a cause for major concern. At this time nothing came of the idea to sell the Neutral Lands in Kansas to help alleviate the growing debt.

In 1848 the Nation was alarmed at what appeared to be an attempt to incorporate it into the United States. In order to combat such action the National Council in 1853 authorized the appointment of a resident agent in Washington to keep careful watch on the affairs of the Cherokees. Steps were taken in Congress in 1854 when Senator Robert W. Johnson of Arkansas proposed a bill organizing the country west of Arkansas into three territories to be named Chalohkee, Muscogee and Chakta. These territories were to become the state of Neosho.

There was much social disorder in the Cherokee Nation because of crime, and to suppress this activity several acts were passed by the National Council in 1852. But crime did not noticeably subside. Therefore, Chief Ross in his annual message to the National Council in October 1859 asked that very strict laws be enacted to discourage existing social and civil disturbance. Despite the social disorder that prevailed and the distressing state of finances, the Cherokee Nation in 1860 had achieved a moderate degree of stability.

In accordance with their Mississippi agreement, the Choctaws after arrival in Indian Territory divided their Nation into definite districts: the Okla Falaya, or Apukshunnubbee, in the southeast; the Moshulatubbee in the north; and the Pushmataha to the west of the Kiamichi River. Soon the Choctaws began to prosper, roads and trails were early established, and settlements sprang up; Boggy Depot became the trading center of the western part of the Nation. In the southeastern part, about a mile from Fort Towson, was Doaksville, the largest town in all Indian Territory. The United States government established a post office in Doaksville in 1832; in Skullyville in 1833; in Eagletown in 1834; in Perryville in 1841; and in Boggy Depot in 1849. These towns were relatively small, but each thrived with hotels, blacksmith shops, stores, produce markets and a newspaper. They were located on important roads where streams of emigration flowed through to Texas or California.

The Choctaws were mainly an agricultural people, and prosperous farms were seen along the Arkansas and Canadian Rivers. The poorer citizens of the Nation lived back in the hills where they cultivated small patches of corn for their food, while their cattle, hogs and ponies shifted for themselves in the woods. Corn, pecans, and large quantities of cotton were exported from the Choctaw country in exchange for manufactured goods. Some citizens did well economically, such as Robert M. Jones, who owned more than five hundred slaves. He had an interest in a trading establishment at Doaksville, and operated a number of steamboats and five large Red River plantations, of which the largest comprised more than five thousand acres.

A council was held in 1835 at Camp Holmes in the Creek Nation, and a treaty of peace was made between the Osages, Comanches, Wichitas, and other native tribes, and the newly arrived Creeks, Cherokees, and Choctaws. The culmination of this intertribal action was the Council of the Five Civilized Tribes at North Fork Town, in the Creek Nation, on November 8–14, 1859. A code of intertribal law was adopted which provided that criminals fleeing from justice might be requisitioned by the Nation where the crime was committed, that citizens of one Nation might be admitted to citizenship in another by the consent of the proper authorities, that a citizen of one Nation who should commit a crime such as harboring a runaway slave from another Nation would be subject to the jurisdiction of the local laws, and that the five Nations would cooperate in suppressing the sale of strong drink. The United States government encouraged these intertribal conferences, hoping thereby to further a project of uniting the wild tribes of the region and all the recent immigrants into a consolidated territorial government.

A new Choctaw constitution was written in 1834, which vested all legislative power in a General Council. A new constitution was adopted in 1838 when the Chickasaws were included as part of the Choctaw Nation. Later, in 1855, the Chickasaws were separated from the Choctaws and again a new constitution was desired. At Skullyville in January 1857 the new document was drafted. There was strong opposition from the conservative citizens and finally a compromise constitution was approved in 1860. After many changes in capital sites, Chahta Tamaha was designated the capital in 1863.

There was very little white immigration during the period from removal to the Civil War. The mixed-blooded ascendancy that had been so prevalent in Choctaw councils just before the removal had declined. The full bloods or third generation mixed bloods carried on the government, for it was difficult for the mixed bloods to obtain an elective office.

From about 1833 to 1861 the history of the Choctaws proceeded in a basically orderly manner. It might well have been otherwise. Living on a wild and remote frontier, the Choctaws had adopted an alien religion, taken over an educational system utterly foreign to their traditions, accepted a constitutional and legal system completely unrelated to their racial experience, and had altered their farming and business practices to suit the requirements of a complex economic system. Yet so eagerly had they accepted these changes that they had become fundamental to their total way of life.

The majority of the Chickasaws came to Indian Territory in the winter of 1837–38. They arrived at Fort Coffee and Doaksville in four companies which had been organized for expediting tribal business and the payment of annuities. This Nation was the wealthiest of the Indian Tribes when they emigrated from Mississippi. A large national fund from the sale of their lands had been invested under government auspices to bring in an income to be paid out in annuities for the benefit of all the Chickasaws. The influential mixed-blooded families were wealthy in slaves and other property and Pitman Colbert, an enterprising trader, had six mules and a special wagon to haul his money (in gold loaded in kegs) from Mississippi to Doaksville.

The Chickasaws first made their homes in Choctaw Districts as the recently organized Chickasaw Districts lay west in the region where hostile Comanche and other plains tribes had their villages. The United States established Fort Washita in 1842 for the protection of the Chickasaws, but another decade passed before there was any extended permanent settlement in their District. The Chickasaws did not like their political situation for they were outnumbered in the General Council and had little power in their governmental relations with the Choctaws. They were also afraid that the Choctaws would eventually control tribal finances.

Soon two factions arose. Isaac Alberson, who had been elected, was serving as Chief of the Chickasaw District with its own laws, officers and schools. His opponents, led by Pitman Colbert, objected to the appropriation of money from the national funds for the establishment of schools and advocated the observance of the old tribal customs. When the time came for the annuity payments, Agent William Armstrong would not turn the funds over to the members of the Chickasaw Commission but paid out the money to the individual members of the tribe.

More political unity seemed to appear in the Chickasaw Nation with the election of Edmund Pickens as the Chief under the constitution adopted in 1848, and the negotiation of several treaties. Provisions aimed at the settlement of the problem concerning the national funds were secured in a treaty made at Washington in 1852. The 1855 treaty with the Choctaws defined the boundaries of a district wherein the Chickasaw secured the unrestricted right of self-government and full jurisdiction over persons and property. The Chickasaws and Choctaws also were to receive from the United States the sum of $800,000 for the Leased District[3] to be divided between them in the ratio of

---

[3] An area west of the ninety-eighth meridian, in Indian territory, leased to the United States for the settlement of other Indian tribes by the terms of the Choctaw-Chickasaw Treaty of 1855.

three to one. A convention was held in August 1856 and a new constitution was drafted and adopted. The Chickasaw Nation was organized with legislative, executive and judicial departments. Cyrus Harris was elected the first governor and the capital of the Nation was established at Good Spring and named Tishomingo City. The manuscript of the constitution was lost on the way to Texas to be printed, so a special session of the Council in August 1857 was required to provide a redraft of the constitution and laws before the new order could be established in Indian Territory.

In the twenty-five year period before the Civil War the Creeks were remarkable for their adaptation to new conditions and for their general progress. They were also unusual for the maintenance of their National government, which had been interrupted by war among themselves and with the United States, and for the manner of their removal west. The land selected by the delegation sent out by the McIntosh Creeks in 1826 had not been surveyed or patented, and in 1828 it was included in lands granted to the Cherokees. The Creeks were indignant at the idea of abandoning the farms they had just improved, but the United States commissioners called the leaders of both tribes to a council at Fort Gibson in 1833 and succeeded in making a compromise.

The Creeks were generally industrious. Even during the first years they raised a surplus of corn. Soon they had plantations and ranches, each a busy industrial unit providing for the needs of a large body of workmen and producing corn and cattle to be shipped to district markets. With the exception of the wealthy mixed bloods, such as Benjamin Marshall and members of the McIntosh families, the people of the Lower Creek settlement north of the Arkansas River were less thrifty and prosperous than the Upper Creeks on the Canadian River. Both groups still worked their communal fields, and the few tools that they owned were usually the property of the town. Food, clothing, implements and other necessary supplies promised by the United States government were long delayed after the arrival of the Creeks, and frauds in government contracts were notorious. In taking care of widows and other dependent members of the tribe the custom of individual planting grew up beside the communal agriculture procedure. Thus developed an increasing tendency for each family to establish its domicile in the midst of its own fields.

Trading posts licensed by the government were established at convenient locations near the large Creek settlements. The smuggling and sale of intoxicating liquors from the border states flourished. Drinking and drunkenness were frequent occurrences at ball games, ceremonials and council meetings, although these conditions violated the United States Intercourse Act of 1834, which prohibited the introduction and sale of liquor in Indian Territory. The missions and schools operated by Protestant denominations also opposed these practices. Commerce between the Creek country and the outside world was carried on by steamboats that ran up to the vicinity of the Three Forks near the confluence of the Arkansas, the Verdigris and the Grand Rivers. Considerable amounts of produce were exchanged for manufactured articles at New Orleans. The most important overland routes were the Texas Road and the California Trail.

Politically the Upper and the Lower Creek divisions were united but they remained aloof from each other until after the Civil War, except for meetings of the Creek General Council. The written laws of the Nation, compiled before the removal in 1826, were approved by the General Council in 1840. The Creeks adopted a short written constitution about 1859 and undertook to make their officers elective, and by 1861 they had a fairly complete criminal code. The Creek Nation was the meeting place of numerous intertribal councils attended by delegations from the plains tribes as well as the Five Civilized Nations. These councils helped to foster a spirit of international cooperation through the years.

The Seminoles faced three major problems after finally being removed to the West. One problem was the status of their former slaves and the free Negroes who had lived in the Seminole country. Another problem was the status of the Seminoles in the Creek Nation, namely, their legal right to land, the location of their dwellings, and their civil liberties in regard to government. The third major problem was the uncertainty that surrounded their contracts for subsistence and even annuities from the United States. Instead of economy and efficiency in the letting of contracts and in their administration, partisan politics and the narrower concerns of individual profits were often the decisive factors. For example, corn, beef and pork were brought from the port of New Orleans or from St. Louis at considerable expense, whereas the nearby Cherokees and the Creeks, with an ample supply of livestock and grain, were in need of a market for their surplus products.

The Blacks were considered a problem of peculiar significance to these Florida Indians. Many of the Blacks or Negroes in the Seminole country, although descendants of fugitive slaves, had been free for several generations. In addition, nine-tenths of the Negroes had surrendered to General Thomas Jessup in Florida under the assurance of freedom in Indian Territory. He therefore sought measures of protection for them against capture or sale. The promise made to the Creek Indian veterans from the Florida War that they could keep all slaves that they captured threw into the complicated situation a further element of confusion. General Jessup was never successful in his effort to simplify or solve the problem.

In 1845 a new treaty with the Creeks started the removal of the scattered Seminole bands on Creek and Cherokee land to one district between the North Canadian River and Little River, an area west of their previous territory. This permitted the Seminoles for the first time since their removal to have a national life. Since their town government still had to be under the general laws of the Creek Nation, the Seminoles desired another treaty. About a decade later a treaty between the United States and the Creeks ceded a part of the Creek country to the Seminoles, in which they were to establish their own government and laws. The settlement of the Seminoles on the tract ceded by the Creeks in 1856 and the organization of their government were under way by 1859. By 1860 the Seminoles were slowly improving their situation, moving on the land assigned them, building homes and making an effort to organize their government.

Education and Religion

After the establishment of homes the Five Civilized Nations began to build their school systems. The Choctaws were noted for their educational system and schools, which became the pattern for similar institutions established by the Creek, Chickasaw and Seminole Republics. The initiative for establishing a school system for the Choctaws was taken by the Presbyterian missionaries of the American Board of Commissioners for Foreign Missions. They received no salary but their maintenance was provided by the Board. The United States government made a small appropriation and friends made donations, but the main expense was borne by the Choctaw Nation.

The Choctaws also made an arrangement with Colonel Richard Mentor Johnson by which he established an academy in Kentucky under the patronage of the Baptist General Convention. The Choctaws supported this institution enthusiastically from the entrance of the first group of twenty-five boys in the fall of 1825 until the fall of 1841, when they decided to discontinue their support in favor of schools in their own country.

Some of the well-known missionaries in the Choctaw Nation were Cyrus Kingsbury, Alfred Wright, Cyrus Byington, and Ebenezer Hotchkin. The Reverend Mr. Kingsbury was called the "Father of the Choctaw Mission" because he established Elliot Mission, the first mission station among the Choctaws in Mississippi. He moved west with the Choctaws and died in their midst in 1870. Progress came rapidly and in 1830 there were eleven schools with twenty-nine teachers and an enrollment of 260 children. Between 1832 and 1837 no less than ten mission stations were located in the Choctaw Nation by the American Board. When the Chickasaws came west in 1837 they settled among the Choctaw missions of the American Board, and not as a separate people. Of the missions in the Choctaw Nation, Bethabara (1832), Clear Creek (1833), Bethel (1832) and Bok Tukle (1834) did not prove permanent, but Wheelock (1832), Pine Ridge (1835), Greenfield, also known as Lukfata (1837), Mountain Fork (1837), and Goodwater (1837) were all in operation in 1840. Seven mission schools were being conducted at these stations at this time, with a total of 213 pupils in attendance.

There were more mission stations and a larger force of workers in the Choctaw Nation than in any other part of the Indian Territory before the Civil War, yet after 1842 practically every school in connection with them, especially the boarding schools, was largely supported out of the Choctaw national funds. An annual appropriation of $26,000 was provided for education in the Choctaw Nation by its General Council, beginning in 1842. As a result Spencer Academy was organized in 1844, and was located about ten miles north of Doaksville. At about the same time Fort Coffee, located about five miles from Skullyville, was opened; Armstrong Academy in the Pushmataha District, and New Hope, near Fort Coffee, were opened in 1846. The General Council also appropriated money for the support of Pine Ridge, Stockbridge, Goodwater, and Wheelock, which had been established earlier by the American Board. The Choctaws had nine boarding schools by 1848 supported by tribal funds. They were usually operated under a contract with a mission board which furnished the teachers and paid their salaries. With schools established in their own country, the Choctaws no longer supported the academy in Kentucky. They now began the practice of sending a number of selected graduates from their boarding schools to attend colleges in the United States at public expense, and several future Choctaw leaders received degrees from Dartmouth, Yale and other colleges.

Day or neighborhood schools were also established in the various communities. In the beginning these were financed by local enterprises or missionaries but very soon they were supported by public appropriations. The Choctaws reported five hundred children enrolled in these neighborhood schools in 1860. The boarding school attendance brought the total enrollment for 1860 to nine hundred. The Sunday Schools made provision for adult education. Entire families came and camped near the church or schoolhouse, attended school on Saturday and Sunday, and received instruction in the first steps of arithmetic, reading and writing in the Choctaw language. Most adult Choctaws became, at least so far as their own language was concerned, a literate people before they had been in their new home for a generation.

Publications in the Choctaw language were to a large extent religious. Besides the New Testament and portions of the Old Testament, these publications consisted of hymn books, moral lectures, biographical sketches of pious Indians, the Westminister Catechism, and doctrinal tracts such as Jonathan Edwards' *Sinners in the Hands of an Angry God*. By 1837 a total of 30,500 tracts had been published in the Choctaw language. The American Board also compiled and published in the Choctaw language a dictionary, spellers, arithmetics, and a collection of Bible stories for children. A Choctaw almanac was issued from 1836 to 1843 which contained a variety of statistical information about the Nation. The New Testament in Choctaw was published in New York by the American Bible Society under the direction of Byington and his assistant, Alfred Wright, but nearly all the other material was printed at a press that had been set up in the Cherokee Nation soon after they emigrated to the West. Although there were many publications in the Choctaw language, all the regular schools were conducted in the English language.

The Choctaw schools were under the control of a board of trustees by 1842. This board consisted of one member from each district, appointed by the district chiefs. Each trustee was responsible for the establishment of neighborhood schools. An act passed in 1853 provided for a superintendent of schools who should be ex officio president of the board, and who with the trustees should be elected by the General Council for a four year term.

There was close cooperation between the Choctaw government and the mission boards in the management of their schools. This relationship made it inevitable that Choctaw conversion to Christianity would parallel the development of their educational system. Although an anti-Christian party settled in the northern district, under the influence of Moshulatubbee, the Choctaw Nation was basically Christian by 1860. Twenty to twenty-five percent of the people were members of Presbyterian, Methodist or Baptist churches. Sunday observance was general, and sessions of the General Council opened and closed with prayer. Many of the native preachers and Choctaw leaders were temperance workers, and temperance societies were organized in connection with the churches and schools.

The first written law of the Chickasaws in 1844 provided for the establishment of an academy. The first school that opened in the Chickasaw District was a day school in connection with the Methodist mission station at Pleasant Grove, near Fort Washita, in 1844. Many Chickasaw families living in the Choctaw districts sent their children to the Choctaw schools conducted in connection with the various mission stations. From fifteen to twenty-five boys were also sent each year to the Choctaw Academy in Kentucky. After this academy was closed, a number of boys were sent away to eastern academies, some of whom later entered notable colleges. In each instance, unless an individual boy's expenses were paid by his parents, which happened in only a few cases, all education was paid for out of national funds.

In 1845 money was allocated to the Reverend William H. Goode for the Chickasaw sub-agency at the Boarding Spring Council Ground near Fort Washita. At that time the Chickasaw Council appropriated a substantial amount for the erection of buildings and an annual sum for the maintenance of a tribal academy to be conducted under the auspices of the Mission Board of the Methodist Episcopal Church, South. The Reverend Wesley Browning, appointed as its first superintendent, supervised the construction of the building and establishment of the farming operations in connection with the institution, which was opened in 1851. The Chickasaw Academy was opened with the Reverend John Robinson as superintendent, its site being two miles east of the present town of Tishomingo. The first name given it by the Methodist Indian Mission conference in its report of 1847 was the McKendree Manual Labor School, but it was soon known as the Chickasaw Manual Labor Academy. Subsequent appropriations up to 1858 provided for the erection and maintenance of Wapanucka Female Institute, Bloomfield Seminary, Burney Institute and Colbert Institute.

Missionary work began in the Creek Nation when John Davis came to the Arkansas-Verdigris settlement in 1829. The following year, the Baptist denomination allowed him $200 for expenses. In that same year the Presbyterian missionaries of the American Board organized a church, some members of which had been Baptist or Methodist converts in the East. Both the Baptists and the Presbyterians sent missionaries to reside in the Creek Nation by 1832, and regular missions were established. A certain amount of Creek school work was carried on in connection with these missionary activities. Most of the schools were conducted by the wives of missionaries. Attendance was irregular because of lack of interest, insufficient food and clothing, and numerous cases of malaria.

The Creeks' language difficulty was also a serious problem. As a step toward aiding the situation, John Fleming, of the American Board managed with the help of young James Perryman to develop a written form of the Creek language. In 1835 Fleming's *The Child's Book* was published by the recently installed printing press at Union Mission. Another Creek primer and St. John's Gospel in the Creek language was also made available.

By 1836 several churches had been established in the Arkansas-Verdigris River settlement. John Davis, the Baptist missionary, lived among the Upper Creeks, but the coming of a large number of Creeks hostile to the missionaries in that year made their presence unwelcome. Because of this and other reasons the Creek Council at Fort Gibson in 1836 decided to expel them. The Council also imposed a penalty of fifty or one hundred lashes upon any Creeks who should attend Christian services.

About fifteen young Creeks were maintained in the Choctaw Academy in Kentucky by the $3,000 set aside for education under the removal treaty and the $1,000 provided by the treaty of 1833. After the expulsion of the missionaries the Creeks finally consented to use a portion of this money for the employment of government teachers in their own country. Davis for a time taught one of these schools at North Fork Town, but for several years the only one conducted at the Creek Agency was by a roving white man who was afterwards sent to prison as a counterfeiter. A though the Creek agent, James Logan, had become convinced that the English day schools were failures, the Creeks insisted that their money be spent at home. The agent then urged them to contract with missionary societies for the establishment of boarding schools in their own country.

The first boarding school was opened at Coweta in 1843 by a Presbyterian minister, the Reverend Robert Loughridge. He was accepted by the chiefs by promising to confine his preaching to the mission buildings. By 1845 Baptist and Methodist missionaries were openly working in the Creek country. The next year the Reverend Mr. Loughridge persuaded the chiefs to lift the ban on his preaching and in 1848 the official opposition to Christianity was lifted. In 1847 two more boarding schools were authorized by contracts with the Methodist and Presbyterian mission boards. The Methodists located their school near North Fork Town and named it Asbury after their old mission in the East; the Presbyterians chose a site in the Arkansas settlement and gave the school the old Creek name of Tullahassee. Both schools were completed by 1850, and each accommodated from eighty to one hundred pupils.

In general, it was only the mixed bloods who attended the boarding schools, and their training increased the cleavage between mixed bloods and full bloods that was already apparent within the Nation. Several small day schools were conducted in the heart of the full-blooded settlements by Methodist and Baptist missionaries whose salaries were paid by the United States government out of Creek educational annuities. The native language project was not revived and the instruction in English proved to be beyond the capacity of many children who spoke only Creek at home.

In 1856 the Seminoles bought from the Creeks a portion of land and secured large additional annuities and complete control of their educational funds. They then established seven day schools under the administration of a native superintendent in each of the two settlements, and several graduates of Tullahassee received appointments as teachers. They then had a national system of education with the possibility of bridging the gap between the progressive and conservative members of the Nation. The Seminoles had asked for schools for their children when they began locating in Indian Territory. Their first school was opened in 1844 under government auspices, the teacher being John D. Bemo, a Seminole with a remarkable career and the advantages of schooling in the East. In 1848 the Reverend John Lilly began mission work among the Seminoles under the auspices of the Presbyterian Board of Foreign Missions. The next year a mission school was opened at Oak Ridge by Lilly, and by 1856 the Reverend James Ross Ramsey had entered the field.

The year 1841 witnessed the establishment of a public school system for the Cherokees with the Reverend Stephen Foreman as national superintendent of schools. These schools were supported by appropriations of the National Council from the Cherokee educational funds provided in the treaties with the United States. The establishment of mission schools was limited by law in 1841 in the Cherokee Nation. Dwight Mission was moved from Arkansas in 1829 and remained the outstanding school of this class among the Cherokees. Teaching was carried on at some of the earlier mission stations for a time, including new Springplace, a Moravian mission near the present village of Oaks in Delaware County, at Fairfield Mission, near Lyons in Adair County, and at Baptist Mission near present Westville in Adair County. By 1843 there were eighteen public schools in operation. Two seminaries for higher learning were opened to Cherokee students in 1851, with the National Female Seminary located three miles southeast and the National Male Seminary one and one-half miles southwest of Tahlequah. Because of inadequate funds operations were suspended before the close of the decade and were not resumed until after the Civil War.

Slavery and Abolitionist Activity

The "peculiar institution" of the southern states existed also among the Five Civilized Nations of Indian Territory. Population figures reveal that as early as 1839 there were nearly six hundred slaves among the Choctaws; about one thousand among the Cherokees; and about four hundred in the Creek Nation. Not long thereafter the Seminoles had one thousand Negroes, many of whom had been adopted into the tribe in Florida. Both the Choctaws and the Chickasaws had come from Mississippi and Alabama, where the culture of cotton made Negro slavery profitable. Among the Choctaws who settled in the Red River region were a number of slave owners who opened up extensive plantations along the river and grew wealthy, principally from the cultivation of cotton. Some of the larger slave holders were Robert M. Jones, David Folsom, Pitman Colbert, Peter Pitchlynn, and Robert Love. Few of the full-blooded Choctaws owned slaves, for most of these people settled in the woods and on the edges of the prairies of the uplands and depended upon their stock for a livelihood. Likewise, among the Chickasaws a few of the mixed bloods were well known for their wealth in slaves. Because they were rich in tribal annuities the proportion of slave holders in this tribe was large, so that nearly every Chickasaw family owned a few slaves even if for nothing more than personal servants.

Many of the mixed-blooded Cherokees were also slave owners. But the Cherokees were a race of mountaineers, and as Negro slavery never flourished in mountain regions, comparatively few of the full-blooded members of the tribe became slave owners, especially since the cultivation of cotton was not commercially important north of the Arkansas River. Among the Cherokees noted slave owners were Joseph Vann and John and Lewis Ross.

The Creeks owned many slaves although they did not engage extensively in the production of cotton. Daniel McIntosh and Opothleyahola were large slave owners. A considerable number of free Negroes were citizens of the Creek Nation after removal, and these people lived in several separate settlements. Locally there was a sharp line of distinction between free Negroes and other members of the tribe as in various other sections of the United States.

The Seminoles also had slaves. They were accompanied to Indian Territory by a number of refugee Negroes who had fled from slavery in the United States and had been adopted as members of the tribe while it was located in Florida. Although there is a divergence of opinion regarding the treatment of Negro slaves in Indian Territory, it is generally thought that slavery never existed in the form that characterized it in the southern states. The worst features of slavery were not known to the slaves of the Five Civilized Tribes.

Abolitionist activity was not welcomed in Indian Territory although it was carried on in connection with mission work. The first public expression against the abolitionist movement arose in the Choctaw Nation in 1836 when its General Council passed a law compelling any missionary or preacher or person who was found favoring the doctrines of abolitionism to leave the Nation and stay out of it. The teaching of slaves to read and write or sing without the consent of the owner, or allowing a slave to sit at the table with them, was sufficient ground to convict persons of favoring the principles of abolitionism.

When the Presbyterian mission headquarters at Boston put pressure upon the missionaries openly to oppose slave holding by the Indian people among whom they were working, some of the missionaries defended the slave owners and withdrew from the American Board. Others became so outspoken in their anti-slavery sentiments that it became expedient for them to leave the country. Finally, the American Board of Commissioners of Foreign Missions withdrew its support from the missions, first in the Choctaw Nation in 1859, and then in the Cherokee Nation in 1860. Although the Methodist Episcopal Church divided along sectional lines in 1844–1845 because of the slavery issue, there was no contention among their members in the Five Nations for the reason that they all belonged to the Southern branch of the church. Though there were Southern Baptist and Northern Baptist in Indian Territory, the Baptist mission work under the direction of the Reverend Evan Jones and his son, the Reverend John B. Jones, made no secret of its propaganda for abolition.

In 1859 the Reverend Evan Jones was the dominant spirit in the inception of the secret Keetoowah Society, organized among the full-blooded Cherokees and reputed to be hostile to the mixed-blooded members of the tribe, as well as strongly in favor of abolition. The tribal Indian agents appointed by the United States government during the years immediately preceding the Civil War were all from the South, and several of them were keenly apprehensive of the influence of the antislavery missionaries working among the Indians. At the same time it was charged that a secret society, known as the Knights of the Golden Circle, was actively pushing its pro-slavery propaganda in Indian Territory.

Civil War

The position of the Five Civilized Tribes on the border, the southern sympathy exhibited by the Indian agents, the fact that the Southern states held most of their investments in the form of bonds, the "peculiar institution" within Indian Territory, and the abandonment of the area by the United States at the outbreak of the Civil War seemed to recommend alliance with the Confederate States of America. The Choctaws and Chickasaws reacted more favorably than the other three Nations to the Confederate call for secession. The Cherokees, Creeks and Seminoles were more divided. The Cherokee mixed-blooded faction in sympathy with the South was led by Stand Watie, brother of Elias Boudinot and the southern Creek sympathizers were led by D. N. McIntosh. Opothleyahola, the elder statesman of the Creek full bloods, felt that the interests of his Creek people bound them to the North and to the protection implied by their treaty guarantees in spite of the fact that the United States government had given them little reason for adherence. Billy Bowlegs and John Chupco headed the Union faction of the Seminoles while John Jumper headed the Confederate faction. In contrast to the abandonment of Indian Territory by the

Federal government the Confederacy offered through Commissioner Albert Pike various inducements for alliance, including the promise of annuities at that time past due. Subsequently at North Fork Town representatives of the Choctaw and Chickasaw Nations and the McIntosh faction of the Creeks on July 10 and 11, 1861, entered into treaties with the Confederacy. Pike then went to the Seminole Agency and made a treaty with the faction headed by Jumper.

After the defeat of the Union forces at Wilson's Creek near Springfield, Missouri, on August 10, 1861, the surge of Confederate sentiment was so powerful in the Cherokee Nation that Chief Ross was no longer able to maintain the neutral position he had advocated. On October 7 and 8, 1861, at Tahlequah he negotiated a formal agreement with the Confederacy.

When the Creek full-blooded leader, Opothleyahola, and his followers learned that their names had been attached without authority to a Creek treaty made with Pike, they withdrew to themselves and camped near North Fork Town. The Creek Confederate faction with about fourteen hundred men, including some Texans, planned to attack them. Opothleyahola anticipated them and on November 5 began to move his followers, hoping to take his people out of danger. This was the beginning of the exodus from Indian Territory of nearly half of the Creek tribe; they were also joined by the Billy Bowlegs and John Chupco element of the Seminoles.

Opothleyahola's band was initially attacked by a group of Confederate Indians and Texans at Round Mountain on November 19, 1861, but the Federal faction held their own, and went on to Bird Creek where on December 9 another engagement took place. Again Opothleyahola's people escaped and fled northward toward Kansas but on December 26 in combat action at Chustenahlah they were compelled to retreat with great loss. Despite much confusion many succeeded in keeping together and escaping into Kansas. As most were on foot, without shoes and thinly clad, their trail was crimson from bleeding feet. Numbers of them froze to death and their bodies, covered with snow, were left where they fell. A number of women gave birth to children on the snow. The band reached a point on the Verdigris River in Kansas by the middle of January 1862 and there they continued to suffer intensely during the winter months that remained.

In the meantime, on November 22, 1861, the Confederate War Department organized all of Indian Territory as a military department with Brigadier General Albert Pike as commander. Almost two months later, Indian Territory was attached to the Trans-Mississippi District under Major General Earl Van Dorn. The principal event of 1862 that affected Indian Territory was the Battle of Pea Ridge in northwest Arkansas. The defeat of the Confederates was complete and exposed the country above the Arkansas and Canadian Rivers to invasion from the north. To offset his retreat from Fort Davis, near Fort Gibson, General Pike established Fort McCulloch, just north of the Red River. He kept Cherokee, Creek and Seminole regiments in the area above Fort McCulloch as advance guards to raid and harass the Federals.

To offset this situation the United States army organized from Opothleyahola's band the first regiment of Indian Home Guards, composed of eight companies of Creeks and two of Seminoles. They were merged into what became known as the First Indian Expedition, which functioned in two brigades and included also organizations from Kansas, Indiana, Ohio and Wisconsin under the command of Colonel William Weer. Federal authorities now planned an invasion of Indian Territory in March 1862. During the invasion a third Indian regiment was organized under the command of Colonel William A. Phillips, bringing the total number of invading soldiers to about six thousand.

Colonel Weer's regiment finally moved southward on June 23 and pursued a Confederate Cherokee force and a larger unit of white soldiers under Colonel J. J. Clarkson. The Confederates were defeated and surrendered ammunition wagons, mule teams and provisions. Weer then marched his troops to Tahlequah and at Park Hill arrested Chief Ross and placed him on parole at home. The Union forces did not feel their position secure and their officers considered withdrawal to the north. Weer accepted the view but soon reversed his decision and ordered his officers to take up a permanent position at Fort Gibson. Colonel Frederick Salomon, second in command, then ordered Weer's arrest and took the responsibility of withdrawal upon himself. In the ensuing general court martial, Brigadier General James G. Blunt dissolved the court and restored Weer to his rank as colonel. Chief Ross was arrested a second time and was carried to Fort Scott with the Federal troops. From there he was sent to Washington and finally permitted to remain in Philadelphia for the duration of the war.

When Salomon withdrew the Union regiments from Indian Territory he left Indian troops on the Verdigris River to watch developments. Colonel Phillips, placed in command of these soldiers, performed remarkable services with the Union Indians. Under conditions of extreme disorder, with raids and counterraids sweeping the country, he gave much needed protection to Indian families that had elected to stay in their homes. Despite Phillips, nevertheless, Indian Territory became a wasted, desolate region of terror and despair.

Minor engagements occurred in 1862 on Cowskin River and Spring Creek in which the Confederates were defeated. During the latter part of that year General Pike was relieved of his command after a prolonged quarrel with Confederate officials. From the Confederate defeat in the Battle of Prairie Grove, Arkansas, on December 7, 1862, Colonel Phillips marched 1,200 Federal Indian troops and two white companies supported by artillery to the Arkansas River near Three Forks. He then crossed at Frozen Rock Ford and captured and burned Fort Davis, opposite Fort Gibson.

In February 1863 the Union Cherokees held a council at Camp Ross on Cowskin Prairie in which they repudiated the Confederate alliance and affirmed their loyalty to the United States. At the same tribal council all Cherokee slaves were freed in accordance with President Lincoln's January 1 Emancipation Proclamation. In April Colonel Phillips drove Colonel Watie out of Fort Gibson, but in June 1863, at Cabin Creek, Watie attacked a supply train sent to Fort Gibson from Kansas. The Confederates were defeated and fell back to Honey Springs, their supply depot about twenty-three miles south of Fort Gibson.

Anticipating that Brigadier General William Cabell would soon join Brigadier General Douglas H. Cooper at Honey Springs for an attack on Fort Gibson, Blunt hastily constructed boats with which to cross the Arkansas River. Cooper's forces were established for battle on both sides of Elk Creek. The engagement was begun in the morning of July 17 by artillery on the prairie north of the present Oktaha, about three miles north of Honey Springs. The Confederates soon fell back into

the timber along Elk Creek, where their withdrawal became a
retreat and soon turned into a rout. Only the effective rear
guard action of Cooper's cavalry units prevented complete disas-
ter. The Honey Springs battle, in which nearly nine thousand
men were engaged, was the most important military action in
Indian Territory during the Civil War because it paved the way
for Federal occupation of much of the area. There were other
Confederate attempts made on Fort Gibson in August and skir-
mishes at Perryville and North Fork Town, but the Southerners
were defeated and their supplies taken, and Fort Smith fell to
Federal forces six weeks after the Battle of Honey Springs. For
the remaining months of the Civil War northern Indian Territory was in Union hands.

Colonel Watie, who was commissioned a brigadier general before the war ended, was a persistent and implacable enemy of
Union Indians. He raided at Tahlequah after the Confederates
defeat at Honey Springs, and his band destroyed the house of
Chief Ross at nearby Park Hill. In September 1864 he captured a
large Federal wagon train at Cabin Creek near the place
where his forces had met defeat earlier in the war. The raiders
captured seven hundred mules, one hundred wagons and vast
quantities of war materials.

In February 1864 Colonel Phillips led 1,500 Union soldiers
into southern Indian Territory to end Confederate resistance in
the Chickasaw and Choctaw Nations. He distributed copies of
Lincoln's Amnesty Proclamation to Confederate Indians and
their leaders along the route of march. He was hopeful of
obtaining formal repudiation of the Confederate treaties but his
mission met with only limited success. Gradually, however,
the southern Indians learned that their alliance was with the
losing side. General Robert E. Lee surrendered at Appomattox
on April 9, 1865, and President Jefferson Davis was captured on
May 10. Watie was the last of the Confederate generals to lay
down his arms when he surrendered at Doaksville, deep in the
Choctaw Nation on June 23, 1865.

Indian Territory was important as a source of food, cattle,
horses and manpower for both armies during the Civil War. At
the beginning of the war there were ample supplies of potatoes,
corn, beef and pork, with smaller amounts of cereal grains such
as wheat, barley and rye. The Five Civilized Nations had quantities of food commandeered by both the United States and

Confederate armies. Cattle and horses were also indiscriminately seized. But suffering at the hands of Caucasian government was not a unique experience for these courageous people.

Summary

The removal of the Five Civilized Tribes involved the relocation of sixty thousand Indians from the southeastern United States. The vast majority of these people made the trip to Indian Territory under the supervision of the United States government from 1830 to 1840, although some came later. Even in the deep South these Indians had been distinguished by their application of and adjustment to Anglo-Saxon institutions. Four of these Nations (Cherokee, Choctaw, Chickasaw and Creek) inaugurated representative government similar to that of the states surrounding them, but while they acquired the institutions and culture of white men they also acquired their vices. These tribes considered themselves Nations and operated as sovereign republics. They were agriculturally oriented, establishing farms, raising herds of cattle, planting varied crops and weaving cloth for clothing. They laid out roads, built mills, engaged in commerce, owned slaves and sent their children to schools conducted by missionaries.

Removal to Indian Territory was necessary because others coveted the land that these Indians owned. Only a few whites understood the grief and desolation that overcame them when they left behind most of their cherished possessions and started on their tragic journey westward. The haphazard removal policies of the United States government indicated that little thought and attention had been given to this operation. Of all the Five Civilized Tribes the Chickasaws suffered least during removal.

Upon arrival in Indian Territory no one completely escaped pioneering hardships, but some suffered more than others even within the individual Nations. Gradually between removal and the Civil War these Indians began to adjust and progress even in an atmosphere beset with difficulties. Many of their problems were created by the expedient policies of the United States. A favorite and often repeated government procedure was to deal with a minority of a tribe and then declare that the whole was bound by their action. This process caused long periods of dissension, extending especially within the Cherokee and Creek Nations until well past the Civil War. The effort to compel the Creek and Seminole Indians to live together, as well as the Choctaws and Chickasaws, hampered development to some extent.

The unkept promises of the removal treaties created problems that lasted well into the 1880s. But the patience, hard work, ingenuity and good sense exhibited by the Indians, their slaves, some of the Indian agents and the missionaries in a large measure paved the way to the economic, political and social position enjoyed by the Nations on the eve of the Civil War. But these Indians became involved in this tragic war, an event that disrupted and destroyed for them most of the material achievements they had realized since their immigration to Indian Territory.

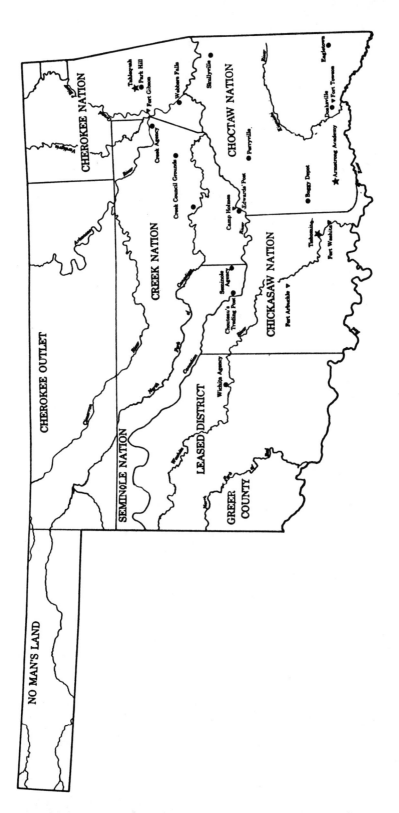

Indian Territory on the Eve of the Civil War

Chapter Two

EARLY PROBLEMS OF
RECONSTRUCTION

When the Civil War came to Indian Territory, the task of reconstruction began. Opothleyahola, the elder statesman of the full-blooded Creeks loyal to the United States, introduced the problem to President Abraham Lincoln during the first summer of the war:

> Now I write to the President our Great Father who removed us to our present homes, and made a treaty, and you said that in our new homes we should be defended from all interference from any person and that no white people in the whole world should ever molest us . . . and should we be injured by anybody you would come with your soldiers and punish them. Now the wolf has come. Men who are strangers tread our soil. Our children are frightened and the mothers cannot sleep for fear. This is our situation now. When we made our Treaty at Washington you assured us that our children should laugh around our houses without fear and we believed you. We, your children, want it to be so again and we want you to send us word what to do. Your children want to hear your word, and feel that you do not forget them. . . . It was at Washington when you treated with us, and now white people are trying to take our people away to fight against us and you. I am alive. I well remember the treaty. My ears are open and my memory is good.[1]
>
> Fort Smith, Arkansas
January 5, 1866

---

[1] Opothleyahola to President Abraham Lincoln, August 15, 1861, cited in Annie H. Abel, *The American Indian as Slaveholder and Secessionist* (Cleveland: The Arthur H. Clark Company, 1915), pp. 245–246n, hereinafter cited as Abel, *The Indian as Slaveholder and Secessionist.*

Oktarharsars Harjo, Mikko Hutke, and other leading Creeks, together with a few Seminoles and Chickasaws, met with Creek agent George Cutler at LeRoy, Kansas, in November of 1861 to explain the hopelessness of their situation. They were subsequently sent to Washington, where they recounted the story of their loyalty. They explained that their homeland was surrounded by secessionists and that the Creek people were not strong enough to hold out against them. They were informed that their treaties would be respected, and assured that help would be sent as soon as possible.

During the fall of 1861 the loyal Creeks determined not to allow themselves to be intimidated by the secessionist elements in their Nation and placed themselves under Opothleyahola's direction. They gathered for protection in a great camp near the junction of the North Fork and the Deep Fork Rivers. Here they were joined by a number of Seminoles and Negroes.[2] About twelve hundred Indians and approximately three hundred Negroes made up Opothleyahola's band. When threatened by Confederate Indians and Texans under Colonel Douglas Cooper, Opothleyahola moved northward toward friendly Cherokee country, but attacks came on November 19 at Round Mountain and on December 9 at Caving Banks on Bird Creek. Both times the loyal group fought well and slipped away and withdrew to the north. But on December 6 at Chustenahlah, Cooper overcame Opothleyahola's forces when their ammunition ran low. A scene of indiscriminate slaughter followed in which women and children were butchered, families were separated in the confusion, and many were captured; but other families succeeded in keeping together and escaped to Kansas. Many froze to death while making the journey, while some died later or lost limbs due to exposure.

The Exiles

Many of these exiles had been well-to-do farmers before they left home, but by the time they reached Fort Roe on the Verdigris River in southern Kansas they were all reduced to complete destitution. Superintendent William Coffin of the Southern Superintendency had little to give to the exiles and

---

[2] Negro is used instead of black, for during this time any reference to a person of color as black was usually resented.

even with the aid supplied by Major General David Hunter, then commanding the Department of Kansas, the loyal Indians suffered acutely from the need for shelter, food, clothing and medical attention.

The exiles from Indian Territory spent the winter of 1861–1862 at Fort Roe on the Verdigris River, but with the coming of spring it was evident that the Indians would have to be moved, as the stench was terrible from numbers of dead ponies, and the water was contaminated. The Creeks were accordingly moved to a location near the town of LeRoy, Kansas, situated on the Neosho River about thirty miles from the Verdigris River. They were placed by permission of the owners on land belonging to the whites. The Creeks numbered about forty-five hundred including men, women and children, while on the Verdigris River. The removal of so large a number of people, many of whom were sick and helpless, was tedious, laborious and expensive. By September 1862 the number of deaths among the Creeks since their arrival in Kansas was nearly four hundred.

Many complaints were made by these exiles encamped on the Neosho River, as a large number were deprived of shelter, food and clothing. Only the sick, upon requisition by a physician, could obtain coffee, sugar, vinegar or pepper. Each refugee received about a pound of flour per week and a scanty supply of salt. The bacon used had been condemned at Fort Leavenworth and many who ate it became ill. Virtually no cooking utensils, axes or hatchets were to be found. By October 1862 white settlers were demanding that their land be vacated and Union officials wanted more efficient and inexpensive supply methods. When the Sac and Fox tribes, twenty–five miles north of the Neosho River valley, offered part of their reservation for refugee use, everyone was relieved but the refugees. Although Opothleyahola led the tribes in bitter opposition, he was persuaded to agree to removal in the fall of 1862. He died soon after reaching the new location.

Notwithstanding all their hardships and disappointments these people exhibited courage and endurance, and breathed the spirit of fidelity to the United States. But they desired to be restored to their farms, and to rebuild their cabins, renew their fences, plant seed and obtain from the soil a subsistence by means of their own industry.

The restoration of the refugees to their homes commenced

about the middle of May 1864. The returning Creeks reached Fort Gibson the latter part of June too late to plant anything for that year. The provisions were inadequate and the cattle supply, which had been deemed almost inexhaustible, was growing shorter every day due to the activity of cattle thieves. The larger portion of the country was still held by Confederates. The Creeks were disappointed that they were not taken directly to their own country instead of to Fort Gibson in the Cherokee Nation, and they desired the government to give them protection in their own homeland as soon as possible.

The loyal Creeks were still living in and around Fort Gibson early in 1865. They would have settled entirely on their own lands but it was dangerous to be very far removed from the protection of the garrison stationed at Fort Gibson. They continued to look forward to harvesting their crops and removing to their own lands, on the south of the Arkansas River, in time to make themselves self-sustaining for the coming year. Return was slow however. During the fall and winter of 1868 and 1869 another group of Creek refugees (Confederates this time) finally returned from their wartime residences in the Choctaw and Chickasaw country and in Texas. A number of disaffected loyal Creeks under the leadership of Spokokogeeyahola, who declared himself to be the successor of Opothleyahola, remained in the Cherokee country until January and February 1869 when the greater portion of them were removed to their own country.

The Cherokee refugees also desired to return to their homes. In addition to the early exodus of 223 Cherokees into southern Kansas, about two thousand had moved on to their Neutral Lands some twelve miles south of Fort Scott, Kansas, during August 1862. The beginning of 1863 found the majority of the loyal Cherokees in southwestern Missouri, for near the end of the previous year General Blunt, without consulting Superintendent Coffin, had moved the refugees found around Fort Scott to near Neosho. These Cherokee refugees were settled on a portion of their own tribal land but it was within the limits of Kansas. Since Neosho was a secessionist stronghold in Missouri, it was almost impossible for supplies of any kind to reach the refugees, except at great expense and under heavy military escort. Superintendent Coffin sent Justin Harlan and A. G. Proctor as agents to assist the Cherokees at Neosho. The Southern Superintendency continued to supply necessities as best it could, supplemented to a degree by the military, but the conditions of the refugees remained miserable until March 1863.

With the first indication of the passing of winter Colonel Phillips, then in command of the Army of the Frontier, recommended the return of the refugee Cherokees to the Cherokee Nation. He reported that the country was clear of Confederates and that no hindrance stood in the way to prevent the movement. Military protection, seeds, and agricultural implements were promised. The Indians and Colonel Phillips reached Tahlequah at about the same time in the month of April but the country was not clear of Confederates. Before a crop could be raised the troops and refugees were driven into Fort Gibson.

With no crops and the high cost of transportation, plus roving bands of Confederates and bushwhackers, Coffin wondered how the seven thousand destitute Indians, with the number constantly increasing, would subsist during the winter if the Confederates were not driven from the Arkansas River. He also hoped that the water would rise so that supplies could be shipped to Fort Gibson. He further felt that they should be returned to southern Kansas, where ample provisions could be obtained at low prices. He hoped that they could be returned in the spring of 1864 in time to raise crops. As the summer advanced the wants of the restored refugees grew, and they were in a pitiable state mentally and physically, with little prospect of amelioration. The tide turned when Major John Foreman reached Fort Gibson with reinforcements on July 6 after having been engaged by Watie's Confederates in a skirmish near Cabin Creek on June 30. The condition of the Cherokees in 1863 was the most pitiable imaginable. Before the war they had been the most powerful, wealthiest and best educated Indians in the United States. Now their power and wealth were gone and they were humbled, disgraced and impoverished.

Loyal Seminole refugees, numbering 919, received some relief in the way of food and clothing from General Hunter when they reached Kansas. The Seminoles were moved to LeRoy on March 6, 1862, and to Neosho Falls on April 24. They were to have been taken as far north as the Sac and Fox Agency, but when they reached LeRoy they became obstinate and refused to go any farther. They were restless and complained of the government's use of their annuities to feed and clothe them; further, they had not been protected according to treaty stipulations. Much of the goods they were allocated was not suitable. A large proportion of the fine woolens and bleached muslins received by them had to be traded off for green corn, chickens and eggs for less than one–fourth of their cost.

About sixty Negroes came with the Seminoles and over one hundred others from the Seminole Nation joined them later in Kansas. Agent G. C. Snow reported that they were generally intelligent and spoke the English language. They understood how to do farm work, though it was evident that they had not been brought up to labor in the same manner as the slave Negroes who had lived in the United States.

Much sickness had prevailed among the Seminoles since their arrival in Kansas and at least ten percent of their number had died. Most of the deaths were attributed to the exposure suffered while enroute to Kansas. The Seminoles continued to experience poor health and even in 1864 their mortality exceeded eighty, among whom was Principal Chief Billy Bowlegs.

By October 1865 about one–half of the refugee Seminoles had been returned to Indian Territory but they were located upon the Creek and Cherokee lands near Fort Gibson. The remainder, about five hundred, consisting mainly of the families of those who had volunteered in the Union Army, remained in Kansas near Neosho Falls but they were to be moved soon to Creek land south of Fort Gibson. Their own country was too disturbed for them to return at this time.

Since the Choctaw and Chickasaw Nations joined the Confederacy almost en masse, their number of loyal exiles was relatively small. The Chickasaw refugees numbered about three hundred in 1863, and the Choctaws about one hundred in that same year. They were given subsistence at the Sac and Fox Agency under the direction of the agent, Isaac Colman. When Colman arrived at Fort Smith, he found in the Federal lines about three hundred more Choctaws who were in want of provisions and clothing. He also issued to them rations of flour, beef, salt and tobacco. The loyal Choctaw-Chickasaw refugees increased in number to about two thousand by October of 1865. Even as late as the early part of 1867 there were destitute Chickasaws in and near Fort Gibson.

The Choctaw and Chickasaw Nations had been fairly free from want or distress as these areas did not suffer seriously from military devastation. Many of the Confederate Cherokees and Creeks settled in camps on the Boggy, Blue and Kiamichi Rivers where they remained until the end of the war. These additional people brought about a distressing food shortage for the

Choctaws. In September 1865 when the peace conference met at Fort Smith, help from the Washington government was desired by some six thousand southern Cherokees in the Choctaw and Chickasaw Nations in the vicinity of Red River.

The Confederate faction of the Seminoles also appealed to the United States government during the peace conference at Fort Smith. They pleaded that they were poorer than ever and that the Confederate States had for two years fed their people who were unable to feed themselves. Now since the cessation of hostilities this situation had changed, thus placing them at the mercy of the Federal government.

In January 1864 the Senate Committee asked J. P. Usher, the Secretary of the Interior, for his opinion as to whether conditions would not allow a return of the loyal tribes to Indian Territory in time for raising a crop. General Blunt, who was in Washington, was also asked for his opinion and he responded favorably to the idea, mentioning that the lack of military protection was the major delay. With this knowledge and favorable information from the Secretary of War, Edwin M. Stanton, there seemed to be no reason why the refugees should not be returned. Senator James Lane availed himself of this opportunity to introduce on March 3 a joint resolution calling for refugee removal from Kansas. He gave their number as 9,200 and the monthly cost of their maintenance as $60,000. The bill became law in May.

The removal of the refugees was primarily Superintendent Coffin's responsibility but adequate military aid had to be forthcoming to insure a successful venture. When he applied for an armed escort he found that Major General Samuel R. Curtis, now commanding the Department of Kansas, could furnish one only to the border. Coffin telegraphed Commissioner of Indian Affairs William P. Dole, hoping that he might be able to get an order for troops directly from the War Department, but the Red River Expedition in Louisiana was in progress and no troops were released at that time. Finally, on May 26 Brigadier General William Steel, commander of Indian Territory, was directed by Secretary Stanton to furnish an escort from the Kansas border onward. After wagons and teams were obtained, the procession of wagons, people and animals journeyed to Fort Gibson. The advance guard reached there on June 15, 1864, but while enroute their progress had been hampered by cattle thieves and thunderstorms.

Fort Gibson was not the Mecca that was anticipated. There were already about nine thousand people there to be fed, and the new arrivals added another seven thousand. There was discord between white and red people, both inside and outside the army, and there was discord between civilians and soldiers. The bickering that arose between the white officers and the Indian rank and file soon became notorious. It was caused chiefly by the disputed ownership of ponies. There were complaints directed at the food contractors, who were accused of delivering inferior goods. There were also criticisms of army practices. In April General Blunt had issued an order restraining the Indians from selling their stock; he also ordered the seizure of nearby salt works, and the Indians resented both of these orders, particularly the latter. As the Indian crops matured the soldiers, without regard for Indian needs, helped themselves to the product of the labor of women and children. In addition it seemed that some military authorities were involved in the illicit cattle traffic.

The end of the Civil War in Indian Territory marked for many the loss of the fruit born of the years of hard struggle between removal and the war. How heartbreaking it must have been to have suffered through the war years as so many did, only to return to desolation, despair and abject poverty. Battles fought in Indian Territory, though not altering significantly the course of the war, did lay waste the country and so thoroughly impoverished its inhabitants that Secretary of the Interior James Harlan declared that thousands would inevitably perish during the winter unless the government provided for their relief.

Yet there were those in Congress who repudiated the idea that any responsibility for the Indians rested upon the government's shoulders, and indeed as the Senate debated the condition and treatment of the restored refugees, the Indians were being mistreated. They had been returned to Indian Territory lacking almost everything with which to commence life again, except personal energy. Consequently, they appealed to the government for subsistence until they could raise enough to support themselves.

Cattle Thieving

Now that the war was over and treaties of peace and amity were being worked out with the United States, each Nation had to focus attention on problems peculiar to itself resulting from that war, problems that could not easily wait until formal peace negotiations with the United States were consummated. But cattle thieving, returning refugees, lack of food, clothing, shelter, finance, the disruption of educational, civil, and social agencies and the questions involved in establishing the status of the freedmen were problems common to all.

One of the first major problems facing the Five Civilized Tribes and the Southern Superintendency was illegal cattle driving from Indian Territory. Upon Superintendent Elijah Sells' arrival at his headquarters in Leavenworth, Kansas, he found communications from George Reynolds of the Seminole Agency and Milo Gookins of the Wichita Agency on that very subject. After investigation into the matter, Sells was convinced that there was in operation a regularly organized band of cattle thieves with sentinels, scouts, numerous employees and plans so completely systematized that they generally succeeded in driving off with impunity all herds of cattle coming within their range.

Commissioner Cooley was equally convinced from the available evidence that the large-scale illegal cattle driving from Indian Territory could be stopped only by securing the active cooperation of the military authorities, for previous civil attempts had brought no tangible results. He therefore applied for a sufficient force of troops to be placed under the direction of the Superintendent of Indian Affairs or such agents as he might designate. These troops were promptly furnished and ordered to report to Reynolds, the Seminole agent, who at once entered upon his duties under instruction from the Office of Indian Affairs. Reynolds succeeded in seizing Indian cattle in the hands of the "cattle brokers" and he arrested the parties in charge, who confessed that a portion of the cattle had been stolen from the Indians. Several small herds were seized and a portion of the cattle was turned over to George Snow, the Neosho agent, for beef for the Indians, and the remaining cattle not claimed were sold at public auction.

Reynolds maintained in his report to Commissioner Cooley

that since the commencement of the Civil War approximately three hundred thousand head of cattle had been driven from Indian Territory without the consent of the owners and without remuneration. At an average value of fifteen dollars per head this sum amounted to four million five hundred thousand dollars. There seemed to have been two classes of operators connected with cattle driving from the Indian country. The first were those who took the risk of driving from the original range or the owners' homes; this class usually drove the cattle to the southern border of Kansas, where the second class was waiting to receive the stolen property. These cattle brokers met with such unparalleled success that the mania became contagious. Soon the number directly and remotely engaged was so large and the operators so powerful that it was almost fatal to interpose obstacles in their way.

The problem of cattle thieving was immense, and Agent Reynolds operated under a severe handicap. Many people in Western Kansas had large herds of what had once been Indian cattle, and their basic sympathies lay with the cattle thieves. Superintendent Sells on June 15, 1865, also authorized Justin Harlan, agent of the Cherokees, to organize a force sufficient to protect those Indians from being robbed by marauding cattle thieves. Colonel Phillips looked further and accused the Indian agents near Fort Gibson of cattle thieving and robbing the Indians of their small amount of corn. These charges were denied by the Choctaw–Chickasaw, the Creek and the Cherokee agents. Cooley concluded after an investigation that the charges were without foundation.

Other Difficulties Within the Nations

Another problem was the renewed desire for land ceded to the Indians. In 1865 pressure commenced anew for this land and climaxed to some degree when the treaties were negotiated. Superintendent Sells reminded Commissioner Cooley that the Seminole Indians were a branch of the Creeks, spoke the same language and were closely identified by strong ties of consanguinity as well as common interest; therefore they might be consolidated with advantage to both. Since the Creek Nation had an immense tract of land, even after disposing of that portion north of the Arkansas River for the settlement of other friendly Indians, they might adopt their cousins, the Seminoles, let them settle upon their lands and still have a surplus on the south side of the Arkansas River. This arrangement would leave all of the Seminole land to be sold for their joint benefit under a consolidated organization.

Sells further maintained that since the Cherokees still owned a tract of eight hundred thousand acres in the southeast corner of Kansas, it should be purchased by the government for general settlement. The proceeds could be used to benefit the entire Nation and the problem of whites intruding upon the Indian lands would also be solved. It was further suggested that in case it proved impossible for the loyal and southern Cherokees, who were at this time still not reconciled, to live together in friendship, the southern Cherokees could easily make terms with the Chickasaws to join with them.

Early reconstruction problems for the Cherokees were numerous, for about ten thousand five hundred of the seventeen thousand Cherokees had remained loyal, and it was the loyal faction of this Nation as of the Creeks and Seminoles that suffered the most. They became refugees from their homes, leaving them in the hands of the enemy who seemed determined that no trace of the homesteads of their brethren should remain for their return. The southern Cherokees also suffered. Those who went south numbered about sixty five hundred and were also in destitute circumstances. They took refuge in the southern portion of Indian Territory, near or on the Red River, on the Choctaw lands. After the war was over petitions were made to the Federal government in behalf of the southern refugees. The United States established supply depots, let out contracts for the systematic feeding of the destitute and appointed special agents to see that the contracts were carried out in good faith. In this way the indigent were supported during the winter of 1865–1866 and well into the following summer.

Cooley seemingly sympathized with the southern faction of the Cherokee Nation, judging from the manner in which he dealt with confiscations. He pointed out to the Secretary of the Interior that the southern faction was hampered by the sweeping act passed by the tribal council, which took from them every acre of land and all of their improvements. He reminded the Secretary that improvements which had been worth thousands had been sold for as little as five dollars. And when the repentant rebel party had sought to rejoin the Nation they had been offered only the opportunity to go upon new lands and begin the world again, with no hope of any restoration of property.

Agent Harlan asked that the loyal Cherokees be compensated for their losses, as these losses were mostly sustained after the men were in the United States Army and the area had not been protected by the United States as their treaty had promised. Instead, even in 1863, when the Union Army occupied Fort Gibson marauding Confederate parties from their camps on the southwest bank of the Arkansas River crossed over into the Cherokee country and murdered and captured whom they pleased, plundered all the loyal Cherokees of everything they wanted and burned and destroyed everything which they could not carry or drive away. They murdered the old men and boys large enough to aid the wives and mothers in raising crops and threatened the women if they did not abandon their crops. Throughout the whole summer, fall and part of the winter of 1863 these depredations continued. Harlan declared that he never heard of the robbers losing any of their plunder by military pursuit or even being hindered from crossing the Arkansas River to get quantities of loot.

The Cherokee schoolhouses and seminaries suffered in the general destruction which the Nation experienced. Their schoolhouses throughout the area were mostly burned and only the bare walls were left standing. As long as the whole national fund had to be used to supply the destitute with food, education would be neglected. The Cherokees had no means of paying teachers and it would be a long time before they would have, unless the United States government repaid them for some part of their losses. Their churches, heretofore numerous and well-attended, were dilapidated and their attendance severely decreased.

The Cherokee soldiers were mustered out of the United States service on May 31, 1865. Besides receiving their pay nearly three weeks late, they found that it was too late to plant corn. Almost all of the corn was planted by the women and children and all that the men could do after their discharge was to assist in finishing the cultivation. There would not be enough bread because the large surplus was in the hands of a few, which meant that many would have to be specially fed until another corn crop could be raised. In 1865 they raised no wheat at all.

The destitute condition of the Creeks was not alleviated by their annuity funds. In Agent J. W. Dunn's judgment the practice of paying Indians annuities by the per capita cash method was of no advantage to them; he preferred to see the annuities used to supply the necessary equipment for farming. He also shared the opinion of the United States government as to the best method of reconstructing the Indians, and was gratified to learn that all Indian tribes were now to be removed to an Indian Territory. Here they would more quickly adopt the democratic form of government, he thought, than if they were to remain in their scattered tribal condition. On the north side of the Arkansas River Dunn visited the mission that before the war had been a flourishing institution of learning under the care of the Presbyterian Church. The buildings, though standing, were badly abused. No fencing was to be found and fruit trees and shrubbery were mostly destroyed. Naturally education had been neglected during the war years but the people hoped that some provision could soon be made for the education of their youth.

The number of persons comprising the Choctaw and Chickasaw Nations in 1865 was about seventeen thousand in all. They had had a population of twenty-five thousand at the beginning of the war, including five thousand slaves, of whom at least 212 remained loyal. Due to the fact that during most of the war Confederate forces occupied the Choctaw and Chickasaw Nations, and many of the Indians who joined these forces had constantly remained in the vicinity of their homes, they did not suffer destruction to the same extent as the various tribes to the north. But the extensive use of horses and cattle by the Confederate Army reduced the wealth of these Nations, thus leaving about one-third of the people without means of subsistence. Cattle thieving was also carried on to an alarming degree, and droves of cattle were continually passing out of these Nations over all of the public thoroughfares, but more especially over those leading to Little Rock and Fort Smith, Arkansas.

In the southern portion of the Choctaw-Chickasaw land, the Red River country, the crops were unusually good, and enough had been raised during the last year of the war to provide amply for that portion of the people of the area, if only the Confederate Cherokees and other noncitizens of the Nations were removed from among them. This state of things, however, did not exist among the people who were returning to their homes in the extreme western and northeastern portion of the Choctaw-Chickasaw country. Having been away from their homes and in the Confederate Army for nearly three years, they now found themselves in a condition of extreme destitution and actually suffering for the necessities of life.

Agent Colman called attention to the influence exercised over the Indians by the white men who mixed among them by marriage, by adoption and by tacit consent without any direct permission. To these men he attributed the disloyalty of the Choctaws and Chickasaws. They organized and led the Confederate Indian regiments, and Colman firmly believed that the same men who desired to remain in the Nation as traders had been the principal emissaries of the Confederate government, and through their influence had caused the people of the Nation to throw off their allegiance to the government of the United States. Colman held that strict justice required that they should be ordered out of the limits of the Nation and severely dealt with should they return unauthorized.

The Choctaws and Chickasaws deserved praise for the interest they always manifested in the subject of education. In this respect they were far ahead of their Indian neighbors. They had been well supplied with academies and boarding schools, where the children of the wealthier class had been educated, but these were closed during the war years. Colman recommended the establishment of a common school system in the Nation for the children of all classes to receive a liberal education at rates that would be within the reach of all.

Another problem was lawlessness. For a period of time after close of the Civil War it was believed that the people of Indian Territory, and especially those of the Choctaw and Chickasaw Nations, had considerable trouble with Negroes from adjoining states. Some of the landowners of Texas were anxious to rid themselves of their former slaves and they encouraged those of a shiftless and unruly disposition to move to Indian Territory. Settlements were formed by these intruders in the southern portion near the Red River. As there was little demand for labor and the land had been impoverished by the war, the intruding Negroes resorted to stealing.

Meetings of the Choctaw-Chickasaw vigilance committees were held on the prairies or in the woods, with guards being stationed around the area. Scouts rode throughout the country on the watch for suspicious looking persons, and all strangers had to give accounts of themselves. If the individual was a Negro he would generally be seized and whipped and told never to be found where he was not known. In the case of the lawless bands and settlements of Negroes, notice was given them to leave the country within a certain time.

If a horse thief were found upon the range he was immediately hanged from some convenient tree or shot upon the spot. Communication was effective. If a horse was stolen in one part of the country the fact, together with a description of the animal, was known in other parts of the country by the time the thief appeared with the animal. Now and then when the pursuers overtook the thieves pitched battles followed and sometimes there were casualties on both sides. Thus the vigilance committees effectively enforced order by common consent.

The need to curb lawlessness was another reason given by some Indian agents to their superiors in attempting to secure prompt and liberal government action in behalf of the Indians. The general consensus that the Indians must be fed and clothed or their suffering would lead them to steal was communicated from Brigadier General James C. Veatch to Colonel J. Schuyler Crosby when reporting on matters concerning Indian Territory. The principle that it was cheaper to feed than to fight the Indians, or pay for the punishment of their stealing, was illustrated daily in the Territory. The cost of sustaining a small army in the West in a campaign against the Indians or even at military posts, where there was no war, was far greater than the whole annual expenditure of the Office of Indian Affairs.

The Freedmen in Indian Territory

It was but natural that the former slaves should also suffer deprivations. Some of the former slave owners did what they could to assist their former slaves. It was rumored that the Freedmen's Bureau would have contributed more to the welfare of the Negroes in Indian Territory had it not been dominated by persons who were too uninformed of actual conditions to benefit the Negroes permanently. The immigration of freedmen from the border states into the Choctaw and Chickasaw country and the subsequent work of the vigilance committees in these Nations seemingly gave rise to stories that precipitated the United States Government (prodded by the "Radical Republicans") to order an investigation of the condition of the freedmen in Indian Territory. General John B. Sanborn was appointed as commissioner for regulating relations between freedmen in the area and their former masters.

General Sanborn's report was made in the form of three letters. Since historians have interpreted these letters in light of their various frames of references, the full text of the first and third letters (from Sanborn's *Annual Report* of 1866) will be included.

Sir: I have the honor to report that, pursuant to instruction from you, of date November 20, 1865, I have visited the following tribes of Indians, in the Indian territory, which formerly held slaves, viz: Seminoles, Creeks, Cherokees, and the loyal portion of the Chickasaws, under Lewis Johnson, and my report is made out and forwarded at this time, before visiting the Choctaw and Chickasaw nations, for the reason that as the condition of the freedmen in these nations requires the immediate action of the government, there should be no delay on account of any failure of mine to make an early report. The freedmen are the most industrious, economical, and, in many respects, the more intelligent portion of the population of the Indian territory. They all desire to remain in that territory upon lands set apart for their own exclusive use.

The Indians who are willing that the freedmen shall remain in the territory at all, also prefer that they should be located upon a tract of country by themselves. This question has been canvassed much by the freedmen and the Indians, and the freedmen have come to the conclusion that they are soon to be moved upon some tract of country set apart for their exclusive use, and hence are not inclined to make any improvements where they are, or do any more work than is absolutely necessary for their immediate wants.

The spring or warm season commences early in this country, and farmers and planters ordinarily commence ploughing and planting as early as the first of March. Hence you will see that it is of the most vital importance that if lands are to be set apart for this population it should be done at once, and if not they should be so advised immediately, so that they will be induced to make other arrangements. Most of these freedmen have ox-teams, and among them are black-smiths, carpenters, wheelwrights, &c. The sentiments, prejudices, &c., on the part of the Indian nations towards the freedmen at present are as follows, viz.:

The Creek Nation look upon the freedmen as their equals in rights, and have, or are in favor of, incorporating them into their tribes, with all the rights and privileges of native Indians. The Seminoles entertain the same or nearly the same sentiments and feelings as the Creeks.

The Cherokees are divided in sentiment. A portion, and not a very small portion, think the government should move the negroes from their country, as it has freed them; while a portion, including the principal chief, Downing, are in favor of having them retained in the Nation, and located upon some tract of land set apart for their exclusive use; and Colonel Downing says that this policy will obtain in the nation, and that civil rights will be accorded to the freedmen before a great while.

The Choctaw Nation is divided in sentiment, but the pre-ponderance of sentiment is strongly against the freedmen and a violent prejudice exists against them in that Nation, which time alone will overcome. The public men and council acknowledge a change in the relations of the former masters and slaves, while a large portion of the people do not admit any change in these relations, and their action and treatment toward them is much the same as formerly, except in instances where the freedmen are driven away from their former homes by their masters. One freedmen has been killed at Boggy Depot by his former master, and there are rumors of several other cases, and no action has yet been taken by the Government to punish the party guilty. . . . My own conclu-sion is that the public sentiment of this Nation in regard to the freedmen is radically wrong at the present time.

The Chickasaw Nation is still holding most of their negroes in slavery, and entertain a bitter prejudice against them all. They have provided by law for the emancipation of their slaves, and exclude all from the Nation who left it during the war. In other words, all negroes who left the country and joined the Federal army are prohibited from returning. This is also true in the Choctaw Nation. It is reported to me by the chief, Lewis Johnson (of the loyal Chickasaws), that Governor Colbert stated to many people, and publicly, before leaving for Washington, that they should hold the slaves until they could determine at Washington whether or not they could get pay for them, and if they could not then they would strip them naked and drive them either south to Texas, or north to Fort Gibson. So bitter is the feeling against the return of the negroes that have been in the Federal army, that Major Coleman and myself have concluded that it is not safe or advisable for Lewis Johnson and party to return until troops are stationed at Arbuckle.

Many negroes have been shot down by their masters in this Nation, and the Government has taken no steps to punish the guilty.

My conclusion is that nothing can be done to ameliorate the condition of the freedmen in the Choctaw and Chickasaw nations until there is a proper military force stationed at Boggy Depot, Forts Lawson, Washita, and Arbuckle, and that my advent there at the present time, to carry into effect your instructions, would be the cause of much excitement, while nothing would be accomplished, and insults and disgrace be likely to follow.

The first step toward the accomplishment of anything for the freedmen of those nations or even towards enabling the loyal Indians to return with the freedmen associated with them, is the garrisoning of the military posts. It is possible that much more might have been done to change and correct the public sentiment of these nations if all the federal officers brought in contact with them had been decided in their own ideas that these classes were free, and endeavored to impress their views upon the Indians. But with the public sentiment and law of these nations as it is, and the most prominent of the public men absent, I am certain that nothing can be accomplished more than to commence the correction of public sentiment, which I have endeavored to do by circulars. . . .

The condition of public sentiment throughout these two nations is no cause for delay on the part of the government to make provision at once for the freedmen of all the tribes, to go upon tracts of country set apart for their own exclusive use, which is so much desired by the freedmen and all loyal Indians. There are two practicable methods of doing this. The first and most desirable is by treaty stipulation with the respective nations in the treaties about to be concluded at Washington. The second is by congressional enactment, carried into effect as Congress shall provide.

There should be set apart a tract large enough to give a square mile to every four persons, as there is much waste land in the nation.

The tract or tracts of land should be the most fertile in the territory, as the freedmen are the principal producers, and should in all cases touch either the Arkansas or Red River, so that the crops could be run out on flatboats. Reference should be had to timber and prairie as well as bottom and uplands. Persons not freedmen, living now upon lands so set apart, shall be allowed the option of remaining or having the improvements appraised by three disinterested parties, and receiving the appraised value of the same from the government. Sixty days from the passage of the act or approval of the treaty should be allowed such party to signify his choice to the proper officer.

Provisions should be made for the survey of such tracts, at the earliest time practicable, into sections, &c., and the freedmen over eighteen years of age allowed to enter three hundred and twenty acres of the same under the homestead law, or by scrip provided for the purpose, without power of alienation during the life of the party entering the same, or for a definite term of years.

When the tribes know that this policy and course is determined upon by the government they will, in my judgment, submit to it without any open resistance, perhaps without a murmur; and the freedmen will rejoice that at last they have a prospect of a permanent home for themselves and their children.

The freedmen of the Seminole and the Creek tribes believe that the national laws and customs of their tribes are sufficient for their protection, while the freedmen of the other tribes all feel, and say they know, that there is no security or protection for them, either in person or property, without some power or government superior and above that of the Indian nations to which they belong. These views of the freedmen are, in my judgment, correct, and the territory should either be organized into a military district, with martial law in full force, and fully enforced, with a good executive commander who would supervise everything, or a territorial government should be organized to execute the laws.

All the Indian tribes are unanimously opposed to the erection of a territorial government: but such a government, or a military government, is imperatively required by the situation. It cannot be expected that any government would leave ten or twelve thousand of its citizens as the freedmen of Indian Territory now are, while within its own borders without any government or without the full protection and benefits of its own laws and institutions. To hand them over to the laws and customs of the Indian Tribes would be extraordinary and anomalous.

All lands set apart for the freedmen should, whenever practicable, be located east of the ninety–seventh degree of longitude, as the drought is usually so severe west of that as to render the maturity of crops very uncertain. With lands set apart for the freedmen of the Indian nation, and the freedmen located upon them, and a government, military or civil, organized and executed for their protection, they will, beyond doubt, soon become an industrious, intelligent, and happy population.

All of which is respectfully submitted.

I have the honor to be, very respectfully, your obedient servant,

JOHN H. SANBORN,
    Brevet Major General and Commissioner.
Hon. James Harlan,
    Secretary of the Interior.
                Fort Smith, Arkansas, April 13, 1866.

The second letter indicated that General Sanborn had completed his tour through the Choctaw and Chickasaw Nations. Modifications and additions were made to the first report. He noted that a slave code was still being executed, and that the Indians wanted the freedmen moved to a separate area and that the freedmen seemed willing to go. General Sanborn recommended a reservation of thirty-six square miles. He further suggested that a provision be made in form of law that unmarried women with one or more children living with her be given 160 acres of land upon the reservation set aside for freedmen. He felt that since many of these children were half breed or mixed blood, this hampered her chances for marriage. Other recommendations were made relating to schools, territorial government, sectioning and future settlement on Indian land. The third report indicated that between January and April General Sanborn's view of the condition of the freedmen was changed.

Colonel: I have the honor to report that the existing relations between the freedmen of the Indian Territory and their former masters are generally satisfactory. The rights of the freedmen are acknowledged by all; fair compensation for labor is paid; a fair proportion of crops to be raised on the old plantations is allowed; labor for freedmen to perform is abundant, and nearly all are self-supporting.

Only one hundred and fifty have applied for assistance this month, and I think the number will be much reduced the next month.

Much of the assistance rendered is to freedmen that have been taken south by their masters, and who are now returning to their old homes.

Under these circumstances there seems to be little reason for continuing this commission beyond the tenth of next month, unless it should be to correct the few abuses that may arise, and exercise a general supervision over these matters in the territory, and this will probably be more necessary about the time of the maturity of the crops than during the summer months while they are growing.

The necessity or advantage of continuing the commission also depends very much upon the conditions of the treaties about to be concluded at Washington, and the laws passed in pursuance thereof. But it seems that the Indian agents, under proper instructions, could well attend to and perform all those duties that now, or in any event after the tenth of next month will, pertain to this commission.

I therefore respectfully request that you will either grant me a leave of absence of forty days, to take effect from the tenth of next month, or that you will allow me to proceed to Washington at that time and close my accounts, and there wait further orders.

I have the honor to be, very respectfully, your obedient servant.

JOHN B. SANBORN
    Brevet Major General and Commissioner.
Colonel D. N. Cooley

The manner in which the various Nations endeavored to adjust to the articles in the 1866 reconstruction treaties relating to the future status and privileges of the freedmen furnishes some validity to General Sanborn's assessment of the attitude toward Negroes in the five Nations.

Summary

The Five Civilized Tribes in 1865 faced problems of reconstruction for a second time. The loyal faction of the Creek, Seminole and Cherokee Nations in particular had witnessed the bitter irony of having a great republic renege on promises and violate treaties. They had experienced loss of property and life, grief and desolation upon being abandoned by, and sometimes even when under the protection of Union troops. With few exceptions the life of destitute refugees had been the lot of the supporters of the Union, as well as some who sympathized with the Confederacy. Most refugees from all Five Civilized Nations had common conditions with which to contend. The refugees themselves were mostly old men, women and children, for the men of military age were away fighting. There was much dissatisfaction where the refugees assembled, considerable homesickness prevailed, and many suffered an enforced change in their habits of living. Numbers had come from homes of comfort and plenty, but in refugee camps they had suffered malnutrition, overcrowding and bad hygenic conditions. Smallpox alone killed hundreds of refugees. Raiders plundered and robbed at will as long as there was anything left worth taking. Loyal Indian refugees were also apprehensive of what was being charged against their government account, for they from long experience had no illusions as to the white man's generosity, and whisperings of graft and peculations were not unheeded by them. They had been conscious that they had outstayed their welcome in Kansas and that citizens who were not profiting from the expenditure of the relief money were clamoring for them to be gone.

The exiles all desired to go home at the earliest practicable moment. A return in the autumn or the winter would permit them to gather cattle and hogs to furnish meat, and at the same time prepare their fields for a spring crop, thereby relieving the government of the responsibility of feeding and clothing them. They had of course wanted assurance first that their enemies had been removed so that they could venture further than the vicinity of Fort Gibson in order to cope with the abject poverty that faced the majority of them.

Upon their return several problems claimed immediate attention. Homes and farms had to be rebuilt and illegal cattle driving, greed for their land that had been promised in perpetuity, crime and general lawlessness had to be curbed. Tribal government, political harmony, schools, churches and economic prosperity had to be reestablished and activated. The question of how to care for the freedmen and the decision of what his future status would be in Indian Territory was no less perplexing to many Indians of the five Nations than it was to many Caucasians of the Southern states. Evidence does indicate, however, that sentiment in the Creek and Seminole Nations toward the Negro was not as often characterized by violence or other acts symbolizing deep-seated resentment of their presence as that manifested in the other Nations.

Other problems of reconstruction would be solved or alleviated later, but for the present attention had to be turned toward reestablishing political relations with the United States. This major step was to be taken at a peace council called for September of 1865 in Fort Smith, Arkansas.

Chapter Three

UNITED STATES REQUIREMENTS
FOR RECONSTRUCTION

Before the peace council at Fort Smith convened in September 1865 several efforts were made by the Indians themselves to try to prepare for this event. Unsuccessful attempts were made in 1864 to get the Confederate Indians to renew their allegiance to the United States government. But with General Lee's surrender on April 9, 1865, the Indians allied with the Confederacy knew defeat had come. They began to ponder concerning the steps that should be taken to enable them to return to their former association with the Federal Union under the most desirable terms.

Efforts Towards Tribal Unity

Feeling that a united front could best serve this purpose, an Indian Council of all the tribes of Indian Territory was called by the Creek Nation. Council Grove on the North Canadian River, just west of present Oklahoma City, was the site selected. The delegates were to arrive on May 15, 1865; fear of being disturbed by Federal forces caused the Council to move nine days later to Cotton Wood Grove on the Washita River, a site known as Camp Napoleon. Here the southern element of the Five Civilized Tribes and the Comanche, Caddo, Osage, Cheyenne, Kiowa, Arapahoe, Lipan, Northern Caddo and Anadarko tribes entered into a league of peace and friendship. The object of this confederation was to maintain Indian Territory as the present and future home of the Indian race; to preserve and

55

perpetuate the national rights and franchises of the various Indian Nations; and to cultivate peace, harmony and fellowship. It was also declared that the earnest desire of the confederated Indian tribes was that an Indian would not spill another Indian's blood.

General Douglas Cooper and General Watie agreed on the expediency of convening the Grand Council, which had been meeting at Armstrong Academy. To convene the Council at this time seemed wise, and Cooper notified its members that the session was called for June 10. The Grand Council met at Cleata Yamaha, Choctaw Nation, and here the principles set forth at Camp Napoleon were sanctioned. The proceedings were written in the form of resolutions on June 15, 1865. In brief these were:

1. That the wishes and intentions of the Grand Council be communicated to all other Nations of Indians in alliance with the government of the United States and at hostilities with the Nations of the Grand Council, and that those Nations be invited to become parties to the confederation and cooperate with this council in its efforts to contract new friendly relations with the United States government.

2. That the governors or principal chiefs of the Five Civilized Nations, with the consent of their councils, be authorized to appoint one or more commissioners, not to exceed five from each Nation, to represent the interests of each Nation in Washington and with power to negotiate treaties as needed with the United States government.

3. That one or more persons authorized to be appointed may act as proxies for the remainder, should it be out of their power to proceed in person to Washington. The delegates were to be authorized to invite the United States government to send commissioners from Indian Territory to treat with tribes of this confederation who may not be represented at Washington.

4. That no treaty made under the provisions of these resolutions would be binding until ratified by the National Councils of the tribes making these treaties. The delegates were to be instructed to communicate with the proper military authorities of the United States for the purpose of effecting a cessation of hostilities in order that there be time and opportunity to negotiate with the United States government; also, they were to obtain from the military authorities a passport to Washington, and to further urge upon the military author-

ities the propriety of sending no forces into Indian Territory until delegates confer with the United States government for the establishment of permanent peace.

These resolutions were approved on June 6 by the general delegation. A special delegation accompanied by Captain G. Wilcox, the Assistant Adjutant General on General Cooper's staff, went to Fort Smith to call on General Cyrus Bussey, who served as the commander of the Frontier District. Along with the resolutions of the Council they carried a letter from Winchester Colbert, the governor of the Chickasaw Nation. Bussey reported the contents of Governor Colbert's letter to his superior officer, General J. J. Reynolds, but while he waited to hear how he should proceed, a commission from Louisiana, acting under authority conferred by General F. J. Herron, carried on peace negotiations with the Indians. This made unnecessary at this time a journey of the Choctaw delegation to Washington. A commission headed by Lieutenant Colonel Asa C. Matthews effected truces with each individual tribe through its prinicpal chiefs, since the Grand Council that Herron had heard about had adjourned.

The resolutions of the Grand Council for the reunion of warring elements was revived by Watie. About June 28 Watie appointed six delegates whom he instructed to go to Fort Gibson or to any other place where Unionist Indians were congregated and open negotiations for the reestablishment of tribal harmony. The delegates reached Fort Gibson about July 8. Their mood was not conciliatory and their general action was of such nature that Colonel John A. Garrett, who commanded Fort Gibson, grew uneasy and insisted that the secessionists cross to the far side of the Arkansas River and stay there. Only a few secessionist Indians were allowed on the Fort Gibson side each day.

Meanwhile Lewis Downing, in the absence of Chief John Ross, called his followers together in a council at Tahlequah to decide if the southern Cherokee delegation should be given an audience. Amnesty was proclaimed on July 14 and the promised conference with the delegation which took place four days later ended in general disappointment. While the Cherokee were attempting to settle their differences other divided southern tribes followed the example with an even smaller measure of success. Nothing really constructive resulted from any of the midsummer conferences, whenever they were held. This was evidenced by the fact that there was no general solidarity among the tribes or factions when they met the United States commissioners in Fort Smith in September.

There was even controversy as to where the peace council would convene. Washington and Fort Gibson had been mentioned as possible sites. The secessionist Indians protested in favor of Armstrong Academy. They asserted that Armstrong Academy had been agreed upon with Colonel Matthews, that it had been publicly proclaimed, and that it was too late to make a change because the plains tribes had been invited. In addition the Grand Council would be holding its regular session at Armstrong Academy in September, and this would provide an obstacle to the meeting at Fort Smith in the early part of the month. The United States authorities decided upon Fort Smith and did not yield. They too had sent out notices that could not be recalled. After further confusion and contention the secessionist Indians finally decided to convene the Grand Council on August 24 at Armstrong Academy and then adjourn to Fort Smith.

The Fort Smith Conference Convenes

President Andrew Johnson appointed a commission to represent the United States at Fort Smith that consisted of the following: Dennis N. Cooley, Commissioner of Indian Affairs; Elijah Sells, Superintendent of the Southern Superintendency; Thomas Wistar, a leading member of the Society of Friends; Brigadier General W. S. Harney, United States Army; and Colonel Ely S. Parker, of General Grant's staff. James M. Edmunds, Commissioner of the General Land Office, and Major General Francis Herron were appointed, but they both declined. Associated in the capacity of secretary and assistant secretaries were Charles E. Mix, Chief Clerk of the Indian Bureau, George L. Cook, W. R. Irwin, and John B. Garrett. These men left Washington with Secretary Harlan's instructions based upon Senate Bill No. 459 for the organization of Indian Territory, commonly known as the Harlan Bill, that had passed the Senate at the last session of Congress.

The commission met on September 7 at Fort Smith and

organized. Cooley was made president and Mix was to be chief secretary and also take part in the deliberations of the commission as he was connected with the Office of Indian Affairs. The first meeting of the Fort Smith Council found a number of Indians present but all were from the loyal party. They included representatives from the following tribes: Creek, Osage, Quapaw, Cowskin Seneca, the Seneca and Shawnee of the Neosho Agency, Cherokee, Chickasaw, Choctaw, Seminole, and the Shawnee and Wyandott from Kansas.

The United States agents present were Major G. C. Snow for the Osage, Quapaw, Seneca and Shawnee; George A. Reynolds for the Seminole; Isaac Colman for the Choctaw and Chickasaw; Justin Harlan for the Cherokee; J. W. Dunn for the Creek; Milo Gookins for the Wichita and other affiliated tribes located within the country leased by the Chickasaws and Choctaws; and J. B. Abbot for the Shawnee in Kansas. The delegation from the disloyal Indians had not arrived, and the Delaware as well as the Sac and Fox tribes located in Kansas were expected but were not present for any of the sessions.

On the way to Fort Smith Cooley wired Secretary of the Interior Harlan from Fort Leavenworth and asked for instruction on procedures. Harlan replied he should commence by saying the President was willing to grant peace, but that he wanted land for other Indians, and a civil government for the whole Territory. Cooley's report of 1865 embodied practically the exact instructions. Obviously the United States government felt that this was an ideal time for effecting these two pet projects of long standing since the Five Civilized Nations had all signed Confederate treaties of alliance, thus classing them as "rebels" in the sight of the United States government.

The council was called to order on September 8 by Cooley and a prayer was offered in the Cherokee language by the Reverend Lewis Downing, acting chief of the Cherokees, after which Cooley addressed the Indians. In accordance with Secretary of the Interior Harlan's ideas, the tribes were informed generally of the object for which the commission had come to them. Cooley told them that they had as tribes for the most part violated their United States treaties by making treaties with the Confederacy. Because of this action they had forfeited all rights under their treaties with the United States and they must be considered as being at the mercy of the government. There would be shown, however, every disposition to treat them leniently and above all a determination would be made to recognize in a single manner the loyalty of those who fought upon the side of the government and who had endured great suffering on its behalf. When Cooley finished several replies came from the Indians. The general consensus of the representatives of the Five Civilized Nations was that, not knowing the object of the council until that time, they would have to consult among themselves, and they therefore asked time for deliberation.

In the afternoon of the first day Cooley requested the representatives to make replies to the morning address as they might desire. The Five Civilized Nations submitted that they did not have the proper authority to make a treaty or to enter into any arrangement with any of the Indian tribes. Most declared that they thought the purpose of the council was to make peace with the southern element. Robert B. Patton, representing the loyal Choctaw but not a delegate, maintained that he was there to seek certain rights due them under the 1855 treaty.

Beginning the Reconstruction Process

On the second day Cooley acknowledged the speeches made by the various tribal representatives. He made known again that the policy of the government called for the negotiation of treaties with the Nations, tribes or bands of Indians in Indian Territory, Kansas or on the plains west of Indian Territory. Again Cooley named the Nations and tribes who by making treaties with the enemies of the United States had forfeited all right to annuities, lands and protection by the United States. The delegates were also informed that the commissioners were empowered to negotiate with the tribes upon the following propositions:

1. Each tribe must enter into a treaty for permanent peace and amity among themselves as tribes and with the United States.
2. The tribes settled in Indian Territory were to agree, at the call of United States authorities, to assist in compelling the tribes of the plains to keep peace.
3. Slavery must be abolished and measures taken to incorporate the slaves into the tribes, with their civil rights guaranteed.

4. A general stipulation that slavery was henceforth abolished and involuntary servitude would never again exist in the tribes or Nation, except in punishment of crime, must be incorporated in the new treaties.

5. A part of Indian Territory would be set aside to be purchased for the use of Indians from Kansas or elsewhere, as the government might desire to colonize therein.

6. The policy of the government to unite all of the Indian tribes of the region into one consolidated government should be accepted.

7. No white persons except government employees or officers or employees of internal improvement companies authorized by the government would be permitted to reside among the Indians unless adopted by the several Nations.

In these proposals for new treaties not only were the features of the Harlan Bill recognized but also Commissioner Dole's plan for the concentration of all Indians within the territory occupied by the Five Civilized Nations and Senator James H. Lane's bill of 1863 providing for the removal of the Indians from Kansas. The Indians were reminded again that the loyal factions would be provided for and treated liberally.

Most of the Indians continued to declare that they were not authorized to negotiate or conclude treaties with the United States government for they had not been informed before coming to Fort Smith as to the purpose for which the council was called. They maintained the attitude that they represented only a small portion of the different tribes and therefore felt it would be necessary to submit the proposed treaties to the tribes as a whole for acceptance. The delegates from the Union faction of the Cherokees, relying upon the recent assurances of favor, protested against the attitude of the commission. On the fourth day of the council Cooley replied to them and denounced their leader, John Ross, as one who wrote, published and spoke in favor of the Confederate alliance for many months before the treaty was made.

In deference to the number of tribes questioning the third and seventh propositions Cooley announced that there was in preparation a simple treaty of peace and amity for the signature of all the delegates present, leaving all questions growing out of the recent treaties with the so-called Confederate States to be settled at this or some future council. The treaty of peace was read on the fifth day of the council to the predominantly loyal audience; it gave large attention, however, to the allegiance of factions of the tribes to the Confederacy and to the liabilities which this involved. The treaty also recorded the maintenance of Federal military supremacy in Indian Territory, and it spoke of generous and magnanimous intentions on the part of the Federal government. The treaty did not embody the seven propositions that Cooley announced in the beginning. It was only a recognition of allegiance to the United States, and it possessed no reconstruction features.

The United States through its commissioners promised that peace and friendship with all Indian nations and tribes would be reestablished and declared its willingness at this council or at any time in the future to enter into treaties to arrange and settle all questions relating to and growing out of former treaties made by these nations with the Confederacy. In the meantime and in the remaining days of this council meeting, explanations and protestations of various sorts were made concerning the position of each tribe.

The formal signing of the treaty of peace and amity began on the sixth day with the United States commissioners leading the way followed by the Senecas, Shawnees, Quapaws, Seminoles and Chickasaws. The Creeks refused to sign unless a statement exonerating them from all complicity in making an alliance with the Confederacy was accepted for filing by the commissioners. Cooley objected at first, remarking that he saw nothing in the treaty to which any loyal person could take exception, but he later announced that the treaty had been revised to meet Creek objections and they signed later on the sixth day.

It was expected that the Cherokees would sign on the morning of the seventh day, but before doing so, Colonel H. D. Reese, their spokesman, declared that while his delegation was willing to sign the treaty, in so doing they did not acknowledge that they had forfeited their rights and privileges to annuities and lands, for the loyal Cherokees were not guilty. He continued by saying that they wished to sign the treaty under a proviso which would make it clear that the execution of the treaty of October 7, 1861, was procured by the coercion of the rebel army. Upon reassembling for the afternoon session of the seventh day, Cooley read a paper signed by the members of the United States Commission declining recognition of John Ross as Principal Chief. John Ross, who had entered the council room on September 15, E. C. Boudinot and Cooley then engaged in a brief controversy over the position of Ross before the council adjourned.

On the eighth day, September 16, the delegations from Armstrong Academy came to the council room although Governor Colbert, Boudinot, and J. W. Washbourne had been in Fort Smith since the fifth day. The treaty was interpreted to them and at their urgent solicitation time was granted them to consult upon its stipulations. Pending further action by the council Commissioner Wistar addressed the Armstrong Academy delegations, reminding them that the restoration and perpetuation of peace was the purpose at hand.

Soon after the delivery of the address by Wistar the commissioners received a communication from Robert M. Jones, president of the southern Choctaw delegation, and Colbert Carter, president of the southern Chickasaw delegation, and from the loyal Chickasaw delegation to the effect that they had been informed that Colonel Parker, one of the commissioners, was about to leave to visit the Indians of the plains. They requested that his departure be delayed until the business of the council was completed, stating as a reason the fact that, as a member of an Indian tribe and as one of the commissioners of the government of the United States, he had inspired them with confidence as to its desires for the Indian nations and that they were anxious to have the benefit of his presence and counsel in any deliberations or interviews with the commission. General Harney volunteered to relieve Colonel Parker and go in his stead. At this stage of the proceedings the Creeks, loyal Choctaws and southern Cherokees expressed their approval of the request for the detention of Colonel Parker and wished to be considered as parties to it.

The southern Cherokee delegation, represented by Boudinot, presented their credentials, accompanied by a statement which the delegates desired to be read and recorded. On Cooley's seven proposals they gave ready assent to the first, second, fourth, fifth and seventh. Tribal incorporation of Negroes, the general colonization of Negroes and the organization of Indian Territory received serious objections, and they requested time to weigh each of these plans. The document also spoke of the Cherokee dissensions and respectfully suggested that after all the blood that had been shed and the intense bitterness that had been exhibited a division of the country should be in order.

After the document had been read Boudinot proceeded to make some remarks in explanation of the statement and began commenting critically upon the course of certain loyal Cherokees but Cooley, the commission president, stopped him. A short controversy then took place between Boudinot, John Ross and William P. Ross which was ended by Cooley. He then stated that the council would listen to one speech or statement at the next session from anyone of the loyal faction of the Cherokee Nation in order that the commissioners might ascertain the facts of both parties to the controversy in the Cherokee Nation.

On the ninth day, September 18, the loyal Cherokee delegation presented a statement in reply to the action of the commissioners in the case of John Ross. The statement defended Chief Ross, assured the commissioners that he was the real chief and not a pretended one and requested that the commissioners rescind their previous decision. Also on the morning of the ninth day the Creek and Seminole Nations announced their reunited status. The Seminoles expressed a general willingness to consider favorably the terms offered by the commissioners. The southern Creeks, the southern Cherokees and the remaining loyal Cherokees who had not signed previously all signed the treaty.

During the afternoon session of the ninth day the secessionist Choctaws and Chickasaws voiced their opinions. They signed the treaty of peace and amity with the understanding that they were signing a treaty preliminary to the making of a treaty or treaties that would definitely determine their future relations with the United States. At this time Watie of the southern Cherokees also signed. Cooley announced that a joint committee of the loyal and disloyal branches of the Cherokees had been formed to settle their differences. Wistar was appointed to work with the Cherokee committee, and Sells and Parker were to confer with the committee of the Choctaws and Chickasaws in relation to the content of additional treaties.

On the tenth day Commissioner Sells asked for a report from the Cherokee committee. Boudinot from the southern delegation presented a petition calling attention to the destitute Cherokees in the Choctaw and Chickasaw Nations and sought aid from the government to relieve the situation. Sells assured him that if Cooley, who was ill at this time, had no authority to act, the matter would be brought to the attention of Secretary of the Interior Harlan. As far as the work of the committee was concerned it was regretted that the members were unable to suggest an acceptable scheme for the settlement of Cherokee domestic division.

The commission offered resolutions on the eleventh day thanking General Bussey for his courteous attention in providing facilities to aid the work of the Fort Smith conference. Cooley also announced that the action of the commission concerning John Ross was justified and would not be rescinded. On September 21, the last day of the conference, Commissioner Parker reported that the committee of Choctaw–Chickasaw delegates had submitted to the commission certain amendments and modifications of the proposed treaty which the commissioners declined. Parker further announced that the delegations would be furnished with a copy of the proposed treaty as set forth by the United States, and whenever they determined to approve it, by notifying the Commissioner of Indian Affairs, they would be invited to Washington to consummate the treaty. Commissioner Parker on behalf of the commission thanked the various delegations and wished them a happy journey home.

Boudinot, speaking for the southern Cherokees and the Seminoles, remarked that consolidation for all the Indian nations into one territorial government was one of the noblest schemes ever devised for the red man and entitled the author to the lasting gratitude of every Indian. The council was then adjourned sine die. After the adjournment Cooley announced that a treaty had been concluded with both factions of the Osage, ceding the government a large tract of land. Cooley also announced that the terms of a treaty were agreed upon with the representatives of both factions of the Creek tribe for a cession of all their land lying north of the Arkansas River and for a part of the area situated south of that stream.

The United States and the "Indian Problem"

The second reconstruction period of the Five Civilized Nations in Indian Territory paralleled the era when the United States government believed that the "Indian problem" needed a permanent solution, for the question of the proper method of handling Indians had perplexed the United States from the beginning. From the establishment of the Federal government down to 1849 the administration of Indian affairs was conducted under the supervision of a bureau in the War Department but in 1849 was transferred to the newly created Department of the Interior. During the crucial period of reconstruction in Indian Territory following 1865, the advisability of transferring authority over the Indians from the Department of the Interior back to the War Department was being discussed. The army found occasion in the confused situation following the Civil War to demand restoration of the power it had originally possessed. The Interior Department was not willing to surrender its control without a struggle and from 1867 to 1870 the question of a change in control dominated consideration of the Indian's welfare.

In the early years after the Louisiana Purchase of 1803 the United States administrators had arrived at a solution to the "Indian problem" by moving tribes to the West. Though Indians often strongly resisted a location change, as illustrated by some of the Cherokees and Seminoles, it was only following the gold rush of 1849 that the wisdom of settling western lands with Indians began to be questioned. Then the "Indian problem" became really serious. But the country was too preoccupied by this time with the issue of Negro slavery in areas outside of Indian Territory to worry much about these Indians. It was not until the Civil War had ended, and over seven million acres of western land were being sold annually, that the United States government recognized that a permanent solution of the "Indian problem" could not be much longer postponed. Once government reserves were depleted Indians must be permitted to remain either where they were or be moved at once before the last places available for settlement were exhausted. Government officials decided upon removal and concentration as a solution to the problem.

With Indian Territory the gateway to the southwest, and even more after the war than before, the possession of part of it for white settlement seemed desirable. The fact that the Five Civilized Tribes had allied with the Confederacy gave the United States government the excuse to carry out a new Indian policy in restoring political relations with these people. The new reconstruction treaties could easily provide the necessary vehicle for securing additional land for Indian concentration with a consolidated territorial government.

Even during the war legislation was enacted against certain Indians to bring about their removal to Indian Territory. On February 18, 1862, the legislature of Kansas adopted resolutions calling upon the United States to purchase and throw open to settlement the Cherokee "Neutral Lands," and the Osage, Pottawatomie, Kickapoo, Sac and Fox, Ottawa Kansas, Iowa, Sac and Fox of Missouri, and absent Shawnee Indian lands. These resolutions were presented in the United States Senate on March 24 and on that day Senator Samuel C. Pomeroy from Kansas introduced Senate Bill No. 245 for the removal and consolidation of these Indian tribes. On April 16 in an obvious move to secure room for the Indians of Kansas he introduced Senate Bill No. 272 to establish the "Territory of Lanniwa," which would have included the present state of Oklahoma and Texas north of the Red River. Representative Cyrus Aldrich from Minnesota introduced in the United States House on June 2 a bill with the same title. The Senate Committee on Indian Affairs reported both bills introduced by Pomeroy on June 25 with the recommendation that they should not be considered further in that session. Representative Aldrich's bill was not reported at the time by the House Committee on Territories, to which it had been referred.

In reviewing measures reflecting the idea that more Indian land cession consolidations were not new, efforts of the Federal government and especially those of Senator James Lane of Kansas and Senator James Harlan of Iowa, who later became Secretary of the Interior, should not be overlooked. Mention has already been made concerning the 1863 effort to induce the Creek refugees to cede a choice portion of their land to the United States. The portion under consideration had been occupied by the Confederate faction of the Creeks and included the most valuable part of the Creek territory. The Senate amended the treaty of cession but the Creeks did not accept the amendment and the matter was dropped until the end of the war.

Lane introduced a bill in the United States Senate on December 15, 1862, to authorize the President to treat with the Indians of Kansas for their removal. He reported this bill, Senate Bill Number 413, on January 21, 1863, from the Committee on

Indian Affairs with an amendment authorizing the President to secure land in Indian Territory by treaty or otherwise for the Indians of Kansas. This amendment had been suggested by Secretary of the Interior Caleb B. Smith. Lane's bill as amended was attached to the Indian appropriation bill by the Senate on February 25 and three days later the House concurred in this action. Thus the plan of removing the Indians of Kansas to Indian Territory became a part of the law of the land on March 3, 1863.

Early in 1865, on February 20, Senator Harlan of Iowa introduced Senate Bill Number 459 to consolidate the Indian tribes and establish civil government in Indian Territory. This bill was reported by the Senate Committee on Indian Affairs and without delay was considered in the Senate. Although the bill passed the Senate it did not receive consideration in the House of Representatives. The Harlan bill was significant in that it influenced the agreements of 1865 and 1866 with the Nations. This was easily manipulated as Harlan was appointed Secretary of the Interior by President Johnson and he began his tenure of office on May 15, 1865. By January of 1866 Harlan had been replaced by O. H. Browning as Secretary of the Interior, but the groundwork had been laid and Cooley, also of Iowa, was still Commissioner of Indian Affairs and in control of the negotiations of the reconstruction treaties.

Completing the Washington Formulae for Reconstruction

Double delegations representing the Federal and Confederate factions in each of the Five Civilized Nations appeared in Washington in January 1866. Their purpose was to conclude formal treaties with the United States for the settlement of all questions of difference resulting from the war, and for reestablishing the Indians upon their lands under clearly defined provisions applying to all classes of their population. The negotiations were entered into on the part of the government by Cooley, the Commissioner of Indian Affairs, Colonel Parker, and Superintendent Sells, all of whom served on the Fort Smith council commission.

Four principal points came up for settlement:

1. The method of adjusting problems between the loyal and disloyal Indians, a problem applying especially to the

Cherokees where confiscation laws, passed by their National Council, had taken effect upon the property of those who had supported the Confederacy.

2. The relations which the freedmen should hold toward the remainder of the people.

3. Compensation for losses of property suffered by those who remained loyal.

4. Cession of lands by the several tribes to be used for the settlement of Kansas and other Indians. Commissioner Cooley did not list the granting of right of way for railroads as a principal point for settlement but inasmuch as the item appeared in each treaty it should be considered a principal point of settlement.

The first nation with whom agreement was made was the Seminoles. The treaty between these Indians and the United States contained eleven articles and was concluded on March 21, 1866; ratification was advised by the Senate on July 19 and it was proclaimed on August 16. By this treaty renewed pledges of peace and friendship were made and a complete amnesty was granted for all offenses resulting from the war. Slavery was abolished and the freedmen placed upon an equal footing with the remainder of the people. This equality was more easily accomplished in the case of the Seminoles since there had already been considerable intermingling of the races before the tribe removed from Florida; several of the interpreters accompanying the delegation representing the tribe appeared to be of African blood. The Indians ceded to the government the entire domain secured to them by the treaty of 1856, amounting to approximately two million one hundred sixty-nine thousand acres, for which they received the sum of $325,362. They received a new reservation of two hundred thousand acres at the junction of the Canadian River with its north fork for which they would pay $100,000 down with the balance of $225,362 to be paid as follows: $30,000 to establish them upon their new reservation; $20,000 to purchase stock, seeds and tools; $15,000 for a mill; $50,000 to be invested as a school fund; $20,000 as a national fund; $40,362 for subsistence and $50,000 for losses of loyal Seminoles, to be ascertained by a board of commissioners. A right of way for railroads was granted through the new reservation and a sum of approximately $10,000 was to be expended for agency buildings.

The Seminoles agreed to the establishment, if Congress

provided, of a General Council in Indian Territory. This would be convened annually, would consist of delegates from all the tribes in proportion to their numbers and would have power to legislate upon matters relating to the relations of the several tribes resident in the Indian country. The laws passed by the General Council were to be consistent with treaty stipulations and the Constitution of the United States and the council itself was to be presided over by the Superintendent of Indian Affairs.

The Seminoles ratified the diversion of annuities made during the war for support of refugees, but the payments due under their former treaties were to be renewed and continued as heretofore. They granted use of 640 acres of land to each society erecting mission or school buildings, to revert to the tribe when no longer used for its purpose. The treaty was signed by Cooley, Sells and Parker for the United States and by John Chupco, Chocte-harjo and Fos-harjo for the Seminoles. John F. Brown signed as a special delegate for the southern Seminoles.

The fact that a majority of the Seminoles had chosen to suffer incredible hardships on the flight from Cooper's military force rather than repudiate their treaties with the United States had no visable effect upon the treaty makers. The statement in the preamble to the effect that the United States required a cession of land by the Seminoles and was willing to pay a reasonable price cannot be regarded as consistent with the price agreed upon. Fifteen cents an acre was the price agreed upon for the government to pay the Seminoles yet the Seminoles would have to pay fifty cents an acre for the two hundred thousand acres to be purchased from the Creeks.

Perhaps one reason that the Seminoles could negotiate with the government so quickly was that both the loyal and disloyal factions were so stricken after the Civil War that they evinced little concern for political differences. To become settled and to begin the process of reconstruction was possibly the major underlying factor in their reasoning. Their delegates were regarded not as partisan but as national representatives. With respect to the purchase money that would be due from the United States for the Seminole cession the commissioners arranged that no money would actually pass into the hands of the Seminoles. Out of the sale price of $325,362 was to be deducted the purchase price of the new reserve and then all charges for rehabilitation. The disbursement of the surplus of $90,362 was to be divided between relief and repaying the loyal faction for the losses it had sustained.

A joint treaty was next made with the Choctaw and Chickasaw Nations. The Choctaws and Chickasaws started preparation early for the 1866 treaty negotiations. They had selected their delegates in October, the Choctaws through their National Council and the Chickasaws through their legislature, which met for the first time since it passed the secession ordinance in 1861. Ignored in each instance by Choctaws and Chickasaws alike was the loyal minority. Robert M. Jones, Alfred Wade, John Page, Allen Wright and James Riley composed the Choctaw delegation as originally constituted although Chief Peter Pitchlynn took an active part in the negotiations. Colbert Carter, Holmes Colbert and Edmund Pickens were the selected Chickasaw delegates.

The contrast between the Choctaw-Chickasaw and Seminole treaties is of greater historical significance than the similarity. The Choctaws and the Chickasaws had been in the vanguard of the secession movement and with some slight wavering had supported the Confederacy until the end. But they were a powerful group and their leading half breeds were shrewd politicians. They had been well instructed beforehand and had some points of issue ready for bargaining purposes. They were not to cede under any condition any portion of the territory they occupied; if the United States commissioners should insist they were to refer the commissioners directly to the people. They might make concessions regarding the Leased District though they were if possible to exact payment for its relinquishment or seek to retain their ownership of the land while surrendering their jurisdiction. But they were willing if it became mandatory to give up the Leased District without compensation, or surrender all of their tribal monies, or even submit to the settlement of Kansas Indians within their occupied territory. They were also to demand compensation for the emancipation of their slaves; this item could be surrendered in exchange for the undisturbed possession of their lands exclusive of the Leased District.

This treaty contained no preamble like that of the Seminoles and therefore no charge of liability to forfeiture, no statement of indebtedness and no presumptive evidence of guilt. The fifty-one articles were concluded April 28, 1866, ratification was advised with amendment on June 28, the amendments were accepted on July 2 and the treaty was proclaimed on July 10. The usual provisions were made for the reestablishment of peace and friendship, for amnesty and for the abolition of slavery in every form. The Indians ceded to the government the whole of the Leased District, which had been rented by the government for the use of Indians removed from Texas. For this tract, which amounted to about six million eight hundred thousand acres, the government was to pay $300,000 to be invested at five percent interest until laws were passed by the Choctaws and Chickasaws providing full rights, privileges and immunities, and grants of forty acres of land for each of their freedmen. The time limit for the passage of such laws was two years. If the laws were passed, the $300,000 with its accumulated interest was to be paid, three-quarters to the Choctaws and one-quarter to the Chickasaws. If such laws were not passed, then the $300,000 would be kept and used by the government for the benefit of the freedmen.

One of two arrangements was to be made at the expiration of two years with respect to the $300,000 trust fund. If the Indians had provided for their freedmen according to the treaty stipulation then the money was to be paid over to them as the purchase price for their lands. From it was to be first deducted $100 for every freedmen who actually removed himself from the Choctaw or Chickasaw Nations. If, on the other hand, the Indians had not made the requisite provision for their freedmen the $300,000 was to be held by the United States not as the Chickasaw-Choctaw trust fund but for the use and benefit of such persons of African descent as the United States could induce to remove from the Choctaw-Chickasaw country within ninety days from the expiration of the two years. Freedmen who returned or remained subsequent to that time were to be denied the benefits and were to be upon the same footing as other citizens of the United States in the Choctaw and Chickasaw Nations. These two Nations were specifically exempted from adopting the freedmen as full members of the tribes and from admitting them as community sharers in tribal lands, annuities and other monies.

Sectionalization or the division of the land according to the method of the General Land Office had been much advocated even before the war and was now urged upon the two Nations.

It was agreed that within the reserved territory lying east of the ninety-eighth meridian Kansas Indians not exceeding 10,000 could settle and be granted the same civil, political and economic status as was to be conferred upon the freedmen. The United States agreed to pay for the land that they would occupy at the rate of one dollar an acre.

A right of way would be granted for railroads through the reservation from the north to the south and from the east to the west upon compensation for damages done to property. The tribes could subscribe to the stock of the particular company such amount or amounts as they could pay for in alternate sections of unoccupied lands, for a space of six miles on each side of the railroads, at a price per acre to be agreed upon between the Choctaw and Chickasaw Nations and the company subject to the approval of the President of the United States.

The two Nations agreed to accept legislation that Congress and the President might consider necessary for the better administration of justice and the protection of persons and property within Indian Territory provided that such legislation did not in any way interfere with the tribal organization or their respective legislatures and judiciaries, or the rights, laws, privileges or customs of the Choctaw and Chickasaw Nations. They also agreed that a council consisting of delegates elected by each Nation or tribe within Indian Territory should convene annually. The number of delegates would be alloted after a census was taken at the rate designated by the treaty of one member from each nation whose population exceeded 500, and an additional member for each 1,000 Indians, native or adopted, or each fraction of 1,000 greater than 500. This assembly would have power to legislate upon all matters pertaining to the relations of the Indian Nations and tribes resident in Indian Territory. Naturally no law should be enacted inconsistent with the Constitution of the United States or laws of Congress. The Superintendent of Indian Affairs was to be endowed with the title of Governor of the Territory of Oklahoma (this is the first use of the name Oklahoma in a treaty or similar government document).

The organization of Indian Territory as a regularly organized Federal territory had not yet been provided for by law nor was it done in this treaty. But from this point the Choctaw-Chickasaw treaty proceeded as if it were an accomplished fact.

The suggestion that, should Congress see fit to authorize the appointment of a delegate from Indian Territory he should be elected in the council presupposed the existence of an organized territory. The provisions in regard to a General Council were more detailed in the Choctaw-Chickasaw treaty than in the other treaties. Provision was made for a secretary of the Council and for pay of members. A marshal was provided for at an annual salary of $500. There was also a clause which suggested the establishment of an upper house to consist of one member from each tribe.

The United States acknowledged all prewar agreements with these unequivocal secessionists and no prewar guaranties or obligations had seemingly suffered any impairment except that the United States made no offer to reimburse the Nation for their funds lost during the war, as indeed the United States paid no Confederate state, nation or tribe for such losses. Only the loyal factions of the tribes were eligible for reimbursement. Claimants for indemnity were thus few in number so it was an easy matter to provide for them. A commission was to be appointed to consider and determine the claims of such Choctaws and Chickasaws. The report would need to be ratified by the Secretary of the Interior, and his approval would authorize the payment of the amount from Choctaw-Chickasaw funds in the hands of the United States. Licensed traders were also empowered to present their cases to a special commission. The aggregate of the claims was not to exceed $90,000.

There was to be no interference with the continuous occupation of the missionaries established in the Choctaw and Chickasaw Nations. Should any missionary who had been engaged in missionary work for five consecutive years before the date of this treaty, or three consecutive years prior to the Civil War, and who, if absent from the Nations, desired to return, he could select a quarter of land for a permanent home for himself and family. His choice of land could not include any public buildings, schools or seminaries; his quantity of land could not exceed 640 acres, to be selected according to legal subdivisions in one body. No land thus granted, nor the buildings erected thereon, could ever be sold or otherwise disposed of except with the consent of the legislatures of the Nations and approval by the Secretary of the Interior.

The Choctaw and Chickasaw legislatures had the right to select one quarter-section of land in each of the counties in trust for the establishment of seats of justice. They also had the right to select as many quarter-sections as they would consider necessary for the permanent endowment of schools, seminaries and colleges, provided the selection did not embrace or interfere with any improvement of any member of the Nation without his consent. These same authorities should see to it that the proceeds of sale of a quarter-section selected for a seat of justice should be appropriated for the erection or improvement of public buildings in the county in which it was located. In every township the sections of land numbered sixteen and thirty-six were reserved for the support of schools therein. If the particular section had already been occupied by proper persons then the legislative authorities of that nation had the right to select such other sections as would seem proper. Members of these nations were to be received as competent witnesses in United States courts. Criminals taking refuge within their boundaries were to be returned upon requisition, and post offices were to be established in the country.

These various provisions were considered to comprise the major points of the fifty-one articles. The treaty was signed by Alfred Wade, Allen Wright, James Riley and John Page, the Choctaw commissioners who were present when negotiations were concluded. The Chickasaw commissioners who signed were Winchester Colbert, Edmund Pickens, Holmes Colbert, Colbert Carter and Robert Love. Campbell LeFlore served as secretary of the Choctaw delegation and E. S. Mitchell as secretary to the Chickasaws.

The next treaty was made with the Creeks. It was concluded on June 14, 1866, ratification was advised with amendment on July 19, the amendment was accepted on July 23 and the treaty itself was proclaimed on August 11. This instrument was relatively short for it contained but fourteen articles reestablishing peace and friendship and declared amnesty for past offenses. It also established full equality of rights and privileges for the freedman and promised them a share in the national soil and funds.

The adjustment of the Creek treaty sections concerning the status of the freedmen consumed much time. The loyal delegation appeared in Washington first and with them a treaty was made which recognized the status of the freedmen to be one of full equality; about the time this version of the treaty was agreed to, other delegates came representing the southern or

disloyal Creeks. These people constituted about one-half of the
Creeks and they strenuously opposed the consummation of the
treaty on account of this provision. They engaged able counsel
and as the result of their opposition the treaty was revised. It
appeared at one time as if all negotiations would fail and the
commissioners, knowing the necessity of a settlement and the
relief needs of the Creek destitute, were disposed to urge the
delegates to yield the point for the present. But the Federal
Creeks held out firmly for the freedmen, urging that when the
brave old Opothleyahola resisted all the blandishments of the
Confederate emissaries and led a large number of people out of
Indian Territory fighting as they went, they promised their
slaves that if they would remain faithful to the government they
should be as free as themselves. Under these circumstances
the delegates declined to yield but insisted that this pledge be
fulfilled, declaring that they would sooner go home and fight
and suffer again with their faithful friends than abandon the
point. They were successful at last and the treaty guaranteed to
their freedmen full equality.

The Creeks ceded to the government, to be used for the
settlement of other Indians, the western half of their domain
estimated at about three million two hundred fifty thousand
acres of land, for which the government was to pay $975,168 in
the following manner: $200,000 to enable the Creeks to reoccu-
py and restore their farms and improvements, to pay damages to
mission schools, and to pay the expenses of the delegates to
Washington; $100,000 for the losses of soldiers enlisted in the
United States Army and to loyal refugees and freedmen; $400,-
000 to be paid per capita to the Creeks as it would accrue from
the sale of lands; interest on the last two sums at five per cent to
be used for the Creeks at the discretion of the Secretary of
the Interior; and the remaining to be paid to the Indians
annually. The amounts due to the soldiers and refugees were to
be ascertained under the direction of the Superintendent of the
Southern Superintendency and the Creek Agent and reported to
the Department of the Interior for approval. The retained
eastern half of the Creek reserve was promised to them in
perpetuity.

Right of way for railroads was provided, the western boundary was to be surveyed at the expense of the United States, and
an amount not exceeding $10,000 was to be expended by the
Federal government in the erection of agency buildings upon

the diminished reservation. The provisions for a general council were the same as in the Seminole treaty. Annuities as provided in former treaties were to be renewed and continued, and the government promised to pay up to $10,000 for the expenses of negotiating the new treaty.

The Creeks were also cheated slightly in the land transactions as the Seminoles were required to pay fifty cents an acre for the Creek land and the government paid the Creeks only thirty cents an acre. The wording of the treaties made by the United States with the Seminoles and Creeks made them sound guiltier of war disloyalty than the wording of the Choctaw and Chickasaw treaty although it was the latter that cooperated almost wholeheartedly with the Confederacy. Both the Creek and Seminole treaties contained the same insistence that these Indians had incurred the liability of forfeiture due to their alliance with the Confederate States. The Creek commission was composed of Ok-ta-has Harjo, Cow Mikko, Cotch-cho-chee, D. N. McIntosh and James Smith.

The Cherokees, torn by feuds and dissensions, sent two delegations to Washington in 1866, each hoping to be recognized as the rightful one. In October of 1865 the loyal faction had sent a petition addressed to President Johnson in behalf of John Ross in an effort to secure his approval for having Ross officially recognized as head of the Cherokee delegation. In this petition they set forth the fact that they were left absolutely without the support of Federal officials or arms at the opening of the Civil War. On November 7 the Cherokee National Council, relying upon the United States to do full justice to Ross upon a fair and impartial investigation, empowered him to act with the delegation that was sent to Washington. Ross himself felt that his past communications with President Lincoln indicated that he would be exonerated.

Although the Office of Indian Affairs had done nothing to recognize John Ross as the Cherokee chief, the Cherokee executive council remained loyal to him and would not act without him. Seven delegates were provided for by joint action of the National Council. They were Smith Christie, White Catcher, Daniel Ross, a nephew of John Ross, S. H. Benge, John B. Jones, and Thomas Pegg. Lewis Downing, the acting principal chief, had on November 6 given them their credentials which were recognized by the United States government on January 30, 1866. The treaty was concluded on July 18, 1866, ratification

was advised with amendment on July 27, the amendment
was accepted on July 31 and the treaty was proclaimed on
August 11.

The Cherokee southern delegation was also alert. E. C.
Boudinot and W. P. Adair, the first to arrive in Washington,
began at once to lay plans in their behalf. The southern delegation also included Stand Watie, his son, Saladin Watie, and
John Rollins Ridge, who came from California, where he had
lived since about 1850. Before all matters were settled Boudinot
and Ridge became hostile to each other.

More difficulty was experienced in completing the treaty with
the Cherokees than with any of the other tribes or Nations of the
Indian Territory. This difficulty had been previously encountered by the commissioners at Fort Smith in 1865. The trouble
was basically due to a political schism of long standing which
erupted anew during the Civil War. The Cherokee Nation had
long been divided into two factions known as the Ross and
Ridge parties with quarrels going back to the time when the
people lived in Georgia. The Ridge party favored the treaty by
which the removal to the West was effected while the Ross party
opposed; but after the removal the Ross party being the most
numerous, obtained and kept the ascendancy and practically
ruled the Nation. There were many men of intelligence,
education and ability on both sides and old jealousies increased
from year to year. The Ridge party under the leadership of
Stand Watie and others endeavored to secure a division of the
Nation and its funds, which the Ross party strenuously opposed.
The Ridge party readily entered into an alliance with the
Confederacy but the Ross party maintained that it was coerced
into making a treaty with the Confederacy inasmuch as it had
no Federal protection. In 1863 the Ross faction deserted the
Confederacy, reconvened the National Council, emancipated its
slaves and vigorously supported the Union.

The two delegations, representing opposing views, came to
Washington and conference after conference ensued with each
of the parties. Both sides engaged able counsel who appeared in
their behalf when important questions were under consideration. Draft after draft of treaties were made and several sections clearly agreed upon when some new differences would
arise and all arrangements would be overturned. The southern
delegates insisted that their people should be separated from
the remainder of the Nation as they could not and would not

live with the other faction. The other party, operating the national organization, insisted that the Nation should not be divided.

About the middle of June 1866 the commissioners, despairing of a satisfactory arrangement with the Ross party, made a treaty with the Ridge party. This instrument contained a provision that the southern party, though not formally separated from the Nation, should be allowed a certain part of the area for their exclusive use and occupancy. They agreed to sell their right to certain portions of the national domain. This treaty was not laid before the Senate but after another month of negotiation another treaty was finally concluded on July 19, 1866. Although not entirely satisfactory to either party it was the best possible settlement attainable. It partially satisfied the Ross party by continuing the Nation under one constitution and one government and it also protected the other party from the apprehension of persecution by the loyal faction by locating them in a specific part of the domain. The treaty also provided that suits between Cherokees involving people of the opposing parties should be tried in the United States courts.

The Cherokees agreed further in the new treaty to repudiate the alliance made with the Confederacy on October 7, 1861, and were granted amnesty for all past offenses. The loyal faction agreed to repeal their confiscation laws and the Watie party would be allowed to settle in a part of their country known as the Canadian District. Also in this area any of the freedmen could locate on a portion of land set apart for them in parcels of 160 acres for each person. Those who settled in the Leased District could select their own judges, make their own police regulations and elect delegates to the Cherokee National Council. A United States court was to be established in the territory.

Licenses to trade, except in the Canadian District, were not to be granted except by consent of the Cherokee National Council. Slavery was abolished and full civil rights for the freedmen were acknowledged. The right of way for railroads was secured, consent was given to a general council as in the Seminole treaty and land was set apart for church and school sites. Provisions were made for the settlement of friendly Indians of other tribes among the Cherokees either by abandoning their own tribal organization and residing in the more compactly settled eastern part of Cherokee Nation or by retaining their tribal existence and settling further west; in either case land occupied by them was to be paid for at prices to be agreed upon between the United States government and the Cherokees. The Cherokee tract of eight hundred thousand acres in Kansas was ceded to the Federal government in trust, to be surveyed and sold for the benefit of the Indians; the proceeds were to be invested for them in the proportion of thirty-five percent for education, fifteen percent for an orphan fund, and fifty percent for the national fund; this tract could be sold at one time for cash at one dollar per acre.

All sums belonging to heirs of deceased soldiers remaining unclaimed after two years would be devoted to an asylum for orphans of soldiers. It was agreed to give the Reverend Evan Jones $3,000 as a testimony of appreciation for his forty years of service to the Cherokees as a missionary. The United States agreed to pay $10,000 for provisions and supplies furnished by the Cherokees to the Creeks during the winter of 1861 and 1862. It was further agreed to pay to the proper claimants an indemnity for losses of property by missionaries resulting from their being ordered or driven from the country by the United States agents and for the loss of their property taken and occupied or destroyed by United States troops, not exceeding the sum of $20,000. The Cherokee treaty was the last of the series negotiated with the Five Civilized Nations. There were many problems ahead; for the provisions of the reconstruction treaties as established by the government would have to be met, and in some instances within a limited amount of time.

Summary

The attitude of the commissioners toward the loyal faction of the Five Civilized Nations at the Fort Smith peace council was an indication that additional problems would develop. A war not of their making had disrupted every phase of their lives, bringing to them nothing but destruction, tragedy, heartache and general misfortune. Now the "Great Father in Washington" seemed to blame them for a defection in which they had little choice, as appeals to no avail had been made to Washington for protection. Even their land seemed to be in jeopardy for it had been indicated at Fort Smith that a measure of it would probably be lost. It was a bitter price to pay for an involvement not entirely of their choosing.

The Washington treaties of 1866 divided Indian Territory into two almost equal sections. The original area of the Five Civilized Nations had been practically halved by the cessions of the Creek, Seminole, Choctaw, and Chickasaw and the Cherokee agreement to permit the government to settle other tribes in the Cherokee Outlet. Though these two sections were almost equal in land area their subsequent histories were distinctly different. In the eastern section, known as Indian Territory, the Five Civilized Nations resumed their development in peace and under orderly government conducted basically by themselves until tribal dissolution began about 1898. In the western side that became known as Oklahoma Territory, the government settled tribes of eastern origin from Kansas and the nomadic tribes of the southern plains. The story of their civilization was fraught with frequent wars, violence and disorder.

Reconstruction of the Five Civilized Nations in Indian Territory as viewed by the United States seemed to offer the opportunity to secure Indian concentration and a consolidated territorial government. These two goals had been long sought. Too many tribes occupied land needed by western railroads or coveted by settlers to make acceptance of the status quo advisable in the eyes of the majority of the members of Congress. Congressional investigation showed that but two areas remained as possible centers for Indian settlement, the public lands to the north of Nebraska and those to the south of Kansas. The administration of President Grant decided that all Indians must be gathered in these locations. This policy guiding the government's effort to confine Indian settlement within these areas was known as concentration. The popularity of the policy of concentration, the lack of knowledge of most Americans concerning tribal affairs and the apathy of the general public toward humanitarian movements during the period following the Civil War left but few to object to the postwar treaties made between the United States and the Indians.

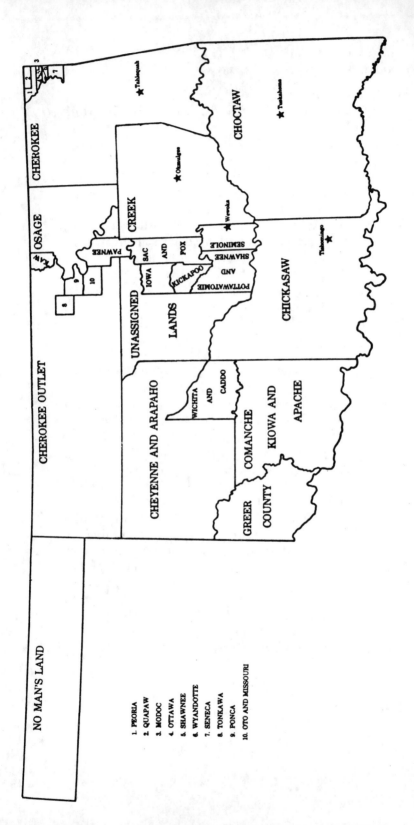

Indian Territory During Reconstruction

Chapter Four

RECONSTRUCTION
IN THE SEMINOLE NATION

The smallest of the Five Civilized Nations was the Seminole tribe and it was the first to reestablish relations with the United States government after the Civil War. Since the war came before the Seminoles were well established in Indian Territory this conflict did not disrupt their life to the degree that it did the other Indian Nations. The Seminole Nation agreed in its Washington treaty of 1866 to cede all of its old reservation to the United States government and accept an area between the Canadian and North Fork Rivers. The eastern boundary of this newly acquired reservation was fixed at the west line of the Creek Nation and it was agreed that their land should extend westward between the rivers far enough to give them two hundred thousand acres. The majority of the members of the Seminole Nation were not yet fully aware of the swindle that had occurred in Washington. But there was at least one protest on record that censured the selling of their land for fifteen cents an acre and the buying of new land for their use with their tribal money at fifty cents an acre. This protest also submitted that the two-hundred-thousand-acre allotment of land was too small, and it voiced resentment at interference with the internal affairs and regulations of the Seminole Nation.

Agricultural and Boundary Adjustment

The southern Seminoles returned to their homes in the fall of 1865 in time to put in crops of wheat, and in the following

83

spring they planted considerable corn. They would as a result be self-sustaining until another harvest could be produced. They also had the advantage of using the cattle that remained to supply themselves with beef. The northern Seminole refugee camp on Cherokee land put in small crops of corn and garden produce which furnished scanty subsistence after July 1866. But this supply was soon exhausted and with winter coming on they would need their annuities and the money provided for them under their recent treaty to keep from suffering.

Most of the Seminoles were anxious to remove to their new reservations, alleged to be admirably adapted to grain and stock raising with an abundance of timber and water. They had long since given up the chase as a means of subsistence and they were anxious to establish new and permanent homes. The supply of farming implements would have to be renewed because the Seminoles were careless with them. They seemed to act upon the theory that when the crop was gathered there was no further use for ploughs, hoes and rakes, and the next season found them with no means to put in their crops. Mass migration to their new reservation occurred during October, 1866, and they commenced at once the erection of cabins and the general preparai on of their land for spring planting. They had brought with them from Kansas and Fort Gibson seed corn and farming implements.

On this land they were told that they must raise sufficient food for their subsistence after the first day of July, 1867, for the government had decided to furnish no more supplies after that time. With the aid of their agent, George A. Reynolds, who secured tools, and by a system of government enforced by Chief John Chupco and the headmen, the Seminoles worked toward self-subsistence. During the winter of 1866–1867 they made more than one hundred thousand rails, carried them on their backs and fenced large areas. They raised about one hundred ten thousand bushels of corn which gave them a large surplus and correspondingly large amounts of vegetables and garden produce. Every man and woman was compelled to work and any negligence exhibited on working days resulted in a fine of five dollars per day. The amount was immediately collected even though it took the last blanket the person slept on or the last penny in the family.

More land was cultivated in 1868 than during the previous year but a drought seriously affected the late corn although enough was garnered until another crop could mature. As the country was well suited for the raising of stock, Agent Reynolds desired that all of their funds be invested in cattle, hogs, horses and farming implements, thus abolishing the system of annuity payments. A number of the southern Seminoles finally moved from the old reservation to the new in the spring of 1869. They were somewhat late in planting as they had to clear the land and build their houses. They grew adequate crops although not as extensively as many produced by those who were permanently located. The statistical statement of farming operations for the various tribes for 1869 showed that the Seminoles had raised an abundance of garden vegetables, more than sufficient to meet their needs. Their personal property also indicated that they were independent and self-sustaining in all that was required to meet the basic wants of life.

Though the Seminole Nation had become self-supporting agriculturally in the time period set by the Federal government there were other problems connected with the land that caused much concern. The Seminoles were realizing by 1870 that they had been defrauded. Even though they were aware that the government had taken advantage of them, they probably would not have complained had the land proven as fertile as had been represented. It was estimated that there were not more than fifty thousand acres of good arable land in their new reservation. Furthermore, their area would have extended at least five or six miles further west had the boundaries been correctly surveyed, and this would have thrown much of the inferior land into the Creek Nation. It was also feared that should their reservation be allotted to individuals there would not be sufficient good land to give each person thirty acres.

There continued to be much uneasiness about the situation concerning the boundary line between the Creek and the Seminole Nations because part of the land to the east, containing Seminole improvements, had been recognized as Creek country. The Creek tribal government claimed authority over the Seminoles residing in this area and many disputes arose over the extent of each tribe's control. Consequently Henry Breiner, the Seminole agent, in 1871 petitioned the Federal government to make provision for any contingency that might grow out of the unsettled difficulty so that the Seminoles would be permitted to remain in their homes unmolested by anyone.

The Seminoles of Indian Territory were also anxious that the members of their tribe still living in Florida be removed to settle on their new reservation. They desired that the government enlarge their reservation to provide the needed land and make the necessary provisions for removal and sustenance until the Florida members could care for themselves. The Nation also requested that the Department of the Interior order a delegation of three to be selected by a general council or their agent to visit Florida for the purpose of advising and assisting in the proposed removal. The Creek-Seminole boundary dispute continued throughout the seventies. Finally on February 14, 1881, an arrangement was made for the purchase of one hundred seventy-five thousand acres east of the Creek dividing line at one dollar per acre. Congress first struck the item from the appropriation bill and it was the next year before money was made available. This settled the issue giving the Seminoles a total of three hundred seventy-five thousand acres of land.

Negotiations for Financial Restitution

The payment of annuities was thought by some to be injurious to the Seminoles because they received very little payment benefit from their per capita payments. In accordance with Article IV of the Seminole treaty a census of the tribe was taken for the purpose of obtaining the prescribed annual payment. The Superintendent of the Southern Superintendency, L. N. Robinson, also followed through in accordance with treaty stipulations and on November 5, 1868, left his office for the Seminole Agency to disburse the sum of $50,000 to the loyal Seminole claimants for losses incurred during the Civil War.

The Seminoles were further dissatisfied with the manner in which their Civil War soldier bounties were being handled. The Seminole government in 1865 authorized John W. Wright of Washington, D.C., by power of attorney, to collect the back pay and bounties due Seminole soldiers for services rendered the United States. To enable Wright to do so, many had given him their discharge papers, but a large number of these had not yet been paid although they had repeatedly called upon Wright in person and demanded their bounties or their discharge papers. They were usually informed that their bounties had not been collected or that they were recorded as deserters. At the same time their discharge papers were either mislaid or not returned from Washington. It seemed that every means was used to keep the Seminoles from their bounties. Many of them, including women, walked a distance of 100 miles to Fort Gibson on hearing that money had been received for the payment of pensions and bounties, only to be informed on their arrival that the money had not been received or that their application papers were incorrect. The Seminoles were gratified in 1870 to learn that their bounties had been taken out of the hands of Wright and they began to hope that in the near future they would receive their money.

They now requested at this time an investigation by the Federal government as to the manner in which their pensions had been and were being paid by T. A. Baldwin, the Seminole agent replacing Reynolds. Because Baldwin felt that per capita payments were a great evil he recommended that the provision of the 1866 treaty be rigidly enforced and that no money be paid except to the heads of families. Baldwin reported that the chiefs had been in the habit of taking out the amount they chose, allowing the balance to be paid per capita. This was an injustice as few received the full amount of their annuities.

Another financial grievance of the Seminoles was that a new mill for which they had made a $15,000 appropriation of their own money had not become an accomplished fact. An old mill had been reconstructed and from its description the Seminoles had cause for complaint. The apparatus for grinding the flour and meal was incomplete as there was no smut machine for cleaning the grain. The bolt and flour receiver had been constructed of green lumber that had shrunk and produced large cracks. The building was one story high and was so constructed as to cover both saw and grist mills. The roof was covered with oak boards that allowed leakage, there was no floor except the ground and the structure was not completely enclosed. The mill was in the possession of E. J. Brown, formerly a trader in the Seminole Nation, who had recently become an adopted citizen. He used the mill for his personal benefit.

Tribal Relations

The population of the Seminole Nation in 1866 was between

two thousand and three thousand individuals. Both the
northern and southern Seminoles, so long divided by the war,
seemed to have a desire to bury the past and come together
again as friends and brothers. Some jealousy and bad feeling
still existed in 1866 and many disputes developed relative to
property rights, but generally the tribal atmosphere was peaceful. Even the intertribal relations remained peaceful although
situated as this Nation was in the western portion of Indian
Territory, next to the turbulent Indians of the plains, they had
frequent cause for complaint. Though there had been depredations committed by parties of Indians attached to the tribes west
of the Seminole Nation, the counsel of the agent advocating
patience and forbearance was heeded and the Seminole Nation
had maintained peaceful relations with the neighboring Indians.

The government of the Seminole Nation remained more
nearly like the old tribal organization than that of any of the
other Indian Nations. For judicial and legislative purposes the
Seminoles were divided into two bands designated as the
northern and southern bands and these units were again sub-
divided into fourteen town bands. Each elected a unit chief and
two lawmakers who represented it in the National Council. The
Council was composed of forty-two members, three from each
of the fourteen towns; twelve of these were Indian towns
and two were towns comprising Negro freedmen. There was
only one legislative body, and in addition to its power as law-
maker it also sat in judgment upon all criminal cases. The head
chief of the northern band, John Chupco, attended to and transacted all executive business and was the principal chief of the
Nation as acknowledged by the Indian agency. The two head
chiefs acted in harmony in all matters pertaining to the settlement of their reservation, the establishment of district schools
and the enactment and enforcement of the laws established by
themselves and the United States. By 1872 the Seminole Council
decided to elect only one chief.

The Seminole laws were few but they were rigorously enforced. In the administration of Seminole justice, the chiefs,
judges and lighthorse police took pride in the speed with which
cases were brought to conclusion. Chief Chupco was an advocate
of rigid law enforcement although Seminole laws were considered harsh when measured by the standards of other tribes. The
Creeks were concerned by the swiftness with which their citi-

zens were tried, judged and not infrequently punished when they were charged with crime in the Seminole Nation. The punishment might be whipping, with a payment of damages in cases where Seminole citizens were injured. The death penalty was common.

Intertribal Relations

The Seminole Nation was also interested in intertribal affairs and attention was turned in that direction through the establishment of the Okmulgee General Council. All the treaties of 1866 negotiated between the Five Civilized Tribes and the Federal government provided that a General Council should be initiated in Indian Territory. In compliance with this provision bills had been introduced in the House of Representatives during the sessions of the Thirty-ninth and Fortieth Congresses. In the Forty-first Congress, Representative R. T. Van Horn of the Kansas City, Missouri, district introduced a similar measure which had been drawn up by the House Committee on Indian Affairs. The terms of this measure aroused bitter opposition among the leaders of all the Indian Nations and strong protests were issued against the bill. It was at this time that the intertribal conference was called to meet at Okmulgee where the first session of the General Council of Indian Territory was organized, with the superintendent of the Central Agency, Enoch Hoag, presiding.

The Van Horn bill was reported to the House of Representatives where a controversy arose between the Committee on Indian Affairs and the Committee on Territories; to resolve the problem the bill was referred back to a special committee consisting of the members of both committees but no further action was taken. Railway construction was quite active throughout the states and territories west of the Mississippi at this time and several lines had been projected through Indian Territory. Railway influence in Congress was very active in an effort to have government land grant subsidies made effective in Indian Territory as well as in the public domain of the United States. It was basically the fear on the part of the Indians that this might be brought to pass that led the governments of the Five Civilized Tribes to call the first delegated meeting at Okmulgee, the capital of the Creek Nation, in September 1870.

Since neither the Choctaws nor the Chickasaws were present at that time, the Okmulgee General Council adjourned to meet again the following December. Before adjourning the members present passed a resolution stating that all tribes signing the Washington treaties of 1866, whether present or not, were bound by the acts which the Council might pass. Before the meeting of the session called for December, Congress appointed a committee consisting of Robert Campbell, John D. Lang and John V. Farwell to attend the General Council. The committee was impressed with the advancement in civilization demonstrated by the tribes.

The adjourned session of the General Council of Indian Territory convened at Okmulgee on December 6, 1870. Two days later Campbell LeFlore of the Choctaw Nation introduced a resolution authorizing the president of the General Council to appoint a committee consisting of ten members to recommend a permanent organization for Indian Territory as contemplated in the treaties of 1866. This committee was appointed with LeFlore as its chairman. Two days later this committee reported, advising that a constitution, republican in form, with due regard for the rights of each tribe under existing treaties, be drawn up and submitted for adoption. This report was adopted with forty-eight delegates voting in the affirmative and five delegates voting in the negative.

Colbert Carter, a delegate from the Chickasaw Nation, then moved that the president of the General Council be authorized to appoint a committee consisting of twelve members for the purpose of drafting the recommended constitution. This motion was adopted and the committee immediately began its work; six days later, on December 16, 1870, it presented its report in part. The consideration of this report was taken up at once and the greater portion of the General Council session remaining was devoted to it. The final vote on the adoption of the constitution as a whole, to be submitted to the several tribes for ratification, resulted in fifty-two ayes and three nays.

The General Council also unanimously offered to mediate a peace with the plains Indians who had been driven to hostility against the United States by the encroachment of white settlers and the destruction of the buffalo herds. It adopted a report prepared by a committee presenting statistical information about the natural resources and agricultural development of Indian Territory. The report also pointed out the importance of homes and cultivated fields to the preservation of the Indian race, and it drew up a strong protest against any territorial plan forced on the Indians by Congress.

The main business of the General Council was the adoption of a constitution for a united government of its choice. The document that the committee formulated aimed to create a federal union similar to that of the United States. It provided for a governor elected by all the qualified voters, a general assembly consisting of a senate and a house of representatives elected from the various tribes to legislate upon intertribal matters and a system of courts with judges appointed by the governor and the senate. It was to go into effect when ratified by tribes representing two-thirds of the population of Indian Territory. The Indians at no time had a free opportunity to act upon the plan, for upon the advice of Secretary of the Interior J. D. Cox, President Grant immediately transmitted it to Congress with the recommendation that it be amended so that Congress would have a veto over all legislation and the executive and judicial officers would be appointed by the President. James Harlan, former Secretary of the Interior, who was again in the Senate, hailed this opportunity to bring the Indians under the control of white men and introduced an amended version of the constitution as the basis of another of his territorial plans.

The delegates to the Okmulgee General Council submitted the constitution in its original form to their tribes. The Seminoles seemed to understand little of political government with respect to the Okmulgee Constitution and the government proposed under it. They therefore thought it best to await the action of the more enlightened tribes on the subject. They were also afraid that the organization of a government under the Okmulgee Constitution of 1870 would force them to submit to the sectionalization of their country. The Seminoles thus decided that they would cooperate with the majority action of the other tribes.

The Cherokees refused to approve the new constitution. The small Chickasaw Nation rejected it generally because it was afraid of the representation given the larger tribes in the General Council. The Creeks ratified the document even though they feared the territorial schemes as much as the Cherokees, but the Creeks evidently believed that the Indians could oppose white entry into Indian Territory more effectively through a union of their own. By the end of 1873 the Choctaw Nation and several small tribes had taken favorable action but the combined population of the ratifying tribes was still 12,243 short of the required majority. Another constitution similar to the first was drafted by the Okmulgee General Council in 1875, but by this time only the Creeks were seriously interested.

Although the Okmulgee Constitution of 1870 was never adopted and the General Council never acquired the powers of a law-making body, it played a significant part in the history of Indian Territory. It helped the people of the civilized and semi-civilized tribes to adjust to the changes which had to be made as the result of their participation in the Civil War. All the 1866 treaties bound the Five Civilized Nations to aid the government in maintaining peace with the plains Indians and to this the General Council made a significant contribution. The difficulty resulting from raids made by the plains Indians on white settlements and the inability of the government to induce these Indians to take reservations was partially alleviated through efforts of the General Council. Meetings were arranged in several instances by the General Council between representatives of the plains Indians and the Five Civilized Nations. Arrangements for settling the plains Indians on reservations were accomplished in some cases. The work of the General Council, however, fell short of the hope of the Congressional Committee charged with seeing the problem through, though it was sincerely felt by the Federal government that the association of the plains Indians with those Indians who had made progress in the ways of the Anglo-Saxon produced a positive impact.

The General Council used its unity to protest through petitions and other forms the Federal government's policy toward the railroads. In 1871 a resolution was unanimously adopted to petition President Grant against changing the pattern of land tenure of the Indians in favor of the railroads and other private interests, including the land seekers. Another petition was submitted by the General Council in 1872. It reviewed the Indians' title to their land as guaranteed by their treaties and showed how the provisional grants in the railroad charters had created powerful inducements to gain title to the land. In 1874 and 1875 the General Council sent similar petitions to the government. It was becoming increasingly apparent to the Federal government that the General Council would not result in the consolidated territorial government with the Indians owning lands in severalty, and in 1876 the government ceased appropriating funds for the General Council. But similar conventions bearing the same name, each convening at Okmulgee, were held annually through 1878. As far as respect for both tribal and intertribal law was concerned, the Seminoles compared favorably with the other nations in Indian Territory. Their civility and general good conduct were proverbial throughout the area.

Reestablishment of Social Agencies

When the Civil War began the Presbyterian missionaries in the Seminole Nation went north and most of the people who had become affiliated with that church found their way to Kansas and other points of refuge. A Baptist missionary, the Reverend Joseph S. Murrow, on the other hand, was appointed as tribal agent by the Confederate government for the Seminoles. The Baptist Seminoles almost to a person joined the Confederacy. Those of Presbyterian faith who allied with the South soon transferred their affiliations to the Baptist Church. Consequently, when the war ended the lines of partisan cleavage in the Seminole Nation were identical with those of religious denominational difference. Two leaders of the tribe, John Jumper and James Factor, had been early converts under the Reverend Mr. Murrow and they carried on his work after the war.

Seminole schools were not reopened nor were churches reestablished by September, 1866. But by the summer of 1867 the Presbyterian Board of Home Missions returned the Reverend John R. Ramsey. The religious element was large among the Seminoles, and many of them were devout members of Protestant church denominations. Sunday schools were established in every neighborhood and the old and the young were instructed in the elements of religious and secular education. The church of the Reverend Mr. Ramsey was reestablished with a nucleus of sixty-six members, and one of this group started a branch station. The Presbyterian mission under Reverend Ramsey was kept open but he was not furnished with necessary funds, although he had been connected with the Seminoles for almost fifteen years. There were Methodists and Baptists in the area but they had no mission. In 1869 John Jumper was the chief proponent of the Baptist church among the Seminoles. The Principal Chief, John Chupco, was a member of the Presbyterian church, as were several other headmen of the Nation.

The Seminole annual report on public schools for the year ending September 30, 1868, stated that four public schools were in operation. School number one was taught by Mary M. Lilley for a seven month term. This was a school for beginners, for few of its students knew the alphabet and none spoke English. The school averaged thirty-five pupils during the year. Reverend Ramsey taught school number two, which averaged thirty pupils. This was also a school for beginners with a term of six months. The progress shown in the children's work and the effort made to attend school regardless of insufficient clothing in severe winter would seem to indicate that there was an intense desire for learning. School number three was taught by Mrs. H. C. Shook and lasted for a term of only three months. This school was located near the old Seminole Agency and the nearby residents were much too scattered for many children to attend; furthermore, many were leaving for their new reservation. School number four was taught by Charles Anderson. The term was six months and attendance averaged twenty-seven pupils. The Reverend Mr. Ramsey, who served as the superintendent of public instruction, reported that the effort of that year was encouraging and he anticipated better schoolhouses and improved conditions in general for the next year.

By October 1, 1869, there were three schools located in the Seminole Nation with sixty male scholars and eighty female scholars in attendance. The superintendent of schools, The Reverend Mr. Ramsey, taught school number one, which had seventy pupils in attendance. There was a degree of irregular attendance on the part of some students but the majority were regular and made encouraging progress in their studies. The school term consisted of eight months, with spelling, reading, writing, arithmetic and geography being taught. School number two with thirty-five pupils was taught by Mrs. Shook, and the length of the school term and the branches of knowledge taught were the same as in school number one. School number three was not in operation during that year due to the failure to build a schoolhouse, although it had been planned that the school would be ready by the winter of 1869–1870. School number four was conducted by Charles Anderson, who taught spelling and reading to thirty-five pupils. Both parents and children in the Seminole Nation seemed genuinely interested in education.

During 1870 there were four Seminole schools in successful operation, two Indian and two Negro. The land which was selected for a Presbyterian mission school in 1867 had never had a mission established on it except on paper. A small mission building was under construction in 1870 but was being made of worthless material and was not at all suited for its purpose. In many cases the influence of the teachers over the children was counteracted by the parents due to lingering prejudice against the customs and manners of the whites. There was the additional drawback of some teachers not being able to speak or understand the Muskogee language and many students could speak nothing but the Indian language. The colored children spoke a jargon English and therefore had an advantage over the Indians in acquiring an education.

It was not surprising that the Seminole Nation showed much progress by 1876, for even in 1869 Reynolds, the Seminole agent at that time, declared that the Seminoles " . . . had complied with the conditions imposed upon them. . . . They took hold of the question of reconstruction and settled it at once practically, and firmly."[1] Seminole progress was significant in all areas. Their schools numbered only five, but steps were being taken to establish two boarding schools and manual labor schools in addition to the day schools. These schools were to be under the supervision of the Baptist and Presbyterian Boards of Home Missions. The amount of funds expended annually for schools at this time was $2,500 but on the establishment of the two boarding schools it was proposed to take out of the money paid per capita the sum of $20,000 and appropriate it to carry on the schools. The Seminoles had reached a degree of prosperity so that they no longer required the $25,000 annually paid per capita among them, and they could afford to use that sum for educational purposes. Some years elapsed before the Seminole academies were established but a female academy sponsored by the Methodist Indian Mission was founded in 1884. Two na-

---

[1] George Reynolds to L. A. Robinson, Seminole Agency, July 25, 1869, *Annual Report*, 1869, pp. 418-419.

tional academies were established by the Seminole Council, one for boys in 1891 (Mekasukey) and one for girls in 1894 (Emahaka).

Summary

The Seminole Nation was the smallest of the Five Civilized Nations and the first to reestablish relations with the Federal government following the Civil War. It was unique also in that it began reconstruction on entirely different land than it had occupied before the war. The delegates of the Seminole Nation evidently possessed neither the cunning nor the power to cope with the sharp and unethical practices of the United States Anglo-Saxon Commissioners; for they ceded to the United States government their old tribal land for fifteen cents an acre and purchased their new land from the Creeks at fifty cents an acre.

The total acres of land purchased by the Seminoles did not prove as good as represented but, with the aid of their agents, their chiefs, their headmen and the industrious labor of the tribe itself, the Seminoles were agriculturally self-sufficient by 1869. Much dissatisfaction resulted from the fact that the land in their new reservation had been incorrectly surveyed and that they had mistakenly made improvements on Creek land. The new reservation designated for the Seminoles was considered to small for both themselves and the tribal members from Florida whom they wanted to join them in Indian Territory. Disgruntlement was evident because of the manner in which their bounties and annuities were being paid, though the bounty claims and annuities of the loyal faction were being paid by 1868. There was also bitter resentment exhibited over the lack of a suitable flour mill that was to have been provided with the $15,000 appropriated for this purpose, and over the fact that the existing structure was being used for the personal profit of the manager.

The general tribal atmosphere of the Seminoles was peaceful following the Civil War. Intertribal relations remained placid although the Indians of the plains gave them cause for complaint. The government of the Seminole Nation was not as complex as that of the other Civilized Tribes, as there was only one legislative body which in addition to its law-making authority sat in judgment upon all criminal cases. The Seminoles' laws were few but rigorously enforced, and the chiefs, judges and lighthorse police speedily brought cases to a conclusion. The Creeks were concerned over the swiftness with which their citizens were tried, judged and frequently punished by the Seminoles.

Major reconstruction barriers in the Seminole Nation were few. Article II of the Seminole treaty of 1866, which abolished slavery and granted full civil rights and privileges to all persons, whatever their race or color, gave the Seminoles less concern than this same provision in the reconstruction treaties of the other Nations. This provision caused little internal, political or economic confusion. Railroads during reconstruction did not bring problems to the Seminoles as to the other Indian Nations, for the first railroad did not come to the Seminole country until 1895.

Though the Seminoles did not comply to the letter of their 1866 treaty provision concerning the establishment of a general intertribal council as the United States government desired, the meetings of the Okmulgee General Council in 1870 were supported by the Seminoles for purposes beneficial to the Five Civilized Tribes. The Seminole Nation was in general terms reconstructed politically and economically by 1869. Agent Reynolds reported in that year that the Seminoles had taken hold of the problems of reconstruction and had settled them resourcefully and firmly.

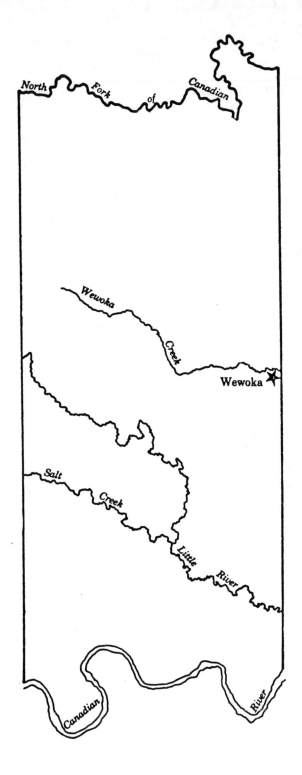

The Seminole Nation

Chapter Five

RECONSTRUCTION
IN THE CREEK NATION

The Creek treaty of 1866 reduced the land area of the Creek Nation to half its original size. The Creeks found their country at the close of the Civil War a desolated area, with their horses, cattle and hogs nearly gone, their farms grown over with underbrush and their homes and fences destroyed or dilapidated.

Agricultural and Boundary Adjustments

The agricultural picture was not good at the close of the war for the Creek Nation was in need of farm implements, a saw mill and a grist mill. The 1866 growing season also had been particularly dry with the southern and western portions of the country suffering the most, for here the corn crop, their principal product, was almost a total failure. Much sickness had prevailed due to the drought and the poor diet it forced upon them. Federal government rations were discontinued on the first of July, 1866, and after that time green corn, potatoes and melons became their only subsistence. The freedmen planted larger crops, attended them more faithfully and were further from want than were their former masters.

To add to the agricultural misery an immense swarm of grasshoppers moved in on the timber land in 1866. In many places they covered the ground like grass withered in the sun. The turnip, cabbage, peach and apple crops were destroyed and even the dry fodder was threatened. The Creeks did not see the end of the grasshoppers in 1866 for in the spring of 1867 a new crop of the insects hatched out and continued the onslaught against all vegetation. Two or three plantings of corn were made by some of the most persevering Creeks and the first growing corn leaves were scarcely visible before they were consumed. The immense numbers of the grasshoppers and their widespread presence made the prospects exceedingly dark. Finally about the middle of May the grasshoppers disappeared. After this the prospect brightened and the people went to work with fresh hope and energy.

The Creeks objected to coal prospecting in their country although it was known in 1866 that coal was abundant. It was seen particularly about the streams and in many places it was visible upon the surface of the soil. To all appearances it was the bituminous variety and could be obtained at comparatively low cost. Limestone was also abundant. Red sandstone was to be seen in some localities but scarcely ever in quantity in a quarry.

In 1868 the crops did not compare favorably with those of the previous year, when every barn was filled with corn. A drought prevailed with considerable severity over the country but in some localities good crops were gathered. The Creek agent F. A. Field reported in 1869 that those who had tilled the soil had been liberally rewarded for corn averaged about fifty bushels per acre, Irish and sweet potatoes were produced in abundance, many kinds of vegetables were planted and the yield was abundant. Field mentioned again that the Creek freedmen seemed to exhibit more energy in farming than the Creeks themselves.

It would seem that by 1869 the Creeks were agriculturally self-sustaining and that any future agricultural misfortune could not be blamed on the Civil War. In 1870 there were more acres of ground cultivated than ever before; besides the old farms new ones had sprung up, and the old farms had been considerably enlarged. Men who had before considered labor a disgrace took hold of the plow and the hoe with zeal. Besides being cultivators of the soil they were excellent stock growers and from appearances in 1870 the prairies would in a few years be covered with all kinds of stock as they had been before the war.

By 1873 the general agricultural picture had improved to the point that about thirty-one thousand acres of ground were tilled out of three million three hundred fifteen thousand acres, as compared with five thousand acres cultivated out of three million two hundred and fifty thousand acres in 1866; five hundred thousand bushels of corn were raised in 1873 as compared with one hundred twenty–five thousand bushels in 1866; one hundred thousand bushels of wheat as compared with two thousand bushels; seventy–five thousand bushels of potatoes as compared with fifteen hundred bushels. Livestock holdings, too, had increased during the same period to the point where there were fifteen thousand horses as compared with thirty-five hundred; thirty-five thousand cattle as compared with four thousand; and ten thousand swine as compared with two thousand.

The greatest obstacle in the way of more extensive cultivation of the soil and the raising of stock was the lack of an example for the Creeks to follow. They desired that the Federal government operate a model farm on the section of land which it reserved by the 1866 treaty for the purpose of erecting new agency buildings. The farm could be operated without the expenditure of government money outside of the amount required to stock it with modern farm implements. The lessons taught and the example given by the enterprise would be of great material advantage to the Creeks as it would place them in a condition to compete with the white farmer with whom they would soon have to come in contact.

The Creeks as early as 1871 desired the formation of an agricultural society for the purpose of introducing and encouraging improvement in methods of cultivation and the introduction of new implements, seeds, fruits and better grades of stock. The Okmulgee Council in 1874 approved an Indian international fair through the influence of Superintendent Hoag as an encouragement to Indian agriculture. The full blood Indians attended mainly as spectators as the fair was basically a white man's project. The fair was successful, however, and they were held annually throughout most of the tribal period.

The Creek Nation had land boundary problems. It was discovered five years after the Seminoles were settled in their new homes that they were too far east and therefore on Creek soil. A formal approach was made to the Creeks to sell the land to the Seminoles in 1873. Earlier attempts had been made to persuade the Creeks to cede the additional land but to no avail. Naturally the Seminoles did not want to move and the Creeks did not want to cede more land. The Creek-Seminole boundary problem was not solved in 1873. But by that time the Creeks no longer trespassed upon the rights of the Seminoles for after the

winter of 1872 a communication came from the Seminole Agency stating that the United States government would hold them
responsible for any depredations committed upon Seminole
property until the right of possession could be settled between
the United States and the Creeks. This seemed to end any
further trespassing. The settlement was finally undertaken in
1881 and consummated in 1882. The United States also located
the Sac and Fox tribe immediately north of the Seminoles in
1869–1870. A similar surveying error was made and the Creeks
refused to sell. Consequently the Sac and Fox tribe was moved
farther west.

Negotiating for Funds Due

In the meantime the Creeks urged upon the United States the
prompt payment of all dues and the early settlement of
claims. There were two claims which demanded immediate
attention. The first of these grew out of the treaty of 1832 by
which there was due the Creek orphans of that date the principal and accrued interest from the sale of twenty sections of land
appropriated for their benefit. This appropriation was to reimburse the orphans for their nonrepresentation in other lands
then divided. The treaty set apart one section of land for each
principal chief and one-half section for every other head of a
family. For the orphans, who were entitled to share in the
division but who had no parents to represent them twenty
sections were granted, to be sold under the direction of the
President of the United States for their benefit. This money was
retained as a fund by the United States and had not been
paid to the claimants.

The Creeks were anxious that their orphan fund money
should be paid over at once. They complained that this fund
had at various times been diverted from its legitimate use and
applied to the support of schools of the Nation and to the
support of orphans not of 1832. The claimants protested this
misapplication of the fund, asserting that it was intended for the
individual benefit of the orphans of 1832 and that it should
not be used for the support or advantage of those who had
previously been assisted by a division of lands in which the
claimants were not permitted to share and in remuneration for

which loss this fund was established. This question had been fully discussed by the authorities of the Nation previous to 1856 and it was decided that this fund was the sole property of the orphans of 1832 and their heirs, and that it could not be used for the benefit of others.

A fund was created by the treaty of 1856 for the support of the schools of the Nation and the misapplication of the orphan fund ceased. The orphans argued in 1867 that this money was due them personally and as the interest was paid out without their permission to the general support of the schools and to other Creek orphans, it now should be paid over with the principal and accrued interest. J. W. Dunn, the Creek agent, urged the appropriation by Congress at the coming session of a sum sufficient to meet this claim in full. D. W. McIntosh, Timothy Barnett, the treasurer of the Nation, and James M. C. Smith were employed in February of 1868 by the claimants interested in the Creek orphan fund of 1832 to secure their payment. They succeeded in securing nearly one hundred and forty-three thousand dollars. The following fall this sum was paid out by Dunn. The orphans were then middle-aged, but they and their heirs received the first payment.

In 1870 the aging orphans received another payment of thirty-one thousand dollars. From this time on the government seems to have made them an annual payment of $4,182.68 as interest on the depreciated bonds. In 1872 Agent F. S. Lyon again called the attention of the government to the adjustment of Creek claims under the act of March 1871. In 1882 Congress made an appropriation of $338,904.39; $70,800 as a value of the depreciated bonds, $106,799.68 to restore the amount misappropriated for refugees, $69,956.29 to return the amount misapplied to general tribal purposes and $91,348.42 as interest. It was provided, however, that the amount used for general tribal purposes should be charged against the Creeks and gradually deducted from their annuities.

The other unsettled Creek claim to which attention was directed was that of the loyal Indians and freedmen of their Nation. By the treaty of 1866, $100,000 was set aside for the remuneration of the loyal Creek Indians for their property losses in the war. Finally in 1869 the Creek agent was directed to pass upon the loyal claims. The Indians brought carefully preserved lists of the property they had abandoned when they fled to Kansas. Although the totals amounted to more than five million dollars only the stipulated $100,000 was prorated in 1870 to the claimants. Consequently there was much dissatisfaction among the loyal Creeks. Exposed and impoverished as they had been during the war, they contented themselves somewhat with the thought that their property lost in defense of the Union would be restored to them. They were encouraged when they were told to make out their claims, but when these were first diminished by the awarding commission to from one-third to one-fifth of their original size and then again by the prorating process to a small fractional part of the award, the Creeks looked upon the whole thing as a farce.

A payment of per capita money stipulated by the treaty of 1866 was made during March of 1867. An enumeration of the population was obtained after considerable time and trouble. It was determined that the number of Creeks, including the freedmen, was 11,445. This number did not include the disaffected band of Creeks located in the Cherokee country, numbering about three hundred and seventy. They refused to share in the money, would not give their enumeration and insisted that the treaty made in 1856 was still their only guide. The payment that began in March of 1867 giving each Creek Indian $17.34 did not include the 1,774 freedmen, for Chief Checote had prevailed upon the Indian commissioner to exclude them from the distribution. But Harry Island and two other Negroes, Ketch Barnett and Cow Tom, went to Washington to protest and in 1868 Congress, with some expressions of indignation against the Indians, set aside $30,882.54 of the tribal annuities for the freedmen. This payment was made in the summer of 1869.

There was dissatisfaction between the northern and southern faction concerning the division of funds. It had been agreed that money should be equally divided between the two factions, to be distributed at their discretion for the payment of their national debt. This was not done. Instead the United States paid all the money to the Government Party headed by Checote. In addition the money that Checote paid over to Oktarsars-Harjo (Sands), Chief of the northern faction, was disposed of in a manner unsatisfactory to many of his own faction.

There were no per capita payments made to the Creeks after

1874 as the Council had voted to retain the fund as a permanent investment. The Nation, however, made payments to individuals for the purpose of relief. A drought and a plague of grasshoppers again in 1874 brought many to the verge of starvation, and two dollars worth of supplies were furnished to about sixteen hundred persons. The Nation also adopted a very humane custom of paying thirty dollars a year to individuals who were blind, aged or crippled who had no other means of support. This form of welfare was continued throughout the remainder of the tribal period.

Railroad Development in the Creek Nation

In the midst of the 1871–72 dissension and dissatisfaction concerning payment for lost property claims and the political disturbances between the Sands and Checote parties, another apprehension arose from the construction of the southern branch of the Union Pacific Railroad through the Creek country. The great number of white men necessarily introduced for the building of the road agitated the Creeks.

To the majority of the Creeks railroad development was not a benefit bringing prosperity and convenience. Most of them felt that their way of life was menaced. The southern branch of the Union Pacific, soon to be known as the Missouri, Kansas, and Texas Railroad, had become a beneficiary of the Congressional land grant system for railroads. The road reached the Kansas line in 1870, crossed the Cherokee Nation, and during 1871–72 was constructed across the Creek Nation following the old Texas Road close to the eastern boundary. Many Indians viewed the coming of the railroad with apprehension as the construction crews were usually lawless, creating disorder, with criminals congregating at each temporary terminal. Usually as the road advanced the more vicious of these individuals departed, but they left behind other intruding opportunists who attached themselves upon the Indian country proving themselves to be speculative, avaricious and unscrupulous.

In an effort to make some profit for the Nation from the railroads, the Creek Council passed a law in October 1870 allowing only citizens the privilege of cutting and selling timber. It was required that others would have to obtain a permit from the district judge and pay a royalty to the Nation. The officer of the railroad ignored this law and purchased construction material from white contractors operating without authority, and the Creeks were forced to see their new timber cut down without receiving any remuneration.

The Council initiated another proposal in an effort to secure profit for the Nation in relation to the railroad. Realizing that most of the Texas cattle would now be driven to the new railroad terminus, a bill was passed providing for grazing and herding of stock in transit during the stock season ending November 30, 1871, in consideration of twenty-five cents per head per month. Not much money was gained, for some cattlemen found ways to evade payment of the tax and others simply ignored the payment. It is evident that many cattle were driven through without payment for by September of 1880 the Captain of the Light-horsemen of the Eufaula post had to appeal to the Creek chief requesting assistance to enforce the act making it the duty of light-horsemen to guard the frontiers of the Creek Nation against entrance of cattle or horses except by railroad from Texas and Arkansas. Creek records of May 27, 1882, indicate that some drovers still refused to pay the tax. By October 16, 1882, an act was passed granting permission to any citizen to apply to United States authorities for permission to graze cattle upon portions of Creek domain ceded to the United States by the treaty of 1866. Although an Act of October 27, 1881 had reduced the tax per head to ten cents, June 13, 1884, found noncitizens driving stock through public domain without paying the tax.

The development of the railroad caused the necessity for alleviating or circumventing other attending economic problems and controlling the number and activity of whites on Creek soil. Citizens were required to secure a permit before employing a noncitizen laborer and persons living in the country under permit were forbidden to employ noncitizens. Improvements effected on Creek soil by intruders were declared to be the property of the Nation. The Creeks tried to prevent the flow of mixed-blood Cherokees to the railroad stations by declaring that the right of intertribal residence had never been recognized except with the consent of the tribe where the settlement was established. One Cherokee citizen was given a special permit to establish a trading center upon the payment of a license tax but such concessions were denied to a number of other Cherokees whose names had been submitted by Chief Downing. The Creeks were greatly troubled at the increase of white traders along the railroad, but this matter was controlled by the Department of the Interior.

Trains crossed the Arkansas River early in 1872 and a new terminal was established south of the river at a station named Muskogee. The usual scene of tents and shacks with the attending speculative excitement followed. Many traders sought to establish themselves there. The stations of Oktaha and Checotah were established and named in honor of Sands and Checote as the lines advanced. Eufaula was laid out in the vicinity of old North Fork Town and many of the local business men moved their stores to the new location. The first trains crossed the Canadian River and entered the Choctaw country in the spring of 1872. By the middle of February, Creek Agent F. S. Lyon had already granted licenses to ten white traders to open stores at Muskogee and Eufaula and more applications were arriving. The Commissioner of Indian Affairs, F. A. Walker, instructed him to refuse licenses except where the need was plainly apparent. Cupidity for land promised to the Indian was intensified by the construction of the railroad. Territorial bills designed to break down the Indian governments flooded Congress. Some Caucasians in the Creek country continued to interfere increasingly in tribal affairs, and Senator Samuel Pomeroy of Kansas forwarded Creek complaints to the Office of Indian Affairs. Many Indians were becoming increasingly apprehensive of their future in Indian Territory with the coming of the railroad and the influx of whites.

Reorganization of Government and Politics

Since there was no recognized government in the Creek Nation from 1861 to 1866, the Creeks were anxious to begin the task of improving and reorganizing their National affairs. Law improvement in 1866 concerned itself chiefly with the security of horses and cattle. As a general rule property within the Creek Nation was more secure than in the states of the Union. Only a few cases of horse stealing were reported. The people were particularly interested in the security of horses and cattle for the possession those animals constituted their chief wealth. Creek Agent J. W. Dunn suggested the establishment of a penitentiary within the territory in which the criminals of the different Nations might be confined at hard labor. He objected to the system of flogging that was currently being used on the grounds that escape was comparatively easy and even in event of apprehension the punishment was light enough to be risked in the prospect of gain. Dunn further felt that branding was likewise not good for it marked the man a felon, and once so marked he usually acted the felon. Work according to Dunn was the answer, for labor to an Indian was painful punishment and confinement was irksome. Once established the expenses of the penitentiary would be small, but even if the institution was not self-sustaining it would be worth the expense. Instead of sending out from its walls a criminal branded and published to his Nation, the man, having learned a trade or occupation while imprisoned, might render useful service to his tribe.

By 1867 the Creeks were agitating for a new code of laws with effective ways of executing them. The laws as then administered required four times the number of officers that should be necessary to execute efficiently a well-established code. The officials were poorly paid and were vague about their duties. Consequently, many urged reform.

In separate and joint council the two Creek factions tried throughout 1867 to reach agreement and build a united Nation. In February of 1867 both groups pledged to unite and live as one nation in peace and friendship. Until this time the Creeks had accepted dual leadership, but a resolution was approved by Sands and Checote that there should be one principal chief elected at a council in May of 1867 and that persons should be employed to build a council house. The proposed election of a principal chief did not take place as scheduled for by that time fundamental governmental changes had been initiated.

In the meantime the completed 1866 treaty was explained to the Creek Council by Agent Dunn, using David M. Hodge, an educated great-grandson of Benjamin Perryman who had fought on the side of the Union, as an interpreter. The Council ratified the treaty and the loyal full bloods believed that under its provisions the United States would reimburse them for all of their losses in the war. Actually articles III and IV of the treaty stipulated that soldiers who enlisted in the Federal army, loyal refugee Indians and freedmen would be paid in proportion to their losses within one year from the ratification of the treaty, or as soon as $100,000 could be raised from the sale of land to other Indians.

The half-breed faction of the Creek Nation was usually termed thé Government Party. This element, long known as the Lower Creeks, was led by D. N. McIntosh, David M. Hodge, Sanford W. Perryman, Coweta Micco, James McHenry and others. They were dissatisfied with the old government and worked to promote the adoption of a new constitution. As a result the National Council of the Muskogee Nation (this name had been applied since the Lower and Upper Creeks united in 1860) met at their council grounds at Black Jack Grove near the Deep Fork River in October 1867. A resolution was passed at this meeting which provided that all subsequent meetings of the General Council should be held at Okmulgee, which was nearer the geographical center of the Nation.

The new constitution was concluded after debate with the Upper Creek faction of the Anti-Government Party on October 12, 1867. Angie Debo declared the constitution to be poorly drafted, while Ohland Morton felt that it showed that much time and thought had been spent in its preparation and that it was well adapted to the needs of the people of the Creek Nation. In general this constitution was similar to that of the United States. It contained ten articles and provided for a thorough reorganization of the legislative and judicial departments. Article I provided for the legislature. The law-making power was lodged in a council consisting of two houses known as the House of Kings and the House of Warriors. The upper house, the House of Kings, was composed of one representative from each town who was elected by a vote of the town represented for a term of four years. The House of Warriors was composed of one representative for every two hundred persons belonging to the town. His election and term of office were the same as that of the representative to the House of Kings.

Each house had the powers ordinarily delegated to all democratic legislative bodies such as judging the return and qualifications of its members, impeaching members for disorderly conduct and expulsion by the concurrence of two-thirds of both houses. Each house elected its own presiding officers and neither house was allowed to adjourn for a longer period than two days without the consent of both houses. The qualifications for the members of both houses were two in number. First, a member must be a citizen of the Muskogee Nation and, second, he must be at least twenty-two years of age.

Article II provided for the executive department headed by an official styled the "Principal Chief of the Muskogee Nation." His term of office was four years and he was elected by a majority of the votes of the male citizens of the Muskogee Nation who had attained the age of eighteen years. Also, a second chief was to be chosen for the same term and in the same manner as that prescribed for the election of the principal chief; in case of the death, resignation, or removal from office of the principal chief, he was to perform all the duties of that officer. In order to be eligible for the office of principal chief a person must be a recognized citizen of the Muskogee Nation and at least thirty years of age. The principal chief was vested with the reprieving and pardoning power and charged with the responsibility of seeing that all of the laws of the Nation were faithfully executed and enforced. The principal chief was allowed a private secretary of his own selection to be compensated out of the national treasury.

Article III concerned the judiciary. A high court was created composed of five competent and recognized citizens of the Muskogee Nation chosen by a national council and compensated out of the national treasury. In order to be eligible for a position on the high court a man had to be at least twenty-five years of age. This court was to meet on the first Monday in October of each year, and it had the power to try all cases where the issue was for more than one hundred dollars. Three members constituted a quorum.

Article IV specified that the Muskogee Nation should be divided into six districts and each district furnished with a judge, a prosecuting attorney and a company of light-horsemen. These district judges were chosen by the National Council for a term of two years. They were to try all cases, civil and criminal, where the issue did not exceed one hundred dollars. Each judge was given the right to summon twenty-four disinterested men, out of which number a jury of twelve men for criminal cases and nine for civil cases might be selected.

Each judge was allowed a clerk, and the judge and the clerk were to be compensated out of the national treasury as provided by law. Any person failing to obey a summons to serve as juror without good reason for the failure was subject to a fine of five dollars. Each juror was to receive one dollar per day for this service to the Nation.

The prosecuting attorney for each district was appointed by the principal chief by and with the consent of the National Council. It was his duty to indict and prosecute all offenders against the laws of his district, and for each conviction he was to be paid the sum of twenty-five dollars. The Light-horse Company consisted of one captain and four privates, elected for a term of two years by a vote of the district. The company was subservient to the orders of the judge. The last six articles of the constitution were relatively short. Article V provided for the selection by the National Council of a national treasurer for a term of four years with the stipulation that no money was to be drawn from the national treasury except to carry out appropriations made by the National Council. Article VI provided for a national interpreter whose term of office was four years. Article VII stated that all officers of the government were liable to impeachment, trial and removal from office for neglect of duty, and that all bills of impeachment were to originate in the House of Warriors. Article VIII, IX and X were general and contained miscellaneous provisions. Article X provided that all treaties should be made by delegates, duly recommended by the principal chief and approved by the National Council; it also provided that treaties were subject to ratification by the National Council and that all treaties should be the supreme law of the land. This constitution was adopted in 1867 and remained unchanged until the end of the Creek Nation in 1907.

After the adoption of this constitution laws were passed for the new government. The powers of all the national officers were clearly defined in a series of laws classed under the title of National Executive Officers. Laws were passed providing for the organization of the Nation in general. The powers and duties of the new judiciary were set out and more fully defined. The six judicial districts provided for in the constitution were created and named Okmulgee, Deep Fork, Wewoka, Eufaula, Muskogee and Coweta.

There followed a series of civil and criminal laws which defined the crimes and stated what the penalty would be in each case of violation. A number of criminal laws already in use in the Creek Nation were approved by the legislative session of the National Council on October 12, 1867. By 1868 the Creeks had published in the Muskogee tongue and in English a portion of their laws and copies were placed in the hands of every officer. The old civil code was reenacted with little change. The first sixteen items were approved on October 12, 1867, and others

were enacted at various times in 1872 and finally approved in
October 1873. They generally contained the same provisions
regarding livestock, debts, wills, and inheritance, the traders'
tax and the employment of white mechanics.

Other laws dealt with education. These provided for neighborhood schools, examination of teachers, teachers' institutes,
mission boarding schools and youth attending school in the
United States. An appropriation of $6,000 in addition to the
amount specified in the treaty was made to rebuild the Tullahassee and Asbury schools. There were also laws governing
elections and practically all phases of life.

All of the acts were approved by Checote, Sands, Micco Hutke
and Pink Hawkins. Hutke and Hawkins were elected as
second chiefs. The action of this council seemed to have fostered
a conciliatory atmosphere between the factions, and everything appeared propitious for orderly governmental development under the new constitution. But launching the new government was not a smooth and simple operation, for there was
considerable political dissension within the Nation. Even before
removal the Creeks were classed as Upper Creeks and Lower
Creeks because of basic differences. The constitution of 1860
had temporarily bridged the gap between the two divisions but
the Civil War had again opened it.

After the adoption of the constitution a party of the Upper
Creeks was formed under Sands. This group refused to come
into the councils of the Nation. They claimed that wrong was
done them in the payment of certain funds made in December
1867, urging that it had been agreed to the satisfaction of
both parties that this money should be equally divided between
the two parties, northern and southern. Inasmuch as the constitution was adopted by an almost unanimous vote, and the
government of Checote was in power by the vote of the majority, the United States recognized the government created by the
constitution of 1867 and paid all the money to it.

L. N. Robinson, the Commissioner of Indian Affairs, felt that
the Checote government was devoted to the interests of the
Nation, favoring religion, education, progress and internal improvement. He and Dunn sympathized with this government
and desired that its authorities be furnished with a force sufficient to put down insubordination or insurrection. Yet trouble
seemed inevitable and there was a notable increase in violations
of the law. More murders had been committed in the year

following the adoption of the constitution than in all the years since the close of the war.

In February of 1868 S. M. Perryman and George Stidham of the Government Party went to Washington to make a new treaty. The Anti-Government Party in some manner learned of their mission and suspected treachery. They reasoned that the treaty of 1866 had returned to them their old laws, which they valued. They felt further that the Creek government had already violated the treaty provisions and they had gone to Washington to have it changed to confirm their illegal actions. Sands wrote at once to the Commissioner of Indian Affairs that their treaty suited them as it stood except that they were unhappy over the land they had been forced to cede.

The Government Party delegates managed to secure a treaty with the Indian administrators. It was signed September 2, 1868, by Commissioner of Indian Affairs Nathaniel G. Taylor and the two Creek delegates. The preamble contrasted the Creek and Choctaw treaties, stated the sharp practice of the Creek-Seminole land transaction, reviewed the inadequacy of the compensation to the loyal Creeks and virtually admitted that the threats of forfeiture had been invalid. It raised the compensation for the ceded land from thirty to fifty cents an acre, made a grant of $650,112 and provided that one-half of this sum rather than the $100,000 of the previous treaty should be applied to the losses of the loyal Creeks. It made restitution for several small claims such as the damage done to the Tulla- hassee Mission property by Federal soldiers. It also provided that no license should be granted to a trader except after approval by the Creek Council.

The Council ratified this treaty in November of 1868 and in 1869 the delegates returned to Washington to urge its acceptance by the United States Senate during the coming session of Congress; but Sands, Cotochochee and Thlothlo Yahola, against the advice of Dunn, managed to reach the city as a rival delegation to oppose it. Although the Federal officials seemed hopeful of ratification the inopportune appearance of the full bloods was sufficient to destroy whatever chance it had.

Political factionalism was intensified by delays in the payment of various claims, and it became increasingly apparent by the spring of 1869 that this division was rapidly leading to a crisis. Lawless members of both parties continued to commit depredations upon their opponents, each relying upon their

faction to protect them from punishment. In June Checote
called the Council to cope with the increasing disorder. There
were protracted debates over proposals for conferences with the
disaffected leaders, and apparently the district judges were empowered to summon citizens to assist in enforcing the law. In
August Sands sent his lighthorse police to the North Fork settlement to arrest members of the other party, intending to punish
them for alleged depredations, and he planned at the same time
to seize the council house and take over the administration.
Checote notified F. A. Field, who had succeeded Dunn as agent,
and Field called on the garrison at Fort Gibson for military
assistance.

Field recommended in 1870 a thorough investigation into the
causes of this constant strife so that the guilty parties could be
punished. Field suspected that recent disorders were partially
due to George Reynolds, a past Seminole agent, who had been
employed by the railroad that would probably profit by the
north-south land grants across Indian Territory. Also in 1870
the Anti-Government Party found another Caucasian friend, Dr.
J. B. G. Dixon, a British subject who took up residence in
the Creek country. At a council held at Arbeka (Sands's town)
in April, he was adopted by this faction as a full citizen of the
tribe, and from this time on he was often employed to conduct
its correspondence and present its cause to the Federal officials.

The Sands or Anti-Government Party was quiet during the
winter of 1870–1871, probably due to their interest in the coming election. It was universally understood that victory by the
Sands faction would mean a return to the old system of government. F. S. Lyon, the agent at this time, was uneasy as election
time drew near for the Sands faction was strong and numerous.
The alliance with Negro voters was an important factor in
Creek politics as it was in some other areas of the South during
this period. It was certain that in the approaching election they
would vote almost solidly for the Sands candidate. Lyon was
almost sure that Sands and Cotochochee were determined to
make a desperate effort to seize the government and reinstate
the old Creek laws.

The determination of each party to win the election became
more fully apparent when, three days previous to the meeting of
the Creek Council in October 1871, groups which had been
quietly gathering in their respective neighborhoods began to
appear in arms around Okmulgee. The day before the Council

was to assemble, three hundred of the Sands faction marched into Okmulgee, drove out those who had charge of the council house, took possession, proclaimed Cotochochee as Principal Chief and proceeded to organize their newly constituted government, keeping possession nearly the whole day. Chief Checote meanwhile ordered the stores to be closed, and noncombatants, with the women and children, were ordered to leave the town. Lyon had previously sent a message to Checote asking that no armed force be used except as the last resort. When Lyon, on his way to the council house, was eight or ten miles away he was met by special messengers from both sides with the assurance that his presence alone could prevent bloodshed. He arrived about six o'clock in the evening and found both forces in camp, with men armed, horses saddled and pickets set.

There were about seven hundred for the defense of the government and about three hundred in opposition. Lyon visited each camp and found a desire for peace, but a determination to maintain at all costs what each considered its rights. Pledges were taken from the leaders that neither party should fire the first shot and these pledges were faithfully kept. The stores were opened the next morning and during the day the regular Council of the Nation met and organized without interruption. Six or eight from each party gathered for a peace conference which assembled each half day for several days.

By determination on Lyon's part to maintain law and secure peace, and by reasoning with the leaders of the groups, a written understanding was procured. It was agreed that all would abide by the constitutional law of their nation as recognized by the United States government. The armed force on both sides was disbanded and business began moving quietly. The Council adjourned to meet again in the middle of the next month. The Anti-Government Party agreed to send their representatives to the Council and all agreed to be brothers and friends. When the votes were counted Checote was declared Principal Chief and Micco Hutke was named the second chief.

The Anti-Government Party loyally observed their agreement to come under the constitution. Sands had taken ill soon after the near-war in October and his enforced inaction may have contributed to the general harmony. Cotochochee called his adherents together as soon as he returned home and advised them to accept Checote as chief and to take part in the new government; but Cotochochee died almost immediately, and his town, Wewoka, was too deeply grieved to hold its election. All the other alienated towns chose their representatives to the Council, which met from November 16 to December 4, 1871. Forty-six towns including three Negro towns, were recognized at this time and the number of members of the House of War-riors was fixed at eighty-three.

On the surface political harmony prevailed within the Creek Nation during the winter of 1871–1872, but additional problems were developing. The decision was reached at one of the insurrectionary council meetings in the spring that Sands and Dixon should go to Washington to call for a new election, but Sands once again became ill and soon died, whereupon Dixon went on alone. Locher Harjo of Nuyaka, who had long been one of Sands' trusted lieutenants, became the leader of the Sands faction. As a result of the activities of Dixon and William Graham, the Commissioner of Indian Affairs, F. A. Walker, or-dered an investigation of the election under the supervision of Hoag. Leaders of both parties testified and it was concluded that Lyon had been imprudent in assisting in counting the votes, but Lyon implored the Indians to await the decision of the Department of the Interior.

Soon after the Hoag investigation Lyon advised the Govern-ment Party to take drastic action to suppress any further disaffection. A special session of the Council was called in Au-gust 1872 and its two houses passed a law outlawing all meetings and secret movements designed to prevent the execution of the laws. It forbade any citizen to petition a "foreign power," to at-tend a meeting for the purpose of subverting the constitution and laws, or to carry any insurrectionary message. It also imposed a penalty of from fifty to one hundred lashes for each offense. The Chief was authorized to increase the light-horsemen and he was instructed to request Lyon to expel Dixon and Charles Wheaton, who had been accused of agitating Negroes and other nonciti-zens. Dixon and Wheaton left for a time but Wheaton contin-ued his intrigues from Kansas and soon both returned and hid in the Negro and full blood settlements. Lyon also attempted the removal of Graham, but Hoag directed Lyon to let him remain.

During the latter part of August and the first of September in 1872 Checote called out about nine hundred assistant light-horsemen to offset any future disaffection. Part of them re-mained in their own districts as home guards but a large body was concentrated at Okmulgee. Locher Harjo collected his forces in the vicinity of the agency. Checote's followers advanced to meet them and a battle seemed imminent. Lyon was temporarily absent, but a garrison had again been stationed at Fort Gibson and its commanding officer, Colonel B. H. Grierson, managed to call the leaders of both parties together and arrange a truce. In the meantime he telegraphed Hoag, who held another conference with the leaders at the agency and again persuaded them to disband. Lyon estimated that the armed demonstration had cost the Nation thirty thousand dollars.

Andrew Williams, a special agent sent by Hoag in 1872 to investigate the election, concluded that the Checote party was clearly in the majority and that a new election would not affect the decision reached the previous year. E. R. Roberts replaced Lyon as the Creek agent in 1873. Upon discovering renewed signs of agitiation between these two parties Roberts urgently requested that the Department of the Interior act upon the 1872 recommendation of the Hoag-Williams Commission and return the decision at once to the Creek Nation. Checote's administration was recognized as the legal and ruling body in June of 1873. The Sands party accepted the situation and sent their representatives to the Creek National Council, taking part under the regular government.

The Creek Nation did not completely utilize its constitution for maintaining law and order. Prisoners awaiting trial were boarded at the house of Timothy Barnett of the Wewoka District, witnesses and jurors traded out their credits at his store and as court clerk he made out scrip to pay himself for his services. He lived with one of his wives in feudal abundance, dispensing hospitality to the whole countryside. He had a second wife several miles away in the Greenleaf settlements. When Barnett learned that another Indian was paying his second wife attention, he murdered him. Judge Nocus Yahola then called out twenty-one special light-horsemen to arrest him. They went to Barnett's home and after a gun battle with his servants, took him into custody. The light-horsemen promised him a fair trial but as soon as they were away from the house they killed him. Authorities made no attempt to investigate this infraction of justice and the light-horsemen received regular pay for their services. This episode might be taken as an example of primitive tribal justice dispensed by Creek law enforcement officers

except that it was the action of a secret society of Creek full
bloods known as the Pins that decreed his death. This society
exerted a strong undercover influence throughout the Creek
Nation. Its political alignment in 1872 was not clearly determined.

But Creek political difficulties appeared to be completely
settled in 1873. Sands, Cotochochee and Ketch Barnett of the
Anti-Government Party had died by September 1872, and both
factions had accepted Checote as the Principal Chief in the
summer of 1873. But dissension became evident after the
election of Locher Harjo, of the old Sands faction, in 1875 over
Checote, who had held office since 1867. The Checote faction
still controlled the legislature and disagreements grew between
the legislature and the Principal Chief which resulted in the
impeachment of Chief Harjo in 1876. Ward Coachman of the
Checote or Government Party served the three remaining years
of Harjo's term.

A major milestone was reached in 1875, for the election of
that year was orderly. Although Checote lost, his farewell address of October 5 expressed gratification over the orderly conduct of the election. He remarked that the campaign was not
characterized by ill feeling or illegal practices, but was dignified
and honorable to all parties. In spite of onslaughts of political
factionalism, the Creek government under the constitution of
1867 stood until tribal dissolution at statehood in 1907.

Political division within the Creek Nation was evident from
the end of the Civil War until tribal dissolution. Much of the
opposition to the Government Party was due to superstition,
ignorance and faith in the United States government. The Indians of the Anti-Government element looked upon the adoption
of the white man's institutions with disfavor. They seemed to
desire the conditions of society and government that existed
prior to the removal of the Creeks to Indian Territory, and this
element followed those who would promise government of that
nature.

Social Agencies Reestablished

As the Creeks returned after the Civil War to rebuild again
on their own soil their missionaries returned to assist in the
growth of the new society. Alice M. Robertson, the daughter of

Ann Eliza Worcester and W. S. Robertson, the Tullahassee educators, described the conditions and problems that faced them upon the return of the family in December 1866. As they came through the Cherokee Nation they saw ruined chimneys marking what had once been great plantation houses; they saw burned-over land where fires had swept through miles and miles of country, killing orchards and destroying fences and cabins; all domestic animals had vanished although wild animals had increased alarmingly. At Tullahassee Mission the well-kept hedge surrounding the front yard they left behind in July 1861 had grown into a mass of tall trees. The weeds were so large that the tall stalks had to be broken and chopped down to make a road for the wagon. The building was windowless and doorless and the large dining room was deep with manure, having been used as a military stable. The kitchen wing in the rear had much of the wall torn down, its brick having been hauled to Fort Gibson during the Federal occupation to make bake ovens for the troops.

Men from both Creek political parties visited and welcomed back the mission family and exhibited renewed interest in education. The freedmen were particularly anxious that their children be educated. Before the war they were not permitted to attend school because they had been slaves but now that they could be educated they seemed determined to profit by it. Already in the districts that had been allotted them, schools had been initiated on their own in anticipation of government assistance. Because they lacked competent teachers, they looked forward also to assistance from the missionaries.

By 1867 the Creek mission schools on the Arkansas and North Fork Rivers were being repaired preparatory to reopening although the sum set aside by the 1866 treaty for their repair was not ample. There were, however, fourteen neighborhood schools in successful operation, instructing probably 500 children and adults. The year 1866 had been a time of severe and necessary labor and every energy of the people was directed to the cultivation of crops and the building of houses. During the winter of 1867–1868 at least six Creek girls served as teachers, conducting neighborhood schools in the crude buildings provided by the communities. By the spring of 1868 Asbury on the North Fork River under the management of the Methodists and Tullahassee on the Arkansas River under the management of the Presbyterians were again in operation. About eighty scholars were taught at each school. They received a common school education with particular attention to their moral advancement. By 1869 the Creeks had an ample education fund and were successfully operating about thirty schools with an average daily attendance at each of perhaps twenty scholars.

Leonard Worcester, the superintendent of the Tullahassee Manual Labor School, reported that an agreement had been entered into between the mission board and the National Council by which the former would furnish and pay the salaries of the missionaries for carrying on the school, with the latter to defray all other expenses. The scholars were to be clothed by their families instead of by the institution as in former years. Under this arrangement the school was reopened in March 1868 with only thirty scholars, fifteen of each sex, in charge of Robertson, assisted by his wife and Nancy Thompson, who had also been connected with the mission before the war. The school began its second session in October 1868 with eighty-one scholars, forty girls and forty-one boys.

The fall of 1869 found the schools in adequate working order but they needed good teachers, for the pay was not adequate for trained personnel to seek employment. Hardly had Asbury Mission been repaired when it was destroyed by fire in 1869 but appropriations were made by the Council to rebuild it. By 1870 all the assistance the Creek Nation required from the United States was for schools, and there was an unusual amount of interest taken by its citizens in education, particularly by those who had previously opposed it.

The Creeks by 1870 had twenty-two public schools located throughout their country under the supervision of a superintendent of public instruction. Each of these schools had one teacher. The average number of children in attendance in each school was about twenty-four; the average daily attendance was about twenty, and the total registered was five hundred and forty. Thirteen of the teachers in these schools were natives, eight of whom were female and five male; all of these, so far as Superintendent J. H. Perryman was able to ascertain, had received their education in the mission schools in this Nation. The nine teachers remaining were white, four of whom were male and five female. Each of these teachers received from the Creek national treasury a salary of $400 for the scholastic year of ten months. Most of these schools had been in operation more than two years.

Superintendent Perryman thought the course of instruction in the several schools was adequate and extensive enough for a sound and practical education. Beginning with the alphabet and its combinations into words and syllables in the primary department, it extended through various elementary branches of instruction, such as reading, spelling, definition, geography, grammar, arithmetic and writing. During the winter months the schools were not as well attended as in the fall and in the spring because some of the children were poorly clothed and lived a great distance from the schools. They often attended school for two or three weeks and then because of severe weather would remain at home until they had almost forgotten what they had learned. But by and large most Creek parents wanted their children to attend school because they appreciated the value of education. Owing, however, to the inadequacy of Creek public school appropriations, which were only $11,000 annually, more than a dozen thickly settled neighborhoods whose residents had made numerous applications for schools did not have their requests granted. In Superintendent Perryman's opinion the schoolhouses were in most cases very crude, inconvenient and poor specimens of architecture. Perryman also declared that if the time, means and thought spent by the authorities of the United States for the purpose of devising a system to bring the Five Civilized Nations into a single territorial government were spent in devising one for educating and preparing these Indians for such a relation with the United States, it would be far more beneficial to these Indians and more honorable and profitable to the people of the United States.

Asbury Mission, destroyed by fire in 1869, was rebuilt by the Methodists with the Creek Nation contributing $10,000 to aid in the process. The burning of this mission was a great loss, not only in money but in keeping eighty Indians out of school for nearly two years. In the meantime Tullahassee struggled along. In 1872 Robertson realized one of his foremost ambitions for the school by establishing a bilingual newspaper, *Our Monthly;* the Creek Council provided funds for the press and some of the type. Young Samuel Robertson, with help from his Creek friend, Joseph Land, was the printer. Ann Eliza Robertson, the wife of W. S. Robertson, was recognized for her linguistic ability and she supplied hymns and passages of scripture in Creek. Robertson, as editor, contributed lessons and other helps for teachers. *Our Monthly* did much to increase literacy and spread information among the Creeks.

E. R. Roberts, the Creek agent in 1873, thought that the

money expended by the Creeks for neighborhood schools was wasted. He recommended that the government establish a normal school for the purpose of furnishing thoroughly trained teachers and then allow only the graduates of such an institution to teach in their schools. He suggested that until the normal school could furnish the Creek Nation with efficient teachers the incompetent ones throughout the Nation should be removed and their places filled with efficient and capable teachers from the United States.

By 1876 Creek schools numbered thirty-three with an aggregate attendance of 500; six of these were for Negro children and cost annually about $425 each. In addition to these public schools there were still only two mission manual labor boarding schools, Asbury and Tullahassee. Each of these schools had a large farm attached on which the pupils were required to work a certain length of time each week under the supervision of an efficient superintendent. From the products of these farms sufficient amounts of vegetables were raised to supply the table of the schools during the year. The success of these two institutions was so great that it was the intention of the Creek Council to establish another to be located on the western portion of their reserve among the full-blooded population.

The Muskogee Female Institute, a Baptist Mission boarding school of forty pupils was established in 1873. During 1875 over $30,000 was spent by the Creeks for educational purposes. Appropriations were made in 1877 by the National Council for two more mission schools, one being for the freedmen of the Nation. Provisions were also made for the support of eighteen young men while they obtained an education in the United States at different institutions. During 1877 Congress made its first appropriation of $20,000 as the beginning of the educational system of the Indian Bureau, and this sum also assisted the Creeks.

Summary

The Creek treaty of 1866 reduced their land area to half its original size. That which was left to them was a desolated area with their farms overgrown with underbrush and their houses and fences destroyed or dilapidated. The agricultural picture was not good at the close of the war but by 1869 the Creeks were agriculturally self-sustaining.

The Creeks were divided politically before the war into two groups known as the Lower Creeks and the Upper Creeks. At the Fort Smith Council on September 18, 1865, these groups agreed to terms of friendship and equal privileges for tribal benefits. In 1867, the same year that the Creek Nation ratified a new constitution, political strife opened between these groups and continued until the end of the tribal period. Political factionalism was intensified by delays in the payment of claims. The alliance with Negro voters was an important factor in Creek politics as it was in some other areas of the South during this period. A great deal of opposition to the Checote or Government Party by the Sands or Anti-Government Party was probably due to superstition, ignorance and implicit faith in the written promises of the United States. The Anti-Government element looked upon the adoption of the white man's institutions with disfavor. They seemed to wish for the conditions of society and government which existed prior to the removal of the Creeks to Indian Territory and this element followed those who promised a government of that nature.

The abolition of slavery and the granting of citizenship, including an equal interest in the soil and national funds to all persons lawfully residing in the Creek Nation if they returned within a year from the ratification of the 1866 treaty, was initiated in part at the ratification of the treaty. Sentiment was divided toward the Negro but the loyal faction supported their various claims. The presence of the Negro, however, did not seem to present as many difficulties within the Creek Nation as it did in the Choctaw-Chickasaw and Cherokee Nations. This reaction was predicted by General John B. Sanborn, who was sent to Indian Territory in early 1866 by Secretary of the Interior James Harlan to regulate relations between the freedmen and their former masters. Sanborn was convinced from a canvass of opinions that the Creek and Seminole Nations would not be adverse to an actual incorporation of the freedmen into their tribes. There was some effort made to eliminate the Negroes from the per capita payments but the freedmen began sharing the fund in the summer of 1869.

The Creek Nation was as concerned with intertribal politics as with tribal affairs. The Okmulgee General Council, an intertribal body, met in the Creek capital in 1870. The Creek Nation was the only Indian Territory Nation in favor of ratifying the Okmulgee Intertribal Constitution drawn up by the Okmulgee General Council. Although this constitution was not generally adopted by the Nations, the Council was significant in the history of Indian Territory. It aided in mediating peace between the United States and the plains Indians; it provided an avenue for issuing protests to the United States government against its railroad policy and any attempt toward the formation of a consolidated territorial government; and it established an intertribal newspaper in the Creek Nation in May of 1876, entitled the *Indian Journal*. The United States government ordered the Council abolished in 1876 after it became increasingly apparent that the Council was not fostering the desired goals of the United States government.

The Creeks, as well as most Indians of the other Civilized Nations, feared the railroads because they considered them a menace to sovereignty. Railroad construction usually brought problems. Construction crews were lawless and disorderly, and criminals congregated at each temporary terminal. As the road advanced it left enterprising intruders within the Nations. The Creeks were particularly troubled at the increase of white traders along the railroad after its construction was initiated in 1871–1872.

A renewed interest in education was exhibited in the Creek Nation after the Civil War though formal education did not begin until about 1868. The freedmen were particularly anxious that their children be educated. Before the war the slave system prevented their sharing the benefits of schools, but now that they were placed on an equality with their former masters they seemed determined to profit by their position. The education of the white children had been neglected in the Creek Nation as well as in the other four Nations. But by 1877 all phases of life in the Creek country had made notable progress.

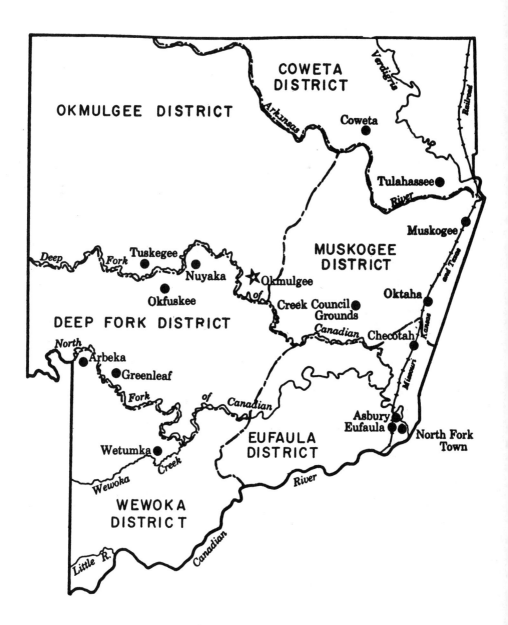

The Creek Nation

Chapter Six

RECONSTRUCTION IN THE CHOCTAW AND CHICKASAW NATIONS

The Choctaw and Chickasaw Nations, though maintaining separate governments and occupying different reservations, were generally classed as one people. Close cooperation had long existed between the two Nations and in 1866 they worked out a joint reconstruction treaty with the United States. The land occupied by the Choctaws and the Chickasaws before the Civil War was left intact in this treaty and they ceded to the government only that area known as the Leased District. Because of their location in the southern section of Indian Territory their country escaped the repeated invasions that had reduced other Indian areas to a desolate waste. Therefore many phases of reconstruction in these Nations, though a difficult process, was not the painful endeavor experienced by the Cherokees and the Creeks.

Agricultural and Natural Resources

By 1867 the Choctaws and the Chickasaws were generally free from want or distress, with the number of cattle, horses and hogs increasing steadily. By 1869 the general state of the country was flourishing; even the crop of oats of that year, which was sown in many instances for the first time, yielded a bountiful harvest. Very little wheat was raised owing to the lack of mills for the manufacture of flour, but the small quantity sown during the 1869 season grew well, a fact which manifested the adaptation of the soil to the production of that grain. The prairie lands produced most crops well with the exception of cotton. The bottom lands on the Red River and its tributaries were well adapted to cotton culture and the 1870 crop was unusually large.

Natural resources were more than adequate within the confines of these Nations. Lead was found in several areas of the country and that taken from the Poteau Mountains near the Arkansas River was pure argentiferous galena. Copper was discovered in small quantities on the Washita River west of Fort Arbuckle. An extensive belt of coal reached north and south from the Arkansas and Canadian rivers to the Red River. Sandstone and limestone were found in regular strata, sufficient for building purposes. Petroleum was in great abundance. Combined with sulphur, it formed the yellowish oil that gave the name to the "Oil Springs" of the Chickasaw Nation, situated near the Washita River not far from the Texas border. These springs also gained a medicinal celebrity for the cure of rheumatism and similar diseases. The Choctaws and Chickasaws had reason to be proud of the mineral content of the land that they occupied.

The first Choctaw laws for the collection of the royalty on timber and coal were declared unconstitutional by the Choctaw Supreme Court in 1875 because they had not been approved by the Chickasaws. Coleman Cole, then Chief, ordered that lumbering and mining operations should cease until the Nations could reach an understanding. The principle that the Chickasaws would receive one-fourth of the royalty was recognized in the Choctaw law of 1880. There were occasions when friction developed when one Nation would try to monopolize collections, but the principle was generally observed that each had the right to legislate exclusively for its own district, although recognizing the right of the other to collect its share of the revenue.

The Question of Sectioning

Governor Cyrus Harris of the Chickasaw Nation foresaw that their land could not be maintained perpetually in common and he therefore advocated allotment or holding the land in severalty. This subject became an issue between the Choctaw and Chickasaw people for Article XI of their 1866 treaty stipulated that the survey and allotment should be made only upon the condition that their legislatures agreed. The Chickasaws, at a called session of their legislature in November 1866, agreed to the measure. The Choctaws did nothing about the matter until March of 1870. At that time a council was called principally for the purpose of deciding the question. The subject was brought before them and was strongly advocated by some, but the full bloods generally opposed the measure. It was then decided by a resolution to lay the matter before the whole Choctaw people at a general election to take place in July 1870. This election was held and the votes cast indicated that the majority was opposed to "sectionizing," as survey and allotment were termed.

The Choctaws continued to oppose the measure, though the land of the Chickasaws was surveyed beginning in the winter of 1870–1871 and the United States government was petitioned by the Chickasaws to allot their land in 1872. The Secretary of the Interior, Columbus Delano, ruled that it could not be done without Choctaw approval. E. P. Smith, the Commissioner of Indian Affairs, maintained in 1873 that in view of the position of the Chickasaw Nation, Congress should provide the necessary legislation to enable the Bureau of Indian Affairs to comply with the request of the Chickasaws independent of the action of the Choctaws, in order that the object of the treaty could be carried out as far as the Chickasaws were concerned.

Even by 1875 the Choctaws declined to request that their land be surveyed for the purpose of allotment. They reminded officials that under the 1866 treaty provision no survey could be made for that purpose until both Nations asked for it, and thus the government took no action against the wishes of the Choctaws. The efforts of the Choctaw Nation, particularly through their delegate to Washington, Peter P. Pitchlynn, delayed allotment until the late 1890's. The Commissioner of Indian Affairs, J. D. C. Atkins, declared in 1886 that the 1866 treaty should be disregarded if necessary to bring about a change. He felt that the Indians had no right to obstruct civilization and commerce and he recommended the forcible allotment of the land in quarter section tracts and the purchase of the remainder for homestead entry. When the bill creating the Dawes Commission was before Congress in February of 1893 a circular letter was sent to the executives of the Five Civilized Nations by their delegates at Washington warning them against the proposed legislation, and they also informed their constituents that the United States no longer considered the treaties binding.

The law creating the Dawes Commission was enacted in March 1893. It authorized the President to appoint three commissioners to negotiate with the Five Civilized Tribes to effect the extinction of their titles to the land, either by cession to the United States, allotment, or any other method, with the ultimate purpose of creating a state or states of the Union. Repeated unsuccessful negotiations were carried on between the Dawes Commission and Choctaw representatives and the commission returned to Washington and reported its failure.

After further negotiations and political changes in the Choctaw Nation an agreement was signed with the United States at Muskogee on December 18, 1896. It provided that the Choctaw chief should deed to the United States the entire tribal domain, which should then be divided equally among the citizens except that each of the freedmen should receive only forty acres. The allotments were to remain inalienable and nontaxable for twenty-five years, although provision was made for the sale of certain portions at stated intervals. The townsites, public buildings and mineral lands were to be reserved from allotment; the proceeds from the sale of town lots were to be distributed equally among all of the citizens except the freedmen. The mineral revenues were to be used by the United States government for the support of education. The agreement was to be valid when ratified by the Congress of the United States and by the Choctaw and Chickasaw Nations.

The Dawes Commission thus succeeded in making an agreement with the representatives of the Choctaw Nation, the first of the Five Civilized Tribes to consent to negotiation. The Chickasaws were opposed to the sale of town lots and they especially objected to the trust plan of conveyance; they insisted that the title of allotments should be made by the executive of the two Nations rather than by the United States. Congress did not ratify the results of this negotiation, but an agreement was later made at Atoka in April 1897. The terms of this agreement were similar to those of the unratified Muskogee agreement in the allotment provisions, although there was some difference in the details. The Chickasaw objection to the trust plan of conveyance was met by the provision that the executives of the two Nations should execute the patents to the allottees.

Financial Negotiations

At the end of the war the finances of the Choctaw and Chickasaw Nations were in a disordered state, as the exact sum outstanding in national warrants was not known and a special wartime issue of paper treasury warrants was unpaid. The negotiation of the 1866 treaty in Washington also resulted in a complicated and confused situation that involved time, money and political strife. The services of H. B. Latrobe, Douglas H. Cooper and John D. Cochrane were obtained to represent the Nations during the negotiations in Washington in 1866. It was believed by many that Latrobe and his associates were employed with the understanding that they would divide their fee with the Choctaw delegates. Allen Wright, as the Choctaw National Treasurer, paid the attorneys $100,000, for which Latrobe gave him a receipt. Latrobe and his colleagues then retained half of this money, which they divided among themselves, and returned the other half to Wright, who distributed it in $10,000 shares among the four acting delegates and the Principal Chief. The delegates also received $2,843 each as the legitimate fee for their services. It was not known for some time that the delegates had participated in the division of the attorneys' fee. When the transaction became public and the Choctaw people realized that Latrobe's fee had been inflated by $50,000 for the benefit of the delegates at the expense of the Choctaw Nation, it created a public scandal.

Wright received the brunt of the criticism in the Choctaw Nation resulting from the scandal. One of the delegates, Robert M. Jones, made a public statement swearing that he never received any of the "return money" or even his regular fee. He also brought out the fact that Latrobe was Cooper's brother-in-law. A printed pamphlet entitled *A Reverend Libeler* reproached Wright bitterly, declaring with wry humor that henceforth he should be called "all wrong instead of Allen Wright."

By 1870 finances had become somewhat stabilized. The Choctaws often found it necessary to borrow money during this period especially to defray the expenses of the council session. These sums were usually obtained by making agreements with the lender to cash for him a specified number of old warrants, usually to the amount of a loan. Wealthy citizens seemed willing to lend their money on these terms and by the cashing of their warrants to exchange an old for a new indebtedness the Nation avoided the payment of exorbitant interest.

The Chickasaws and the Choctaws agreed in the 1866 treaty to pay damages to their loyal Indians but the assessed amount of $109,742.08 was opposed by the Nations. Secretary of Interior

O. H. Browning ruled that the amount should remain as it was and appointed Samuel Smoot special agent to pay the individual claims in the fall of 1868. However, much of the money seemed to have been channeled elsewhere for there were many complaints forwarded to the Bureau of Indian Affairs concerning the amounts received by the individual loyal Indians.

Article 50 stipulated that the commission should adjudicate the claims of the loyal traders who had been forced to abandon their property at the outbreak of the war, provided that the total award should not exceed ninety thousand dollars. The commission honored only the claims of Joseph G. Heald and Reuben Wright of Massachusetts, and between these the $90,000 was divided. The Choctaws made a compromise with these traders by which certain accounts, buildings, and other property were turned over to the Nation to somewhat balance the situation.

The claims arising from the Leased District, the Net Proceeds and the eastern boundary questions were the most extended and intricate of all the negotiations with the Federal government. Article III gave the Choctaw and Chickasaw Nations the alternative of adopting the freedmen and receiving $300,000 for the Leased District or having them removed by the United States at the expiration of two years, in which case the Negroes would receive the Leased District money. Some of the leaders were first inclined to favor adoption. Governor Colbert of the Chickasaw Nation and Chief Pitchlynn of the Choctaws expressed the opinion that the freedmen were needed as laborers; and that if they were removed and colonized in the Leased District freedmen from the United States might settle with them and create a large Negro Nation almost within the borders of the Choctaw-Chickasaw country. When the treaty was ratified in the fall of 1866 the question was postponed until it could be referred to the people through their selection of representatives at the next election. The Choctaw Council that met after the popular mandate requested the Commissioners of Indian Affairs to remove the freedmen as this had been the consensus of the majority. The attitude and action of the majority of Chickasaws was similar to the Choctaws.

In the meantime the United States had not waited for the Choctaw and Chickasaw Indians to negotiate their decision, for Congress in July 1866 appropriated $200,000 to be divided between the two Nations as payment for the Leased District. The Choctaw share, $150,000, was paid to Treasurer Wright and it was rumored that it was from this source that Latrobe received the $100,000 fee that created the basis for the scandal that ruined Wright's political career. Congress also appropriated $15, 000 as interest and even after it had been definitely decided by both Nations not to adopt their freedmen, an additional $15,000 was appropriated and paid in 1869. The two Nations expected that removal would take place at the end of the two year period stipulated in the treaty. When the government did not act it was requested again by the Nations that the terms of the treaty be carried out. No action was taken and the question was left unsettled. For twenty years the freedmen resided in the Choctaw and Chickasaw Nations with no clearly defined status. In general after 1868 they were treated as citizens of the United States subject to the criminal jurisdiction of the Federal District Court in Fort Smith and outside civil jurisdiction. They were given no right in public domain but they were allowed to use necessary land for cultivation.

The controversy over the Leased District involved more than the removal of the freedmen. The tract in question was leased to the United States for the use of Indian tribes by the treaty of 1855 and ceded to the government by the treaty of 1866. It was generally thought that the land was ceded for the settlement of Indians and the colonization of freedmen, but the treaty used the word cede with no statement of purposes although the draft treaty stated that the settlement of Indians was the general purpose. The federal government settled the Kiowas, Comanches and Apaches on reservations in this area in 1867, the Wichitas and affiliated bands in 1868, and the Cheyennes and Arapahoes in 1869. In 1879 Chief William Bryant of the Choctaws inquired of the Secretary of the Interior if the area was still open to settlement by the Choctaw and Chickasaws as it had been under the 1855 treaty. Commissioner of Indian Affairs E. A. Hayt replied that the land had been ceded unconditionally for the use of other Indians and that there was no law which would authorize the citizens of either of the Nations to settle within the Leased District.

The federal government decided in 1885 that land in the Leased District that had not been used for the location of Indians should be thrown open to white settlement; in 1889 the Choctaws passed a law declaring willingness to conform to the desire of the United States to use the Leased District for a purpose different from the terms of the treaty of 1866. Chickasaw cooperation was sought. In response to unofficial notification that the two Nations were ready to treat, the Federal government negotiated for the purchase of that portion of the Chickasaw Nation that was located between the Leased District and the ninety-sixth meridian. After repeated negotiations, an appropriation was made in 1891 for $2,991,450 to be divided between the two tribes in the usual three to one ratio. In the meantime the United States government had induced the Cheyenne and Arapahoes to accept allotments of 160 acres for each citizen in their section of the Leased District, thus opening the rest of the land for white settlement. When the officials of the Choctaw Nation made requisition on the United States for the money that had been appropriated for their use they were put off on various pretexts. President Benjamin Harrison also opposed the payment.

The matter was still pending when the Cheyenne and Arapaho lands were thrown open for white settlement on April 19, 1892. In May of that year the Senate of the United States by a vote of forty-three to thirteen passed a resolution that there was no reason for interference with the execution of the law making the appropriation to the two Nations. The House took similar action. Congress then passed a law which was approved by the Choctaw and Chickasaw Nations providing that $48,800 of the original appropriation should be returned to the United States Treasury to allow for 244 additional Cheyenne and Arapaho settlements. The law also provided that the payment should not be interpreted as a precedent obligating the United States to pay for the remainder of the Leased District.

The Net Proceeds claim[1] was carried over from before the

---

[1] The Choctaws claimed that they had been wronged by the failure of the United States to fulfill the obligations assumed by the Treaty of Dancing Rabbit Creek. They had never been paid for the cattle and other property abandoned at the time of their removal. Those who had paid their own expenses had never been reimbursed, and those who had remained in Mississippi had lost their allotments through the hostility of the United States officials. Since 1853, a delegation of which Peter P. Pitchlynn was head, had been in Washington advancing this claim. They maintained that the government should reimburse each individual Choctaw defrauded in the course of removals, and should pay the Nation the Net Proceeds claim, or the amount realized from the sale of the lands after subtracting the cost of the removals and survey. The treaty of 1885 referred the whole question to the arbitration of the United States Senate, and stipulated that the decision would be final. Acts of the General Council, 1852-1857, pp. 54-55, 74, 91-93, 100-101, 103, Choctaw National Council File, Choctaw Tribal Records, Indian Archives Division, Oklahoma Historical Society.

Civil War. In 1859 the United States Senate appropriated $2,981,
247.30, of which $250,000 was paid to the Choctaws on the eve of
the war and an equal amount in bonds was confiscated when
the Choctaws joined the Confederacy. The delegates appointed to obtain the claim consisted of Peter P. Pitchlynn,
Israel Folsom, Dixon W. Lewis and Samuel Garland. These
delegates first appointed Albert Pike as their attorney, but in
1855 they revoked this contract and employed John T.
Cochrane. It was afterwards charged that the change had been
made because Cochrane had agreed that he would "kickback"
one-third of his fee to the delegates. Latrobe was also involved
in the Net Proceeds claim. He was employed by the treaty
delegation of 1866 to negotiate the treaty and Allen Wright,
who became Principal Chief in the fall of 1866, seemed intent
on having Latrobe assist in negotiating the Net Proceeds claim.
The fulfillment of this desire ultimately cost Wright his political career. By 1870 Folsom, Lewis and Garland had died, leaving Pitchlynn, whom Wright had unsuccessfully tried to remove,
as the only original member of the delegation.

After Cochrane died Pitchlynn and Peter Folsom then employed James G. Blunt and Henry McKee. These new attorneys
were to receive the thirty per cent contingent fee, assume an
obligation to Mrs. John T. Cochrane of five per cent and adjust
the claims of all others who had rendered service in prosecuting
the claim. Latrobe protested to the Secretary of the Treasury
against this arrangement, saying that his contract had never
been revoked so far as the recovery of the bonds was concerned.
He also informed Chief Bryant that Pitchlynn and others were
scheming for the delivery of the bonds so that they might cheat
the Choctaw Nation out of the premium and accrued interest.
Pitchlynn answered by declaring that if Latrobe and Cooper
ever got their hands on the bonds they would claim one-half for
themselves under the settlement made by the delegation of
1866. Allen Wright and the rest had always been so anxious to
have these alleged contracts confirmed by the Council because
they claimed an additional twenty percent for themselves. The
Council had always wisely refused to confirm these contracts,
however.

Chief Bryant informed Pitchlynn and Folsom that they were
the only authorized delegation and that the act of the Choctaw
Council in ratifying the peace treaty did not constitute recognition of the Latrobe contract. Congress again provided for the

delivery of the bonds on March 3, 1871, but Latrobe and the Pitchlynn group both claimed the right to represent the Choctaw Nation. Moreover Lehman and Company brought suit in the Federal courts for the bonds on a requisition claimed to have been made by Pitchlynn and Folsom on April 27, 1871. A special session of the Council then refused to acknowledge any attorney's negotiations or fees except under the Cochrane contract. A court of claims was then created consisting of one member from each district for the purpose of paying the individual claimants and auditing the claims of delegate's attorneys. This method of payment met with opposition on the ground that private claims were not adequately protected. In view of this position agent T. D. Griffith was requested by many citizens to forward protests to the Office of Indian Affairs and the Secretary of the Treasury against the delivery of the bonds on those terms. The Council then passed a law designating the National Treasurer as the proper person to receive the bonds.

Congress next voted to suspend the payment and provided that the Secretary of the Treasury should investigate the liabilities of the Choctaw Nation to individuals and prepare a report indicating the amount of money required to satisfy the claims. Secretary Benjamin Bristow made a full report. Pitchlynn continued to send petitions to Congress and many committees recommended settlement, but the matter was allowed to lapse. During February 1874 a bill was passed revoking the Cochrane contract and all other contracts.

Coleman Cole was elected Choctaw chief the following summer. He believed that the Choctaw Nation should settle all the claims and that the United States government should ignore the delegates and make the payments directly to the claimants. He sent many petitions to Congress expounding this position. During 1875 and 1876 under Cole's leadership the individual claims were handled through a court of claims for each district at convenient places and the claimants were listed under three headings: lost property, self-emigration and land. Under lost property were listed items such as livestock left in Mississippi or lost on the journey, growing crops and such household conveniences as iron pots; under self-emigration was a charge of forty-six dollars and fifty cents for each slave and member of the family, and twenty-five dollars for the rifles promised by the treaty to every Indian man; under land was a list taken from the roll made by the captains and their claimants in 1850 showing the members of the tribe electing to remain in Mississippi who failed to receive their allotments.

When the courts had completed their findings, President Grant was notified that all was ready for the distribution; but payment was not forthcoming and Cole's failure to receive the money lessened his prestige. The Council refused to extend the authority of his courts of claims, approved Pitchlynn's report and brought articles of impeachment against the Chief, but the Senate by a vote of six to four failed to convict him.

The prospects that Congress would act favorably in the matter seemed very remote and consequently Pitchlynn appealed to Congress in 1878 against Chief Cole's wishes, asking that the case be referred to the courts. In 1881 Pitchlynn secured legislation by Congress referring the case to the United States Court of Claims. He died the same year, the last survivor of the original delegates, after devoting twenty-eight years of his life to prosecuting the claim. Blunt had also died and at the request of McKee, John Luce was chosen to assist in the suit. The Court of Claims awarded the Choctaws $408,120.32 for the delayed claims. This decision was appealed by both parties to the United States Supreme Court, which in 1886 reversed the judgment and confirmed the Senate appropriation of 1859.[2]

The Development of the Railroad

The coming of the railroad brought problems to the Choctaw and Chickasaw Nations as to the other Indian Nations. The granting of rights of way for railroads was included in all treaties of 1866 and the Choctaw Council met in joint session in 1869 and gave special consideration to the railroad issue. At

---

[2] United States, *Supreme Court Reports*, Vol. CXIX, pp. 306–321; Acts of the Choctaw Nation, October 28, 1903, and November 16, 1905, Choctaw Tribal Records, Indian Archives Division, Oklahoma Historical Society. The Choctaws had retroceded a large tract of their western land to the United States in 1825, when it was found to be already occupied by whites. The eastern boundary was at that time established on a line beginning on the Arkansas River one hundred paces east of Fort Smith and running due south to the Red River. The treaty of 1855 contained a provision for a new survey, but it was abandoned the next year at the request of the Indian Office. The Nation often instructed its delegates to push their claim, and the eastern boundary question was also settled in 1886. The Choctaws received $68,102. The Chickasaws laid claim to one-fourth of this amount, which was finally paid in 1905.

a session the following spring charters were granted to two railroads, the Choctaw and Chickasaw Central Railroad Company, and the Choctaw and Chickasaw Thirty-fifth Parallel Railway Company. The Choctaws voted to subscribe to stock, paying for it by the sale of alternative sections of land as provided by the treaty. The Chickasaws refused, the Secretary of the Interior also withheld his approval and consequently the enterprise was abandoned.

It was understandable that the Choctaw enterprise was not approved for Congress had passed a law in July 1866, before the treaty was negotiated, which provided that of three specified Kansas railroads the one that should be the first to reach the boundary of Indian Territory would be the beneficiary of the treaties. It made a free grant of the right of way, and a conditional grant of every alternate section in a ten mile strip on each side of the tract whenever the Indian title should be extinguished by treaty or otherwise, provided that the lands became a part of the public lands of the United States.

The winner of the three railroads in question was the Southern Branch of the Union Pacific, known as the Missouri, Kansas, and Texas Railroad, or simply "the Katy." The state line was reached on June 6, 1870. The road crossed the Cherokee and Creek Nations during the next two years, reached the northern boundary of the Choctaw country in the spring of 1872 and crossed the Red River into Texas early in December of the same year. It followed approximately the line of the old Texas Road from Muskogee in the Creek Nation to Denison, Texas, traversing the entire Indian Territory from north to south and cutting across a spur of the Chickasaw Nation just north of the Red River. The year it was completed James Colbert and J. A. Smith located 640 acres of land for town site purposes. Every person who agreed to build a house for a home or business was given a free use of land for that purpose. This town was named Colbert in honor of Frank Colbert. As the road progressed into Indian Territory the usual succession of blustering tent cities sprang up at the temporary terminals, only to be abandoned as the construction moved forward. The whiskey peddlers with their cargo, gamblers and other undesirable individuals came in numbers since the railroad right of way was outside the jurisdiction of the Indian courts and the Federal government rarely bothered to remove troublemakers.

Other problems arose with the coming of the railroad. Upon

entering the Choctaw country the railroad made no effort to pay
for the right of way. It secured exemption from taxation
and it purchased timber and stone from individual citizens in
violation of the law that placed such sales under the control of
the Choctaw Nation. Although the suit was lost to get the
railroads to pay taxes, the principle was established that the sale
of timber was under tribal control and the royalty law of
1871 became the basis of all later legislation pertaining to natural resources. In 1873 it was provided that the money from the
sale of timber should be divided equally between the Nation
and the citizen in possession of the land, and the prices of the
various kinds of timber and lumber were fixed by this and
subsequent acts.

Citizens also complained bitterly regarding their losses when
livestock were killed or injured by the trains. Hog losses were a
particular problem, for the Indians depended upon hogs for
their basic meat supply, and they ran almost wild in the woods.
The excessive freight and passenger charges exacted by the
railroad also aroused much bitter feeling. It cost less to buy a
ticket through Indian Territory than to points within it. Due to
difficulties within the Choctaw Nation between the Indians and
the railroad, the Indians were permitted by President Grant in
1876 to file claims against the railroad with Agent S. W.
Marston. After prolonged hearings Marston ruled that since by
the treaty of 1866 the Indians had granted the right of way to
railroads they were not entitled to compensation, and that by
payments to individual citizens the railroad had settled for the
purchase of construction material. Individual claims to the extent of $1,092.42 were allowed for injured stock and other dam-
ages. The decision was appealed but the Secretary of the Interi-
or sustained the contention of the railroad and ruled that neither the Choctaw nor the Chickasaw Nations were entitled to
damages on any of the claims presented.

Railroad development was closely linked with the development of coal fields. Although a small amount of coal had been
dug and used in the blacksmith shops and for other local needs
before the Civil War, it did not become accessible for commercial development until the coming of the railroads. J. J.
McAlester claimed the credit for being the first to realize the
possibilities of developing the coal fields due to the fact that he
saw a geological report in 1865 that indicated that the best coal
to be found in the Indian country was at the crossroads where

the Texas Road from Springfield, Missouri, to Preston and Dallas, Texas, crossed the California Trail from Fort Smith, Arkansas, to Albuquerque, New Mexico Territory. Acting upon this knowledge, he went to the crossroads and established a store which flourished. He married a Choctaw girl and became entitled to citizenship.

When the Missouri, Kansas, and Texas reached the crossroads in 1872, the station was named McAlester. The advent of the railroads made coal of commercial value so McAlester and other Choctaw citizens formed a company and began to develop the mines in that region under the provision of the Choctaw constitution that granted to a citizen who should discover any mineral the exclusive right to own and work the mine for the distance of a mile in every direction. McAlester and his associates leased their mine to operators from whom they received a royalty. The Choctaw Nation laid claim to this royalty but the Choctaw courts upheld McAlester and his associates. Chief Cole, however, was so opposed to the operation that he ordered the execution of McAlester and three of his associates, but the lighthorse captain, who was also white, allowed them to escape. A compromise was then made by which half of the royalty was paid to the Nation and half to the owners.

Political Readjustment

Although political preferences were shown and campaigns were hard fought, the Chickasaws and Choctaws escaped the intense internal feuds experienced by some of the other Nations of Indian Territory. These factors among others allowed the Choctaws to restore order soon after the war. This was evidenced by the fact that a semimilitary auxiliary force created at the close of the war to aid the civil officers in enforcing the law was abolished as no longer needed by the end of 1866. By the fall of 1867 Chief Wright was able to report to the Council, which had resumed its sessions in October 1865, that every county in the Choctaw Nation had its full complement of officers and that appreciable progress had been made in suppressing crime.

The government of the Choctaw Nation during reconstruction was still based upon the constitution adopted at Doaksville in 1860. This document provided for the separation of the governmental functions into legislative, executive and judicial departments, and specified the powers and duties of each. It included a bill of rights based upon the principles of the United States Constitution and it provided for amendment by a majority of the qualified voters at the general election. The old divisions were preserved in the Moshulatubbee, Pushmataha and Apukshunnubbee districts named for the three great district chiefs who had signed the treaty of Doak's Stand, but they existed mainly as convenient administrative units for school and judicial districts, for the collection of revenue, for the apportionment of senators and for the distribution of members on committees and delegations. At the head of each district was a chief elected by the voters who held office for two years and served as a subordinate local administrator under the direction of the principal chief.

The principal chief was elected by the people for a term of two years under a provision that disqualified him from serving more than two terms in succession. He had to be a free male citizen at least thirty years old, a lineal descendant of the Choctaw or Chickasaw race and a resident of the Nation for at least five years preceding his election. The other executive officials of the central government sometimes termed the "governors' cabinet" were the National Secretary, National Treasurer, National Auditor, and National Attorney. They were elected by the people for two year terms between the gubernatorial elections. These officers were subject to removal by the Council and to the chief's power of appointment where vacancies occurred in elective offices, and this put them somewhat under his control.

The legislative department of the Choctaw government consisted of a General Council of two houses, the Senate and the House of Representatives. The senate consisted of twelve members, with four from each district. They were elected for two year terms during the even years. Senators like principal chiefs had to be of Choctaw or Chickasaw lineage and be at least thirty years of age. The House of Representatives consisted of eighteen to twenty members elected for a term of one year. They were elected by counties according to population, one for approximately one thousand inhabitants. They too had to be of Choctaw and Chickasaw lineage and be at least twenty-one years of age to be eligible to serve. Laws were commonly enacted by a majority vote of both houses and the approval of the principal chief; an executive veto could be overridden by a two-thirds vote. Regular sessions of the Council began the first Monday in October and usually lasted about thirty days. Proceedings were carried on in Choctaw and interpreted into English. The text of the bills were usually in English, but occasionally bills were written in Choctaw.

The capitol of the Choctaw Nation was Armstrong Academy, where it had been established in the fall of 1863 and it remained so for twenty years. It was sometimes referred to as Chahta Tamaha and Choctaw City. An attempt was made in 1876 to remove it to Atoka but the measure was defeated. An amendment proposed to the Council in 1882 was ratified by the people and the capital was relocated about two and one-half miles east of Naih Waya. The name given to the new seat of government was Tuskahoma, meaning Red Warriors.

Elections were held every year in the Choctaw Nation on the first Wednesday in August. The most important elections were held during the even numbered years when the principal and district chiefs, the membership of the Council, the judicial officers and the county officers were chosen. On the odd years occurred the election of the "governor's cabinet" and the members of the House of Representatives. All males over eighteen years of age who had been citizens for at least six months were qualified to vote. Election precincts were established and constantly changed by special acts of the Council. All elections were by ballot, but the voter's choice was a matter of public record as the name of the candidate was written on one side of a piece of paper and on the other side was the name of the voter and a number showing the order in which he voted.

Choctaw law enforcement applied to the Chickasaws living in the Nation by the authority of the dual citizenship arrangement of the 1855 treaty of separation. Citizens of the Creek, Cherokee and Seminole Nations also came under the jurisdiction of Choctaw courts by the compact signed at North Fork Town in 1859. Since the jurisdiction of Choctaw law rested entirely upon citizenship, the laws governing admission into the tribe were significant. Before the war it had been the custom to admit certain classes of whites stipulated in the treaties of 1855 and 1866, and intermarried whites, to membership in the Nation, but the number of these adopted citizens had been small. After the war, with increasing development of natural resources Choctaw and Chickasaw citizenship came to mean an economic privilege that entitled the holder to an equal partnership in the public domain, so citizenship became greatly sought after by many whites. The treaties of 1855 and 1866 provided that the only white persons allowed to enter the Nation were travelers, Federal employees and employees of internal improvement corporations, and others who were authorized by the tribe. One of the first measures used to combat the increasing problem was the establishment of a permit law in 1867, but this provision did not solve the problem.

As Choctaw citizenship was increasingly sought because of the attending economic value inherent therein the Nation was forced to deal with an increasing number of claimants. In 1872 the judges of the Supreme Court were given the power to decide cases of disputed citizenship and the rejected claimants were classed as intruders. The next year the Nation adopted the custom of referring such cases to the National Council, which investigated them through a special committee and legalized the citizenship of successful claimants by legislative enactment.

The Choctaw Nation also enacted a marriage law in 1875 for the protection of its unmarried women. This act provided that no white man should marry into the Nation except under a license from a county official upon the payment of a twenty-five dollar fee and a certificate of good moral character signed by at least ten respectable Choctaw citizens who had known him for at least twelve months immediately preceding his application. The intermarried citizen who deserted his wife forfeited his citizenship, but the death of the wife did not affect his property rights unless he subsequently married a noncitizen. No special restrictions were placed upon the intermarriage of white women. A white woman legally married to a Choctaw man was recognized as a citizen but her citizenship was subject to the same conditions of forfeiture that applied to the intermarried man. The Chickasaw legislature admitted intermarried whites into full tribal membership after 1876.

Criminal cases involving United States citizens were under the jurisdiction of the Federal court for the Western District of Arkansas at Fort Smith. Judge Isaac C. Parker presided over this court from 1875 to 1896. His unusual record and method of allotting justice earned him the appellation of the "hanging judge." The location of this court was very inconvenient for the Chickasaws and the Choctaws and requests were made to the United States to establish courts closer to their country, but no immediate action was taken. Not only was the distance a factor but in many instances the trials were postponed for a year. A witness summoned from the Chickasaw-Choctaw area was often obliged to make three or four trips on horseback before being able to perform his duty. Arrests were usually made by the United States marshals who traveled over Indian Territory collecting prisoners, who were conveyed by wagon by day and guarded in a tent by night. The average jail of the Civil War period was a place of horror and this one was no exception. No decent jail was built here until 1887 and even then it was overcrowded. It was not until 1889 that a Federal court was established within Indian Territory. It was located at Muskogee and had jurisdiction over minor criminal cases and civil suits involving more than one hundred dollars.

Before the coming of Judge Parker and the establishment of the court at Fort Smith there was no court with civil jurisdiction. In business transactions in which one or both parties were United States citizens there was no legal method of enforcing the payment of debts or the fulfillment of contracts. It was risky for wholesale dealers to extend credit to Indian Territory merchants because there was little possibility of collecting payment from the dishonest. People from the United States who wished to defraud their creditors often took refuge in Indian Territory, but there was always the chance that the Indian agent would intervene and take the defaulter with his property to the border, thus placing him again within civil jurisdiction.

A third system of jurisdiction was represented by the authority of the Indian agent. Before any Federal civil jurisdiction was established disputes involving United States citizens were often arbitrated by the agent under a voluntary agreement by both parties. An appeal was always allowed from the agent's decisions to the Commissioner of Indian Affairs. In addition the agent also had a great deal of police power. At first he had to send to Fort Smith for a United States marshal to carry out his orders, but in 1878 a force of Indian police was created to serve under his direction. These men were citizens of the Indian Nations and were selected by the agent on the basis of local recommendation.

The government of the Chickasaw Nation as in the case of the Choctaws was reestablished very quickly after the war. The Chickasaw legislature convened at Tishomingo between the second and seventh of October, 1865. Their governmental machinery was also based on the Anglo-Saxon political experience. Both the Chickasaws and the Choctaws were opposed to a consolidated territorial government and, when the Okmulgee General Council convened in 1870, these Nations did not send delegates. But the Council adopted a resolution which announced that since the machinery of union had been created by the treaties in 1866, all the signatories whether present or not were bound by its acts. The reluctance of the Choctaws to participate in the General Council seemed to stem from their determination not to accept land in severalty and an unwillingness to join in a union with the tribes that had adopted their freedmen. They had decided that if the question of drafting a constitution for a territorial government came up they would invite the Chickasaws to join with them and withdraw from the Council. But they found that they had no cause for worry, for all five Nations opposed the proposed territorial government.

Education and Religion

As soon as the Choctaws settled down after the Civil War they turned their attention to the resumption of their school systems. On November 21, 1866, their Council voted to discuss school matters for an entire day and invited to this meeting all teachers, parents and patrons who were interested. Out of this discussion came a new national educational policy. On December 21 of that year the Council voted to establish schools in each neighborhood of the Nation where there were sufficient numbers of Choctaw children. Teachers were to receive two dollars per month for each pupil in attendance, a salary scale which remained the standard for many years. The exact date that the schools reopened is probably unknown, but by 1868 the public neighborhood school system was well attended. These schools were designed to prepare the children by a primary course of instruction for a collegiate education in the United States.

The superintendent of Choctaw schools, Forbis LeFlore, in 1869 recognized the weakness of teaching the Indian children in the English language and also the need for establishing a greater number of schools. At this time the neighborhood schools were divided into three districts: Pushmataha district had twenty-seven schools with 718 scholars and a term that extended from the first of September, 1868, to March 31, 1869, costing a total of $7,028.45; Apukshunnubbee district had twenty-three schools, 618 scholars, and a school term that extended from the first of September, 1868, to March 31, 1869, with a total expenditure of $6,027.72; Moshulatubbee district had nineteen schools with 511 scholars, the same length school terms as the other districts, and a total expenditure of $6,027.72. Twenty Choctaw children were being educated in the United States under the youth fund treaty provision.

Although the total number of Choctaw neighborhood schools was increased from sixty-nine in 1869 to eighty-four in 1870 the school term was decreased because of limited funds. Attendance in the winter was still very irregular, and because of a lack of knowledge of the English language, incompetent native teachers were being used in many instances. The school system had by 1870 become organized to the point where there were three local trustees over each school. Their duty was to see that the parents sent their children to school regularly and to report quarterly to the district trustees, who in turn reported to the superintendent of public schools, who then reported annually to the General Council. There were no high schools, academies or seminaries in operation in 1870, though Spencer Academy and New Hope Seminary were being repaired. The policy of sending pupils to the United States at national expense continued, especially for college and technical courses.

The eighty-four common schools in 1870 had one teacher each with an average of twenty-one pupils. Teachers were still being paid two dollars per month for each scholar in attendance and the school buildings were generally log cabins erected by the people of the vicinity. About one-third of the teachers were white, the others being natives who had been educated in and outside the Nation. The amount of money spent from the first of October 1869 to the last of April 1870 was $18,886. For the students in the different schools in the United States, $8,300 was spent for the year ending February 1, 1871. Sunday schools both in the Choctaw and the English language were carried on free of expense to the Nation.

The number of neighborhood schools were reduced in 1871 due to the fact that part of the school fund formerly used for that purpose was at that time being directed toward the reestablishment of one male academy, located in the lower part of the

Nation in the Apukshunnubbee district. Spencer Academy had
been a boys' school throughout its existence, under the sponsor-
ship of the Presbyterians, and it was designed to prepare boys
for entering eastern colleges. It also prepared many for the pro-
fessions and business life. Probably at no time was manual labor
stressed as much as it was at Spencer's forerunner, the Choctaw
Academy. The female seminary, New Hope, consisted of fifty
female scholars under the charge of the Methodists. The Nation paid for the teacher's board, and the church paid the
salaries. The course was designed to prepare girls for college in
the United States and gave them training in needlework and
housekeeping.

Among the Choctaw private schools that were established
after the Civil War was the institution started by the Baptist
missionary, the Reverend J. S. Murrow, in his home in Atoka in
1867. It was enlarged and aided by the Baptist Board of
Home Missions in 1887, becoming known as the Murrow Orphan Home. Armstrong Academy, though not private, was reopened as an orphan school for boys upon the recommendation of
Chief Cole in 1877. It continued as a male orphanage until
the end of territorial days. Wheelock Seminary was opened as a
girls' orphanage under the partial support of the Presbyterians.
The Chocktaw Nation took over the entire support and control
of the institution in 1893.

As in the other Nations the Choctaws lacked an adequate
supply of prepared teachers. Yet little effort was made to improve the teachers by association or by normal training until
near the end of the century and even then the attempts were
ineffective until supervised by the Federal officials after 1899.
During the period from the close of the Civil War until the end
of the century the whole school system was supported largely
from interest on Choctaw funds held and invested by the
United States, supplemented by finance from church societies.
Texts were furnished by the Nation though the plan was not so
universal or continuous as in the Cherokee Nation.

The pupils in Choctaw academies and seminaries were boarded at public expense. The communities erected and equipped
their own school buildings. Congressional aid which began in
1904 enabled many Indian children to attend school for the first
time and others to have longer terms and better teachers.
Many institutions that closed during the war never reopened.
Some of these were Fort Coffee Academy, Koonsha Female

Seminary, Chuahla Female Seminary, and Lyanubbee Female Seminary. Goodland Academy, near Hugo, was suspended during the Civil War but the missionaries remained to serve the Indians in any way that they could, and some reports indicated that the staff did a little teaching in the neighborhood. Between 1865 and 1870 Goodland did not exist as a school except for such private teaching as the family in charge of the buildings could handle.

Negroes in the Choctaw Nation were denied school privileges, except for the $3,500 spent each year by the United States Freedmen's Bureau and small sums by the Baptists. It was as late as 1887 before neighborhood schools were listed for Negroes. At that time there were twenty-three for freedmen, with 563 in attendance. Only children of freedmen were permitted to attend these schools and the children of Negroes from the United States had no educational opportunities. The Tuskalusa Colored Academy was probably the only Choctaw attempt to provide a boarding school for Negroes. It was located at Talihina and was coeducational.

The Chickasaw constitution of 1867 provided for a superintendent of education to serve a four year term. It obligated the legislature to make suitable provisions for the support and maintenance of public schools and it also made all school contracts subject to legislative approval. In accordance with these provisions the legislature in October 1867 passed an act to create neighborhood schools. It provided for three schools in each of the four counties and in any community not so selected where as many as ten pupils were available. The superintendent was to be paid an annual salary of $1,500, which was identical to the salary paid to the governor. The superintendent was to let the contracts for school houses or else pay the bills turned in by communities that chose to build their own. This is the exception among the Five Civilized Tribes of common school buildings being erected at national expense.

Teachers in the Chickasaw Nation were paid three dollars per pupil per month for actual attendance. In schools where the attendance was less than thirty, whites could attend by paying tuition. In June of 1870 Superintendent G. D. James reported eleven schools in operation with fifteen teachers. Five of the teachers were Chickasaws. The number had increased to fourteen by 1871 with 482 enrolled. The number remained fairly constant during the next few years, as there were thirteen such schools in 1877. In addition to this system of district schools the Chickasaw legislature provided for sending thirty boys and thirty girls to schools in the United States. Pupils and their parents could select their own schools and the superintendent was to accompany them. These pupils were sent for a three year period.

One unusual feature of Chickasaw education was the custom of paying parents for sending their children to school. Children living over two and one-half miles from school were given seven dollars per month as allowance for board. A legislative act of August 11, 1868, raised the monthly allowance from seven to ten dollars. An act was passed on September 25, 1869, decreasing the monthly allowance to seven dollars but it removed the distance requirement. In 1876 the monthly allowance was fixed at eight dollars for actual attendance of children between six and fourteen years old and the teacher was forbidden to board pupils in the schoolhouse.

Probably one of the weakest features in the system was the plan of selecting teachers. This was left wholly to the superintendent, who was sole judge as to what constituted ability and worthiness. To help assure the Nation of good teachers an act was passed in 1876 which provided that all citizens desiring to teach in neighborhood schools would be required to undergo an examination as to their qualifications.

Soon after the Civil War the Chickasaws cooperated with church societies on educational activity. Most of the time, however, the schools were on a strictly contract basis whereby the national officials dealt directly with individual contractors. The superintendent appointed one trustee for each boarding school, and these two men were the national representatives in management and supervision. The contractor provided board and instruction and usually a good many other items for the pupils. It was not expected that the parents or their children should do anything to share expenses. The process of leasing boarding schools to the lowest bidder was another unique feature of Chickasaw education. The Chickasaws spent more money per capita for educational purposes than any other tribe but the results were meager. Chickasaw girls received more training for homemaking and preparation for college at Bloomfield Academy than anywhere else among the schools of Indian Territory.

Another institute of significance was the Chickasaw Manual Labor Academy. Prior to the war this school was a joint enterprise between the Nation and the Methodist Episcopal Church.

A legislative act of 1870 authorized the repair of the academy and in 1876 another law was passed that a high school should be established at the Chickasaw Manual Labor Academy for boys under the national contract system. Gradually the school began to be called Harley Institute out of respect for Joshua Harley, who came to the Chickasaws in 1868 and started a school in the old academy. He took the contract for the high school in 1876 and with the exception of five years remained there until his death in 1892. By 1889 the Harley Institute had replaced Chickasaw Manual Labor Academy. The act of 1870 also authorized the repair of Wapanucka Male Academy but the act of 1876 changed its status to a special coeducational school for Chickasaw children living in the Choctaw Nation; in 1890 it was changed again to a school for boys.

As a result of the war there were within the Chickasaw Nation many orphan children for whom educational provision needed to be made. A school or home was established for them at Stonewall, known as Lebanon Institute. It was built for an average enrollment of sixty; after this number was reached the remaining orphan children were to be allowed to attend any academy. This institute differed from the other academies in that it was not let out by contract but was under the supervision and control of the governor and the superintendent of public instruction. In 1879 an act was passed changing the name of the Chickasaw Orphans' Home.

It is improbable that any Negro ever received a day of schooling at the expense of the Chickasaw Nation although few other tribes had as many Negroes in proportion to total population. In 1867 the Freedmen's Bureau maintained five schools for Negroes in this Nation. With a little assistance from Baptist mission boards, this was all of the school privileges that these Negroes enjoyed until statehood. Many of the Negroid population were not freedmen and would not have profited educationally had the treaty of 1866 been obeyed.

Freedmen in the Two Nations

The question of what to do about freedmen in the Chickasaw and Choctaw Nations was one that had political, economic and perplexing social overtones, and it was one that remained unsolved for many years. Neither Nation was required to share fully national money or national soil with the freedmen, as they had stipulated within their treaty that the freedmen should receive only forty acres of land and should participate in no division of national money. Slavery was officially abolished in both Nations by legislation enacted in October 1865, but employment of former slaves was regulated by legislation similar to the codes governing the freedmen of southern states. They were required to choose an employer and make a written wage agreement with him before a county judge. Vagrants found without employment were to be arrested by the sheriffs or lighthorse-men and their services sold to the highest bidder, who should compel them to work. The money secured in this manner was put in a special fund for the support of any freed person in need of financial assistance.

Payment of wages began after January 1, 1866, and a standard scale was fixed for eight classes of laborers, including children, with wages ranging from two dollars to ten dollars a month plus specified items of food and shelter. The working day was limited to ten hours in summer and nine in winter, with Saturday afternoon and Sunday as holidays except when forced labor was necessary to save a crop. The wages of laborers constituted a first lien on the crop and the property on the plantation. The former masters were required to make provision in their contracts for the support of the aged, crippled and infirm whom they had held as slaves. The freedmen were guaranteed full protection of person and property and were given civil and criminal protection in the courts equal to that enjoyed by citizens. Former slaves who had voluntarily left the Nation were not to be permitted to return.

The freedmen in the Red River valley were joined by roving bands of Negroes from Texas. It was believed that many of these Negroes, having no other means of subsistence, stole for a living. To check these depredations a secret committee was formed to patrol the country, warning vagrants, hanging cattle thieves and disbanding the most disorderly of the freedmen settlements. It was partially because of this situation and the general attitude of many of the Choctaw and Chickasaw Indians that General Sanborn was appointed in the fall of 1865 as special commissioner to Indian Territory to guard the interests of the freedmen. Considering it unsafe to venture into the Choctaw Nation, he sent out circulars from Fort Smith warning the Choctaws that the freedmen were under his protection. At the same time he sent reports to the Office of Indian Affairs describing the atrocities committed by the Choctaws against the freedmen and advising that the whole country be placed under martial law.

When Sanborn visited the Choctaw country, one would wonder whether he was treated with the utmost consideration, or intimidated, for the tone of his official reports changed completely. He remarked that conditions had never been as bad as might have been inferred from his previous report and that the economic rights of the freedmen were generally recognized and that they were receiving fair wages or rents for their labor on the plantations. In April 1866 he asked to be relieved from duty on the ground that the freedmen were no longer in need of his services. The commission was soon discontinued, leaving the final status of the Negroes to be determined by the Choctaws and the Chickasaws.

The treaty of 1866 gave the Choctaws and the Chickasaws the alternative of adopting the freedmen and receiving $300,000 for the Leased District or having them removed by the United States at the expiration of two years, in which case the Negroes would receive the Leased District money. At first some of the leaders were inclined to favor adoption but the majority of the people favored removal. The Chickasaw and Choctaw Nations requested Congress to remove the freedmen but no action was taken at that time.

There were many petitions from freedmen asking for removal from the Choctaw Nation but on the other hand there were those who desired an arrangement whereby they could stay in the Nation under the special protection of the United States. Some of these petitions were evidently fostered by whites who sought to influence them for their own purposes. V. Dell, a member of the Arkansas Legislature, sponsored a number of meetings of Choctaw freedmen during 1869 and 1870 and secured the adoption of resolutions demanding full citizenship, with equal property rights in land and tribal money, the allotment of the land and the opening of the country to white settlement. The Choctaws destroyed some of the posters announcing these meetings and by threats prevented some of the meetings. George Olmsted, the Choctaw-Chickasaw agent, arrested a Negro who was carrying a letter inviting freedmen to attend a meeting of this nature. The Negroes then demanded the removal of Olmsted for his obvious attitude. Dell used these resolutions to bring pressure upon the government against the Choctaws. Major S. N. Clark, a special agent of the Freedmen's Bureau, also approved of these resolutions.

As the question dragged on the United States government took steps to establish schools for the freedmen. The first school opened at Boggy Depot in 1874 and was supported by the government under contract with the Baptist Mission Board. Some whites living in the area under permit sought to embarrass and intimidate the teachers and many thought that they were responsible for the burning of the school in the fall of 1875. Additional schools were secured at Skullyville, Doaksville, Fort Coffee and other places. The Choctaws continued to petition the United States government for the fulfillment of the treaty of 1866, but when it became apparent that such a policy would never be carried out a sentiment developed in favor of adoption. Beginning in 1875 Choctaw and Chickasaw commissioners met together in attempts to effect a joint settlement, but the Chickasaws stood out against adoption.

The Choctaws then resolved to take independent action. In the fall of 1880 their Council adopted a resolution signifying to the United States their willingness to adopt the freedmen according to the lapsed provision of the treaty, but Congress took no action and the Choctaws were unable to act in the absence of legislation. In 1882 Congress appropriated $10,000 of Choctaw and Chickasaw money for the support of the freedmen schools; it provided that if either Nation should adopt the freedmen it should be reimbursed from the unpaid balance of the Leased District money. This granted opportunity to act without the Chickasaws. The Choctaws then passed a law adopting the freedmen in May 1883.

The newly adopted freedmen were to receive educational opportunities equal to those of the Choctaws so far as neighborhood schools were concerned. Those who elected to remove were each to receive $100 to be paid out of the Leased District balance. Those who would decline to become citizens and fail to remove were to be classed as intruders and subject to removal like other citizens of the United States. In addition the law provided that freedmen should be ineligible for the offices of principal chief and district chief, and that intermarried citizenship should not be conferred upon noncitizen Negroes who should marry Choctaw freedmen. The Commissioner of Indian Affairs objected to those provisions on the ground that they were in violation of the treaty. The Council then repealed the article that made Negroes ineligible to the office of chief and provided for the appointment of two delegates who were to proceed to Washington and work for the adoption of the bill.

J. S. Standley and Campbell LeFlore were selected as delegates and they ably presented the position that the refusal to grant citizenship to intermarried Negroes was not in violation of the treaty. They further maintained that if they could not retain this article they would return the payments they had received on the Leased District and leave the whole question as it had stood in the beginning. Secretary of the Interior Henry M. Teller was convinced and ruled that since the restriction was placed on noncitizens rather than citizens it did not conflict with the treaty. In March 1885 Congress appropriated $52,125 to be placed to the credit of the Choctaws as their share of the balance of the Leased District money.

The Choctaws insisted that under the reciprocal citizenship arrangement of the treaty of 1855 the Chickasaws were bound to grant suffrage and the use of tribal land to Choctaw freedmen living in their district. The Chickasaws had never been as liberal as the Choctaws in interpreting these provisions. While the Choctaws had given absolute political equality to persons of Chickasaw blood living in their Nation, the Chickasaw constitution had stipulated that only members of that tribe were eligible to fill the office of governor or be members of the Council. The Chickasaws were upheld in this discrimination against Choctaw citizens by Attorney General Caleb Cushing, who ruled in January 1857 that the rights of citizenship guaranteed by the treaty of 1855 did not necessarily include suffrage or the right to hold office. The Chickasaws were therefore within their lawful rights when they refused to grant political privileges to the Choctaw freedmen.

Neither Choctaws nor Chickasaws openly mingled socially with the Negroes. When intermarriage became a possibility by the incorporation of the freedmen into the Choctaw Nation, a law was immediately passed making it a felony. The Choctaw freedmen formed a distinct social group. They were usually more thrifty than the other members of their race as they generally cultivated farms of their own or worked as laborers. They lived apart from the whites and the Choctaws and as a rule held themselves aloof from the Negro immigrants from the United States.

Summary

The Choctaws and Chickasaws were confederated for national purposes. They numbered about sixteen thousand and six thousand, respectively, at the close of the Civil War, and they were located on adjacent reserves comprising eleven million three hundred and thirty-seven thousand acres in the southeastern part of Indian Territory. They were shrewd strategists as evidenced by the manner in which they maneuvered the provisions of their 1866 treaty. They had been the most outspoken of the Five Civilized Tribes in their sympathies for the South, yet they received more generous terms and kinder treatment than the tribes who had suffered great hardships for the Federal government. The Choctaws and Chickasaws had a leadership that seemingly better understood the machinations of the Anglo-Saxons than did that of the other Civilized Nations.

Although the Choctaws and Chickasaws cooperated to the extent of making a joint treaty they did not always agree on issues in the treaty. The Chickasaws as early as 1868 endorsed sectionization of their land while the Choctaws were strongly opposed. Both Nations needed to agree to the survey of their land for allotment purposes and, because they would not, this feature of the treaty was not complied with until 1897 and only then through the work of the Dawes Commission. The Choctaws finally decided to adopt their freedmen in 1883, but the Chickasaws never honored this treaty provision as the proportion of Negroes within their nation was large in relation to the number of their citizens.

The basic political structure of the Choctaw and Chickasaw Nations was disrupted no longer than the period of the Civil War. Their tribal councils were activated in the fall of 1865 and again their form of government was similar to that in use in the various states of the Union. Each had a written constitution and both had civil and criminal laws. Their legislative bodies were in the image of the state senates and houses of representatives. They each had their governor or principal chief, and each had a regularly organized judiciary with inferior and superior courts. There were sometimes political incidents between these tribes as well as differences within them but these problems were settled peacefully. The bitter internal political strife or the deep factionalism shown in Creek and Cherokee politics was not inherent in the politics of these people.

The funds of the Choctaw and Chickasaw Nations were paid by the United States to their respective treasurers and then disbursed under direction of the National Councils. The loyal citizens were paid their indemnity in 1868 and the damages due traders Heald and Wright were taken care of in 1869. The Net Proceeds claim, the eastern boundary question and the delayed annuities were all finally settled in 1886. Peter P. Pitchlynn of the Choctaws worked on the Net Proceeds claim from 1853 until he died in 1881. The diplomatic aspects of the Leased District were settled in 1892. The usual division of money between these two nations was based upon a ratio of three-fourths to one-fourth, a percentage derived from the comparative population of the two people.

During the reconstruction period three systems of court jurisdiction were used in the Choctaw and Chickasaw Nations. Before the establishment of a Federal court at Fort Smith there was no court with civil jurisdiction. In business transactions in which one or both parties were United States citizens, there was no legal method of collecting debts or enforcing contracts, though the Indian agent did have a certain amount of authority. Disputes involving United States citizens were often arbitrated by the agent under a voluntary agreement of both parties. It was not until 1875 that a Federal court was established in Fort Smith, Arkansas, which proved to be very inconvenient to many not only in the Choctaw and Chickasaw Nations but in all of Indian Territory. In July 1889 a Federal court was established in Indian Territory at Muskogee with jurisdiction over minor criminal cases and civil suits involving more than one hundred dollars.

Schools were generally reestablished for Indians in the Choctaw country by 1871 and Negroes were given an opportunity for education by 1874. The Chickasaw legislature provided for schools to reopen in 1867 and there was mention in the 1868 report of the Commissioner of Indian Affairs that the neighborhood elementary schools had reopened. The Chickasaws provided no educational opportunities for their Negroes. Before the Choctaws adopted their freedmen and simultaneously provided schools for them, the United States government and the Baptists were of assistance in educating their freedmen. The fact that English was the usual spoken language in schools made comprehension difficult for these Indians who spoke nothing but their native tongue. Consequently, the mixed bloods were the great benefactors of the schools in the Choctaw and Chickasaw Nations and continued academic training in the eastern states. The manual labor type of institution to a degree benefited the full bloods, but they were inadequate in size to enroll all who wished to attend. The Chickasaws spent more money per capita on education than any other tribe in Indian Territory but their system of learning was ineffective for the masses. The fact that they handled their own money kept outsiders from interfering with their educational system in either a positive or a negative manner.

The land of the Choctaws and Chickasaws was generally good and on it they produced cotton, wheat, corn and livestock. The agricultural wealth of these nations attracted white men who often married Indian women in order to become native citizens with full rights to the land. Other white men came to work for the Choctaws and Chickasaws and were able to obtain land and enlarge their holdings. Many whites came to work on the railroads while others came to establish businesses in the many towns that sprang up along the lines. Still other whites exploited the mineral deposits within the area. The Indians generally did not see the railroad as an added convenience or as an aid to advancement for it brought with it many problems that they were happier without. The desire of the whites to open the land to settlement caused a barrage of bills to be introduced in Congress, but the Choctaw and Chickasaw Nations sent numerous memorials to Congress and issued various other protests against the idea of a consolidated territorial government. These Nations suffered less from the horrors of the Civil War because of their geographic location in the southern section of Indian Territory. They also experienced fewer reconstruction problems than the Seminole, the Creek and the Cherokee Nations.

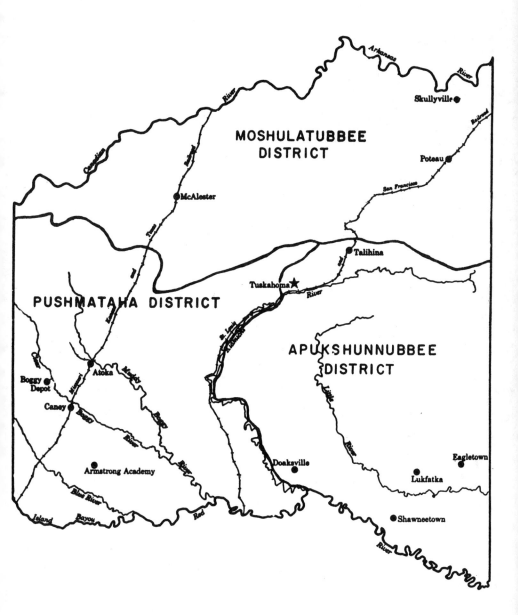

The Choctaw Nation

The Chickasaw Nation

Chapter Seven

RECONSTRUCTION
IN THE CHEROKEE NATION

The task of reconstruction in the Cherokee Nation was an experience that proved to be both heartbreaking and challenging. This proud Nation, once powerful with its established system of constitutional government, with its immense herds of fine cattle and ponies on rich prairie pasturage, with its adequate and often spacious homesteads with its farm buildings, mills, common schools, seminaries and other economic and social aspects of life moving rapidly according to Anglo-Saxon standards, was brought to a standstill by the devastation of the Civil War.

Agricultural Adjustment

Although many of the Cherokee refugees had returned to their own Nation by 1864, comparatively little food was produced that year even though the weather was good. The militarily unprotected condition of the country made it extremely hazardous for the civilian population to attend to agricultural production. In attempting to do so a number of Cherokees had fallen victim to the Confederate bands who infested their land. Many women attempted to raise crops but the spring was far advanced before seed of any kind could be obtained, agricultural implements were scarce and in bad repair, and supplies of every kind were scant.

The Indians in the Cherokee Nation were mainly dependent upon the United States government for a year following the Civil War. In addition a number of former slave owners refused to recognize that the freedmen were no longer slaves. How-

ever the Cherokees were blessed with peace and quiet and an
abundant crop for the year 1867. Many of the southern Cherokees living in the Choctaw and Chickasaw country returned to
their old homes and brought what cattle and hogs they could
procure from those people. Although the number was small it
helped to restock the Cherokee country. By 1869 ample crops
had crowned their labors and herds of cattle and horses had
replaced those lost in the Civil War.

New Uses for Cherokee Land

Articles XV through XX of the treaty of 1866 were concerned
with various transactions and usages of Cherokee land. It
became necessary, as a result, to prepare for the removal of
various Indians to land both east and west of ninety-six degrees
west longitude. In November 1866 the Cherokee National
Council authorized the appointment of a commission to treat
with a delegation of Delaware Indians from Kansas whereby
that tribe might select lands either east or west of the ninety-
sixth meridian. A conference of the delegations was held and on
April 8, 1867, terms were reached and on June 15 these
terms were ratified by the Cherokee National Council. The
Delawares agreed to purchase 160 acres for each member of
their tribe at one dollar an acre. The census taken for this
purpose showed a few more than one thousand and 985 of these
people removed to the Cherokee Nation. The land was to be
selected in aggregate east of the ninety-sixth meridian. They
were to pay into the Cherokee national treasury a sum propor-
tionate to the Cherokee per capita amount then in the treasury
in accordance with the treaty provision. A census of the Cherokees was to be made in order to determine the exact amount to
be contributed to the national fund. The Delawares were thus
to be incorporated within the Cherokee Nation and to share
alike in Cherokees' citizen rights and privileges.

Delawares began in December 1867 to remove to their lands
on the Verdigris and Caney Rivers. Nearly all had reached
their new homes by June of the next year, but conditions soon
developed that caused dissatisfaction. Some had gone too far
west and settled on land later purchased by the Osages, others
complained that the Cherokees were already on the most desirable land. Noting the confusion, the Quapaws attempted to in-

duce them to come into their area and buy head rights from them. Caucasian citizens of the United States were also reported among the Delawares offering to negotiate in withdrawing Delaware funds from the common Cherokee-Delaware treasury in order to buy land elsewhere in Indian Territory. These disturbances gave rise to correspondence between a Delaware headman, John Sarcoxie, a signer of the agreement of April 8, 1867, and Chief Lewis Downing. A letter from Downing to Sarcoxie indicated that Sarcoxie had asked that the Delawares be allowed to cancel their arrangement with the Cherokees and remove west of the ninety-sixth meridian and set up their own government. Downing advised him to give up the idea and invited Sarcoxie to come to Tahlequah, where the National Council was then in session, and lay any grievances he had before that body. This advice helped induce the Delawares to remain an integral part of the Cherokee Nation.

For almost fifty years the Shawnees had lived on a rich reservation in Kansas. In 1854, surrounded by whites, they relinquished all of their lands except 200,000 acres which had been allotted in severalty. An agreement was reached and approved in June of 1869 whereby about seven hundred and seventy Shawnees moved to the Cherokee Nation. Terms regarding funds, the length of time for registering for lands, and immunities and privileges as Cherokee citizens were provisions incorporated in the agreement.

Meanwhile a part of the Cherokee country west of the ninety-sixth meridian had been assigned to the Osage and Kansas Tribes. The treaty of 1865 with the Osages made certain preliminary arrangements for their removal to Indian Territory. An act of July 15, 1870, provided for the selection of a reservation for them, and in 1871 this selection was made in the Cherokee territory west of the ninety-sixth meridian. The Cherokees felt that they were wronged by the valuation of that portion of their land assigned to the Osages, as these lands were priced at only fifty cents per acre. The Cherokees finally received for all of the land in the tract east of the Arkansas River two dollars per acre, and one dollar and fifty cents per acre for the land west of the Arkansas River. By an act of June 5, 1872, all the Cherokee territory between the Arkansas River and the ninety-sixth meridian was set apart for the Osage and the Kansas tribes. The plan of treating with the Indians had been changed during these removals. An act of March 3, 1871, affirmed the

validity of all previous obligations but declared that henceforth
no more treaties should be made with the Indian tribes. Accordingly, after that date reservations were set apart by statute
or by executive order and not by agreements with the tribal
authorities ratified by the United States Senate.

One issue of great concern pertaining to Cherokee land involved the Neutral Lands in Kansas. The Cherokees had wanted
for a long time to dispose of the Neutral Lands. Their
treaty of 1866 authorized the United States to sell this land and
in August 1866, after the treaty had been concluded, Secretary
of the Interior Harlan had entered into a contract with the
American Emigrant Company, a corporation of Connecticut
with headquarters at Des Moines, Iowa, for the sale of the
Neutral Lands at one dollar an acre. This company was a
combination devising ways and means whereby they might purchase the lands in a body at one-tenth of its real value. When
O. H. Browning succeeded Harlan as Secretary of the Interior
he inquired into the sale, found it to be illegal, and had it
declared null and void. Secretary Browning then proceeded to
make his own contract for its sale with James F. Joy of Detroit,
Michigan, a relative. In order to make valid the disposal of the
Neutral Lands the Cherokee delegation entered into a treaty
with the United States on April 27, 1868, which was ratified by
the Senate and proclaimed on June 10. The former contract
with the American Emigrant Company was reaffirmed and Joy's
contract of October 9, 1867 was cancelled. Then Joy was assigned the former contract, assumed its obligations and entered
into a new contract by which he agreed to pay $75,000 to the
Secretary of the Interior upon ratification of the treaty and the
remainder of the purchase price in installations.

When the transaction was completed approximately twenty
thousand settlers and a few Cherokee families lived in the
Neutral Lands. William A. Phillips, chosen by the Cherokees,
and John T. Cox, agent for Joy, were authorized to appraise the
improvements that had been made on the land in order to
compensate these individuals. The Cherokee Nation had at last
realized some benefit from the Neutral Lands.

The eastern or North Carolina Cherokees also presented a
problem to the Cherokee Nation. The main body of Cherokees
came to the West in the thirties, but there remained in the East
a considerable number who had fled to the hills where they
lived in hiding. The Federal government and the Cherokee

Nation considered their status following the Civil War and in 1868 a treaty was concluded, though never ratified, which contained a provision for the removal of the Cherokees residing in North Carolina. Those who should come to the Cherokee Nation within three years from the date of ratification were entitled to all its privileges; after the expiration of three years those removing could be admitted to citizenship only by established action of the National Council. This agitation for removal after the Civil War seems first to have been started in 1866 by a communication from D. M. Morris, a North Carolina Cherokee, which initiated negotiations that lasted for years.

Since the Civil War left the North Carolina Cherokees impoverished many of them considered moving to Indian Territory. In 1869 the Cherokee National Council passed a joint resolution by which an invitation was extended to them to do so. The result of this was the removal in 1871 of 130 under the direction of J. D. Lang, an official from the Office of Indian Affairs, who was also a member of the Board of Indian Commissioners created by President Grant.

The Cherokees remaining in the East in 1874 were settled on the former William T. Thomas holdings[1] and in June of the next year an agent was sent to them. Their condition though improved was still far from satisfactory. Upon learning of the land sales being made in the West under terms of the treaty of 1866, many desired to move to the West in order to share the proceeds. Others wished to leave for different reasons. The Commissioner of Indian Affairs in 1876 asked Chief Charles Thompson if the invitation of 1869 was still open. Chief Thompson replied that it was if the eastern Cherokees could pay their own removal expenses. The newcomers would also be extended no civil rights unless they should become members of the Nation. Nearly one hundred removed within the next four years.

Dennis W. Bushyhead became Chief in 1879 and he took an interest in the North Carolina Cherokees. It was Bushyhead's

---

[1] Cherokee agent William Thomas, acting with power of attorney for members of this band, purchased certain land with Indian funds on which they might live. Thomas took title to the land, leaving the Indians without a valid claim. In 1859, after Thomas became insolvent and insane, the land was sold to satisfy his creditors. This injustice was eventually corrected by action of Congress and the Federal courts. Annual Report, 1881, pp. LXVIII–LXV.

belief that as long as there was a contest between the two groups the Nation itself would suffer. An invitation to the North Carolina Cherokees was again extended to the National Council on December 3, 1880, to join the Nation in the West and in 1881 nearly two hundred removed. Among those removing was a John Ross, Chief of the North Carolina band. The Cherokee National Council by an act of December 16, 1881, provided a relief fund amounting to sixteen dollars per capita for those recently removed, and approximately one hundred and eighty benefited by this act.

Eastern Cherokees Seek Finance

Although the Office of Indian Affairs had urged the North Carolina Cherokees to move, the sum due each for removal and subsistence was not immediately forthcoming and intense suffering resulted. As a result a special appeal was made to President James A. Garfield charging fraud and graft on the part of the Federal agents involved.

The eastern band were also interested in the distribution of proceeds from the sale of Cherokee land occurring since the 1866 treaty. Not being able to obtain satisfaction by having attorneys prosecute their claims, the eastern Cherokees in September 1875 sought an injunction against the payment made by the United States to the Cherokee Nation. This case came before the Supreme Court which held that it had no jurisdiction in the matter. On November 17, 1876, an appeal was made by a convention of the eastern Cherokees to the Cherokee Nation to join in an attempt to unite the two bodies, to settle all difficulties, and to adjust payments so that the eastern Cherokees would be the recipient of a one-seventh share.

It developed that no settlement of claims could be made between the eastern Cherokees and the Cherokee Nation and the matter then became one for Congressional action. Bills were introduced in Congress both to induce the courts of the United States to recognize the North Carolina Cherokees as a part of the Cherokee Nation and to allow them to bring suit in the Court of Claims for the settlement of claims against the Cherokee Nation. Because of this a law of 1882 authorized the Secretary of the Interior to investigate and report to Congress a plan for settlement of all matters of dispute existing among the

Cherokee Indians. Courtland C. Clements of Richmond, Indiana, was appointed by the Secretary of the Interior to accomplish this.

Congress passed another law in March 1883 authorizing the eastern Cherokees to bring suit against the United States and the Cherokee Nation for settlement of claims, with the rights to appeal from the Court of Claims to the Supreme Court of the United States granted to each party. The eastern Cherokees then brought suit in the Court of Claims seeking a one-seventh share of $214,000 which had been created by commuting certain annuities arising from the treaty of 1835, and in the proceeds of the land sales made by the Cherokee Nation, so stipulated in the treaty of 1866, including the Neutral Lands in Kansas. The decision favored the United States and the Cherokee Nation. The Court of Claims maintained that those eastern Cherokees who remained in North Carolina were not to be considered members of the Cherokee Nation as they had dissolved their connection with their Nation when they refused to accompany the body on its removal. The eastern Cherokees appealed to the Supreme Court where the decision was sustained.

The Cherokee Nation then realized that a decision would have to be made on the claims to the right of citizenship on the part of those who had removed to Cherokee land in Indian Territory. As a result Chief Bushyhead in his annual message to the National Council on November 2, 1886, requested that a special commission be created to dispose of these claims as rapidly as possible. As irregularities were expected Bushyhead suggested that the full bloods and others not less than half bloods, if approved by such a commission, be admitted to citizenship but that cases of all others be most carefully investigated. The Chief approved on December 8, 1886, an act which created a special commission of three to pass on the applications for citizenship of those claiming Cherokee blood. In 1888 a new commission was created to complete the work and report to the Chief. Those who were found eligible for certificates of citizenship had to locate permanently in the Cherokee Nation before they could receive the document.

North Carolina Cherokees now living in the Nation established an organization for the purpose of securing whatever rights they might have had with the United States. Joel M. Bryan, one of the Old Settler group of Cherokees, was employed by them to push their claims and to represent them in any action. With the aid of the Cherokee delegation at Washington, Bryan was instrumental in inducing Congress to appropriate $20,000 to pay those who had removed and were yet due certain funds as well as those who should remove at a later date. In 1906 Congress made an additional appropriation as a result of decisions by the Court of Claims a few years earlier.

Old Settlers Seek Funds

While the eastern Cherokees were involved in suits for claims, the Old Settlers group of Cherokees were seeking unpaid funds long overdue from the United States government. After 1846 all political distinctions legally ceased to exist among the Cherokees in the Nation. They constituted one political body and consequently the Old Settlers were without means to petition—either the United States government or the Cherokee Nation—except as provided for by the treaty and then only on matters of business pertaining to themselves. Meeting in Council from time to time until the outbreak of the Civil War fostered no plans by which to secure their claim. An Old Settlers Council was called at Tahlequah in 1867 but nothing substantial could be done without the consent and aid of the Cherokee National Council. In 1874 the National Council authorized a committee to examine any papers in the interest of the Old Settlers, and an act was passed by the Cherokee legislature which instructed the Washington Cherokee delegation of 1874–1875 to give to the Old Settlers group all possible aid, not inconsistent with the general interests of the Cherokee Nation, in obtaining any funds yet due them.

Many attorneys were employed in this case, but John A. Logan and W. W. Wilshire were the first to make progress. In 1878 they prepared an argument to be used in prosecuting the claim, setting forth a balance of $1,072,371.46 due the Old Settlers. An act of August 7, 1882, authorized the Secretary of the Interior to investigate and report to Congress certain matters relating to the Cherokee Indians. C. C. Clements, a special agent for the Secretary of the Interior, made several reports pertaining to Cherokee affairs. He found that money was due both the Old Settlers and those removing under provisions of the treaty of 1835. The Old Settlers were due, according to his report, $421,653.68 with interest at five per cent from September

1852. As a result of this report Congress authorized the Court of Claims to examine all records in the case and then report its findings to the Senate Committee on Indian Affairs. The court reported in February 1885 but could not determine the questions of law involved in the claim. The Senate Committee recommended the passage of a bill authorizing the Court of Claims to try the claim of the Old Settlers and the Cherokee Nation. The claim of the Old Settlers was then referred to the Court of Claims by an act of February 25, 1889, granting the right of either the Old Settlers or the United States to appeal to the Supreme Court. The decision was favorable to the Old Settlers.

The United States appealed the case. It was argued on December 13 and 14, 1892. A decision was rendered on April 3, 1893, awarding the Old Settlers $212,376.94, with interest at five per cent from June 12, 1838, at which time a supplemental treaty was signed providing for payment in addition to that stated in the treaty of 1835. The Old Settlers also received $4,179.26 as payment for land and their improvements made on the reservation in Arkansas given up in 1828. Because of the decision of the Supreme Court an act was approved on August 23, 1894, by which $800,386.31 was appropriated to cover the claims allowed. The Secretary of the Interior was instructed to withhold thirty-five percent for expenses and legal fees, the amount set aside by the Old Settlers council of 1875. The net amount was to be distributed among the Old Settlers and their descendants.

Other Financial Negotiations

The financial affairs of the Cherokee Nation were of great importance since the success and prosperity of schools, the administration of justice, the faithful enforcement of the laws and the progress of public improvements were all dependent upon it. The success of the merchant, mechanic, professional man and farmer all depended upon the promptness with which the national obligations were met. Therefore the Nation realized the importance of attending the treaty of 1866 stipulations that concerned their financial situation; they also desired that the United States honor its commitments in articles III, XXIII, XXIV, XXV, XXVIII and XXX.

Accordingly, the United States appointed two commissioners in August 1868, S. R. Ketzschmar for the United States, and Spencer S. Stephens for the Cherokees, to appraise the property and improvements lost to the Confederate Cherokees by confiscation on the part of the Federal Cherokees. This report was submitted in December 1868 and suggested restitution amounting to a total of four thousand six hundred and seventy-five dollars. Those Cherokees who had lost property due to raids by both armies and by expropriation by the Union armies negotiated with another commission in 1867. Reimbursement was made on November 12, 1867, to those who had issued supplies to Opothleyahola. Claims for bounties and pensions for the Federal Cherokee soldiers and their heirs were being paid by September 1872.

Although trade was profitable in the Cherokee Nation the Cherokee authorities were able to keep out the majority of white merchants; some were in the Nation, but less than in any other Nation except the Seminole. The native businessman was therefore able to initiate a respectable establishment. After the Civil War questions arose over the application of the Indian Intercourse Act of 1834, but the Cherokee government maintained the right granted them in Article VIII of the treaty of 1866 to license traders within the Nation so long as those making application were citizens of the Nation, whether they were adopted whites, Indians, or any others.

Another interesting and significant financial transaction was the Cherokee Tobacco Case of 1870 involving the collection of internal revenue taxes. E. C. Boudinot and Stand Watie in 1868 initiated the establishment of a tobacco factory within the Nation. Nearly five thousand dollars was invested. The underlying strategy seemed to have been based upon a clause of the treaty of 1866 granting the authority to manufacture and sell tobacco products within the Cherokee Nation free of the Federal excise tax ordinarily involved, but Collector of Internal Revenue Columbus Delano informed Boudinot that revenue would be collected and later had all the tobacco and the factory seized for overdue tax payments.

When the case went to the Supreme Court of the Untied States, four judges concurred and two dissented. Many tobacco manufacturers of the southwest had given support to the prosecution of the case in the hope that this factory would be eliminated since it threatened their sales in Indian Territory. Boudinot and Watie lost the factory after doing everything possible to have their business declared legal. Daniel W. Voorhees, Senator from Indiana, sponsored a bill in Congress to compensate them for their loss. After a struggle of two years the bill was indefinitely postponed but Boudinot was eventually allowed compensation by the Court of Claims in 1883.

The Cherokee Tobacco Case aroused unusual interest among the principal tribes of Indian Territory, for the decision clearly stated that from this time a treaty was not to be considered as binding as heretofore and that the Indian Nations were subject to Congressional legislation virtually the same as if their people were citizens of the United States. Alarmed at these possibilities the second general council of Indian Territory petitioned Congress not to be unmindful of the promises that the United States government had made and not to exact laws that would affect their status without the most careful consideration.

Railroad Development in the Nation

A major issue in the economic development of the Cherokee Nation after the Civil War was the provision concerning railroads provided in Article XI of the 1866 treaty. According to this provision the Cherokees agreed to the construction of two railroads through their lands, one north and south, the other east and west. However, they feared the intrusion of whites and the ultimate occupation of their lands. The assurances of Agent John B. Jones in 1871 did little to allay their fears and apprehension for they were aware of the rumor that the land they possessed was a veritable paradise and they also knew that numerous bills had been introduced in Congress seeking the establishment of a territorial form of government which would ultimately result in Caucasian settlement. Naturally the Indians were highly suspicious of railroads. Many believed that nothing could prevent the loss of their land.

The southern branch of the Missouri, Kansas and Texas Railroad, known as the Katy, entered the Cherokee Nation on May 21, 1870. It was constructed from a Kansas border town (Chetopa) across the Cherokee Nation and entered the Creek Nation, continuing southward near the Cherokee-Creek boundary. The Atlantic and Pacific Railroad, later known as the St. Louis and San Francisco (the Frisco), was authorized to build east and west through the Cherokee Nation. It entered through the Shawnee reservation and connected with the Missouri, Kansas and Texas Railroad at Vinita in 1872. The builders of the railroads immediately proceeded to ravage the country of timber which was already scarce. Although this was done in accordance with law the loss of the timber increased the dislike of railroads on the part of the Indians. While these railroads brought the Cherokees into closer contact with commercial development, giving markets for their cattle and farm products, they also brought a group of undesirable individuals into their Nation.

The enforcement of Article XXVII presented many problems for the Cherokee Nation. With the coming of railroads into the Nation the intrusion of whites increased, not only because of easier transportation but also because of enlargement of general business interests; Indian Territory was advertised as an area capable of great development and general travel into the West and the Southwest was encouraged. While many whites brought material benefit into the Cherokee Nation others were of little value and some were criminally inclined.

Among the criminals were whiskey peddlers who realized possibilities of easy money. They promoted the liquor traffic which continued to expand as long as the Federal law remained unchanged. A frequent practice of Federal law enforcement officers was to arrest a whiskey peddler who, tried and found guilty but unable to pay the fine, was released upon turning state's evidence against another peddler who had property. This second offender was then arrested by the officer who, according to the law, received half of the confiscated property and fees for the arrest. This vicious cycle was an example of how the law could be used to benefit some of the non-Indian residents.

Fort Gibson was a rendezvous for liquor peddlers and the fact that it was an army post complicated the situation. Sometimes incidents occurred between army personnel and the Cherokees. There is on record a case in 1869 wherein two Indians killed a soldier. When the matter was reported to Chief Downing to have the Indians arrested and punished, the Chief reminded the Army authorities that under the Indian Intercourse Act of 1834 the case was not in his jurisdiction but was one for the Federal courts.

The section of the Indian Intercourse Act of 1834 which prohibited the introduction of intoxicating liquors into the Indian country for any purpose whatsoever was opposed by some of the Cherokees. In view of this hostility to the measure John W. Craig, the Cherokee agent, recommended that druggists under bond be allowed to sell liquor for medicinal purposes only. Nothing came of this recommendation. Craig believed the United States was powerless in the attempt to suppress the traffic in whiskey but that the Cherokee authorities could do so if they were disposed to aid. It was generally thought during the reconstruction period that the great source of crime originated with whiskey sold by persons who held licenses from the United States government. As late as 1886 Cherokee agent Robert L. Owen maintained that ninety percent of the crimes committed by Indians could still be traced to whiskey.

Other Economic Aspects of the Nation

The land of the Cherokees east of the ninety-sixth meridian was no more than sufficient for their support. Three-fifths of their land was rocky and suitable only for timber or pasture. Pecan trees flourished and the Cherokees ordered a fine of five dollars against anyone who destroyed one. There was building material in abundance and good clay for making brick was found near Tahlequah and other places. A rich yellow sandstone, marble, limestone, flintrock, and black slate were also found. Coal mines yielded well in the northern part of the Nation and these were worked by Cherokees who employed white men as miners under lease from the Nation. The coal, which was of excellent quality, was exported to Kansas. By 1869 Cherokee business comprised four steam sawmills, three water power sawmills, four mixed grain and sawmills and two tobacco factories. There were three stores at Tahlequah, six stores at Fort Gibson and about six others at various places in the Nation. By 1877 the Cherokees numbered about nineteen thousand. They were strictly an agricultural people and depended entirely upon the products of their lands and the sale of their herds of cattle. Business had increased to twenty-four stores, twenty-two mills, and sixty-five smithshops that were owned and controlled by the Cherokee citizens.

The Cherokees opposed allotment of their land and a consolidated territorial government as they did railroad construction, for they felt that the initiation of these three processes would ultimately lead to the dissolution of their tribal government. When the 1870 meeting of the Okmulgee General Council convened at the Creek capital the Cherokees sent fourteen delegates, more than any other Nation or tribe. When the constitution was drafted the Cherokees did not adopt it. W. P. Boudinot, the brother of Elias and editor of the *Cherokee Advocate*, favored the Okmulgee Constitution and allotment of land but was opposed to white settlement and the bills then being introduced into Congress proposing to organize Oklahoma Territory. In this he differed from Elias, who earnestly sponsored these measures. The Curtis Act of 1898, which provided for allotting the land and terminating the governments of the Five Civilized Nations, surmounted all objections and delaying tactics that the Cherokee Nations possessed through this Nation, as well as the other Indian Nations, fought the territorial government plan of the United States government for about forty years after the Civil War.

Internal Problems

Immediately after the Civil War the Cherokees were threatened with serious internal dissensions growing out of animosities between the full bloods and the faction who had sympathized with the Confederate States. When Chief John Ross died in 1866 Lewis Downing, assistant Principal Chief, served as Chief until the National Council could meet and select a successor. The nephew of Chief Ross, W. P. Ross, was chosen on October 19, 1866, to fill the unexpired term. The National Council had been in session prior to his selection and had appointed a committee to prepare necessary amendments to the constitution called for by the treaty of July 9. On November 8 Chief W. P. Ross was authorized to call a "General Meeting of the People" at Tahlequah on November 26 to ratify the amendments and to hear the treaty read. Riley Keys was chosen president and Budd Gritts secretary for this assemblage. The amendments were approved and adopted by the Cherokee people on November 28. On December 7, 1866, Chief Ross issued a proclamation declaring the amendments to be part of the constitution.

The adoption of these amendments brought about many changes in the government of the Cherokee people. For example, the upper house, heretofore called the national committee, became the senate; the lower house was still known as the council. Representation in the council was to be based upon the number of voters in each districts and no district, unless it contained fewer than 100 voters, would have less than two members. A census was provided for in 1870 and thereafter every ten years. Prior to 1867 the National Council met annually on the first Monday in October, and now it was to meet the first Monday in November. Freed slaves and free Negroes were declared citizens and entitled to vote and hold office. The judicial system was modified by substituting a different procedure in the selection of judges and by a change in the term of office. Civil officials in the Canadian District were allowed to continue in office until their successors should be elected and commissioned in November 1867.

After the National Council convened in November 1866 a delegation to represent the Cherokees in Washington was appointed which consisted of W. P. Ross, Riley Keys and Jesse Bushyhead. All the proceedings of the National Council were watched by the southern Cherokees who were not pleased with the state of affairs. A convention of southern Cherokees was called at Brain Town schoolhouse on December 31, 1866, in the southern part of the Canadian District to hear the reports of their delegates who had returned from Washington and to conduct certain other business. John Porum Davis served as the presiding officer of this meeting which lasted about two days. Not trusting the delegation chosen by the northern Cherokees this convention selected W. P. Adair, J. A. Scales and Richard Fields to represent the southern Cherokees in Washington. Adair the spokesman, kept W. P. Boudinot and Stand Watie well-informed.

Recognition of the southern Cherokee delegation was established on January 22, 1867, by Lewis V. Bogy, Commissioner of Indian Affairs, and successor to Cooley. This delegation complained that the southern Cherokees were not fairly represented in the National Council and they maintained that the northern delegation included none of their selection. Adair, Fields and Scales tried very diligently during the next few months to serve their constituents by obtaining a more significant voice in the administration of Cherokee affairs.

Meanwhile in the Cherokee Nation it was becoming evident that John Ross's successor, W. P. Ross, did not have the ability to lead the politically distracted Cherokees to unification. The possibility of new political alignments were recognized by the two Baptist missionaries, Evan and John B. Jones, and by Lewis Downing. They saw them in a union of certain leaders of the Treaty Party, and the southern Cherokees generally, versus those of the full bloods who had been followers of Chief John Ross. Evan and John Jones exercised a powerful political influence in the Cherokee Nation and their strength was with the full bloods among whom they had served as missionaries. Therefore many of the full bloods were Baptists, but in the case of the Cherokees denominational affiliations had little effect on the creation of a new party. Lewis Downing, himself a Baptist minister, was one of the early converts of Evan Jones.

Downing, although not a full blood, was classed as such. His intense feeling that past grievances should be forgiven for the sake of unity seemed to make him just the right man to head the new full blood party. This combination of Downing, representing the full bloods who had heretofore followed John Ross, and the influential Joneses was the embryo of a party that was long to rule the Cherokee Nation. They now undertook to effect an alliance between Lewis Downing, assistant Principal Chief, and the southern Cherokee leaders. Their efforts bore fruit and a new organization was formed known as the Downing Party. W. P. Ross, who had broken with the Joneses, led the opposition. This faction became known as the National Party. One of the terms of agreement between the Downing full bloods and the southern Cherokees was that the nominee for chief should be a full blood.

The new political alignment began operating during the winter and spring of 1866–1867 while the southern Cherokees were suspicious of the northern Cherokees in control of the government. The southern Cherokees desired to break the power of Ross's National Party both in the Nation and in Washington. Leaving Scales and Fields to finish certain business relative to the care of destitute southern Cherokees, Adair returned to the Nation in June 1867 and plunged into the political campaign, feeling that the chances of defeating Ross for chief were excellent.

Ross was defeated in the August election and Lewis Downing and James Vann, who had been president of the national committee for a number of years, were elected respectively principal chief and assistant principal chief. Much bitter feeling developed during the campaign and even after the election there was evidence of violence. A treaty was drawn up in the summer of 1868 by the Washington delegation and N. G. Taylor, Commissioner of Indian Affairs. Though never ratified, this treaty proposed to settle most differences which had existed within the Nation. It contained provisions by which certain claims against the United States were to be adjusted; other provisions called for modification of the judicial plans as provided in the treaty of 1866; and still other provisions proposed to settle boundary controversies. This proposed treaty was a comprehensive attempt toward eliminating irritating differences between the Cherokee Nation and the United States government.

Believing that political relations in the Cherokee Nation would be more peaceful if there were no longer two delegations in Washington, Chief Downing appointed Adair and Scales as members to the previous all-northern Cherokee delegation. By 1868 the Cherokees were on a fair way toward unification. From that date the Nation as a whole seemed more concerned about relations with the Federal government than about political division within the Nation.

Both the 1867 and 1868 reports from the agents for the Cherokee Nation mentioned the peace and quiet of the Cherokee people. The 1868 report emphasized that the treaty of 1866 had been highly effective in healing the breach between the southern Cherokee and the loyal Cherokees. Nevertheless, when the National Council elected W.P. Ross chief upon the death of Downing in 1872, bitterness again prevailed in the Nation. Social and political unrest present by 1873 resulted in a crime wave. Murders became common and Chief Ross was looked upon as the cause by his political opponents despite the fact that no one person could be held responsible. John B. Jones, Cherokee agent at the time, informed Washington about the situaation:

It has been repeatedly charged that crime has greatly increased in the Cherokee country within the past few years. This charge, I am compelled to admit, is true. It is also true that the representations of this increase of crime have been exaggerated and distorted. The disturbance which occurred at Coody's Bluff on the election day in August has been greatly misrepresented. It was the occasion of telegraphic dispatches representing the political parties of this nation as arrayed in action and armed hostility to each other. The facts in the case are that a set of bad men made a wanton attack on

one Jordan Journeycake, a Delaware citizen. Their victim
fled into the room where the voting was in progress. The
ruffians followed him into the room firing pistols and making
other demonstrations of violence. The sheriff's force, who are
the custodians of peace, did not interfere; the voting stopped;
the judges and clerks of election fled. No one, however,
was killed. Journeycake escaped unhurt. The judges and
clerks of election afterward got together and opened the
polls, and soon after closed the election. The desperadoes
then went to the houses of two peaceable citizens, destroyed
furniture, broke windows and committed other depredations.
But the men are unsustained by any political party; none
regret the occurrence more than the members of the party to
which these men belong. They were soon after arrested by a
party of citizens and turned over to the sheriff. A part of them
are now awaiting trial for these crimes before the Cherokee court, while others are in jail at Fort Smith, Arkansas,
awaiting trial before the United States district court for the
western district of Arkansas, on charge of other crimes previously committed. None will defend themselves except in a
legal way before the several courts where their cases are to be
tried. This is about all there is of the great war among the
Cherokees reported by telegraph and published throughout
the country. Although this and other cases have been exaggerated, yet the fact remains that crime has increased, that we
are compelled to deplore a greater insecurity of life and
property. This state of things results largely from the existence of organized cliques and parties, said to be pledged to
defend each member when arraigned for the violation of law.[2]

The Downing party had been deeply aggrieved at the selection of Ross as Chief and consequently some of its radical adherents were ready to charge him not only with murder but also
with neglect of duty. So serious had the contentions between the
factions become that Commissioner of Indian Affairs Edward P. Smith reported to the Secretary of the Interior that had
it not been for the garrison at Fort Gibson the factions probably
would have engaged in war.

In the meantime, hostility had intensified between the Cherokee Nation and the United States. For some years since the Civil
War the operations of the United States deputy marshals were a
source of great complaint and discontent among the Chero-

[2] John B. Jones to E. P. Smith, September 20, 1872, *Annual Report*,
1873, p. 206.

kees. These Indians regarded the marshals as usurpers and consequently entertained for them the hatred which a people usually have for foreigners exercising over them an oppressive authority. With this matter was connected the whole subject of the jurisdiction over the Indians of the United States District Court for the Western District of Arkansas. It was a common occurrence for innocent men to be arrested by these marshals and taken to Fort Smith, Arkansas, and compelled to give bail in a city of strangers whose language they did not understand, or in default of bail to be jailed until the court met. Agent Jones recommended the establishment by Congress of a United States Court in Indian Territory in accordance with Article XIII of the treaty of 1866.

The riot at Going Snake Court House in 1872 heightened the difficulty between the United States authorities in the Western District of Arkansas and the Cherokees. Many whites had been adopted into the Cherokee Nation and the Indian authorities claimed the same jurisdiction over these adopted citizens as was accorded by law to persons of Indian blood. This right seemed to be denied by the United States court having jurisdiction over the territory, and questions of jurisdiction were continually arising. Upon this occasion an Indian, Ezekial Proctor, shot his brother-in-law's wife, Polly Chesterson. The Indian was arrested and held for trial for the murder of the woman under Cherokee law. During the trial the court was interrupted by a posse led by deputy United States marshals who shot the prisoner and his counselor, Moses Alberty. About eight of the marshals' party were killed, with three wounded, and about three of the other group were killed, with six being wounded. The foreman of the jury, Arch Scraper, and Ellis Foreman, a juror, were arrested and put into prison though they were innocent of instigating the riot. Others lived in the brush to avoid arrest. This and other unfortunate occurrences increased the hostility between the United States and the Cherokees.

In 1874 both the National (Ross) and the Downing parties held conventions in preparation for the election of the next year. The Downing people met in August and adopted a platform of sixteen articles which contained the usual demands for economy in government, equal administration of law to all classes of citizens and an equal share in the public domain; unqualified opposition to the establishment of a territorial form of government by the United States was also emphasized. The National Party met in Tahlequah in November and set forth their principles, which differed but little from those of the opposition.

The election of 1875 resulted in the choice of a full blood, Charles Thompson, as Principal Chief, and David Rowe as Assistant Principal Chief. W. P. Ross and James Vann were candidates on the National Party ticket. Thompson, having the point of view of the full bloods, made it somewhat difficult for those who favored a liberal policy in dealing with the whites who were beginning to come into the Nation as laborers. So many issues had been before the Nation during the seventies that it was practically impossible for the parties to continue along the old lines of division.

Freedmen Seek Citizenship

The subject of citizenship was a confusing and perplexing one in Cherokee history. After 1866 it intensified until understanding was impossible between the Nation and the United States government. Charges were frequently made by representatives of both sides. The principal difficulty was that of determining who was an Indian, who had Indian privileges and by what authority this was to be determined. Three definite racial groups were involved, the Negroes, the whites and the Indians. The "Negro problem" arose from the abolition of slavery and related provisions of the treaty of 1866. The whites who intermarried with the Cherokees were accorded certain civil rights and the protection of the law but beyond that lay a field of doubt. Many whites who came into the Nation for valid reasons created even greater disturbance. Much confusion arose even when exiled Cherokees themselves sought citizenship and the North Carolina Cherokees who had never lived in the Nation constituted an additional problem. Readmission to citizenship could be secured only by petitioning the National Council. Each case was taken up on its merits and there were hundreds of cases involving thousands of persons. The question of citizenship cost the Cherokees, directly and indirectly, millions of dollars and created no end of political and domestic disorders.

The Cherokee Nation contended for the right to determine its own citizenship by citing justification in treaties, interpretations and instructions. Consequently, in December 1869 the National Council passed an act empowering the Supreme Court of the Nation to sit as a Court of Commissioners to pass on claims of persons seeking citizenship. It was evident by 1876 that the work was too heavy for this body and that another method had to be devised. The names of persons declared intruders were then submitted periodically to the Chief who in turn reported them to the superintendent of the Union Agency in Muskogee. From there these lists were passed to the Commissioner of Indian Affairs with the request for the removal of the persons from the Nation. These requests were in accordance with treaty provisions of long standing.

Citizenship for Negroes involved much controversy. The treaty of 1866 had abolished slavery but the abolition of slavery did not end the problem for the Negroes or the Nation. By Article IV the Canadian District had been set aside in part for the freed slaves of the Cherokees and all free Negroes who resided in the Cherokee Nation prior to June 1, 1861. Those Negroes who desired to locate in this area were allowed two years in which to do so. The residents of this district were empowered by the fifth article of the treaty to exercise the functions of citizens, elect officials, control local affairs and administer justice as long as there was no inconsistency with the constitution of the Cherokee Nation or laws of the United States. This fifth article also applied to southern Cherokees, for many lived here for a time before occupying their former homes in other districts of the Nation.

Trouble grew out of the ninth article of the treaty. The Nation agreed to the provision that all freedmen who had been liberated by voluntary act of their former owners or by law, as well as all free Negroes who were in the country at the beginning of the Civil War and who were residents of it when the treaty was agreed upon, or who might return within six months thereafter, and their descendants, should have all the rights of native Cherokees. The tenth article guaranteed every Cherokee and freed person the right to sell products without restraint except for such tax as might be levied by the United States on taxable goods sold outside the Cherokee Nation. Thus by treaty the freedmen in the Cherokee Nation were to become a part of the Cherokee citizenship but law on paper and law in fact, then as now, were not always congruent.

The slaves were also refugees of the Civil War. Because some escaped and went north or camped near army headquarters, while some under the control of their masters were taken south of the Arkansas River or even into Texas and neighboring slave-holding states, it was impossible in the limited time permitted by the treaty for notification to be publicly given whereby the widely scattered freedmen of the Cherokee Nation might return and become citizens. Many who learned of the provision returned without their husbands, wives or children, within the six-month period in order to take advantage of the opportunity. They hoped to bring them at a later date. This pattern created much confusion and agents were called upon to remove as in-truders those who came in after the return of the first members of the family in case the six month period had lapsed. When this was done the family would be separated. Some children had been sold and separated from their parents. There were cases where minors had been bound for service until they should reach maturity and these persons could not return. John Craig, agent for the Cherokees, reported in 1870 that many freedmen were detained in virtual servitude in Texas for one or two years after the war or until they escaped. Cherokees not wishing to receive these technical intruders were within their treaty rights but it seemed an unfair hardship upon many freedmen.

By a law of December 3, 1869, the Cherokee Supreme Court sat as a court of commissioners and passed on the claims of freedmen. In cases where no law or treaty covered certain points the court made its own rulings. According to a report made in June 1871 forty-seven were admitted to citizenship and 130 were rejected as intruders. The Office of Indian Affairs instruct-ed the Cherokee agent not to remove the freedmen who were classified as intruders. Chief Downing recommended in 1870 and 1871 that the freedmen be adopted as citizens but bills providing for this failed to pass. Therefore they were living in the Nation without legal status, as were those in the Choctaw and Chickasaw Nations. To this group of freedmen were added those from the United States and Indian Nations who had intermarried with Cherokee citizens. Judges of the Cherokee Supreme Court held that laws governing intermarriage of Chero-kees and whites did not apply to these cases.

Freedmen who were former slaves owned by well-known Cherokees and who had not returned to the Nation within the six-month period also sought citizenship. On October 31, 1874, before the meeting of the National Council, twenty-four of these freedmen petitioned for the rights of Cherokee citizenship. The petition bore such surnames as Vann, Foreman, Alberty and Scales. The Cherokee Senate prepared a bill whereby those freedmen who had not returned in time to accept citizenship, and those who might yet return within a limited time, were enabled to present themselves before the Chief Justice of the Cherokee Supreme Court and offer proof of their claims. If satisfactory, they were then to be granted certificates of citizenship provided that they should make application to the Chief Justice within one year from the passage of this act. The bill, however, failed to pass.

Chief Thompson in his annual message to the National Council in 1876 recommended prompt and definite action regarding Cherokee citizenship for the freeedmen. He felt that either the freedmen should be adopted or rejected. He further urged that an act should be passed requiring the United States to remove the rejected from the Cherokee Nation. The National Council decreed such an act unnecessary, declaring that it was already the duty of the United States to remove intruders. Since there were many citizenship cases to be settled other than those of the Negroes, the National Council decided that it was too burdensome on the regular courts and consequently provided for the appointment of a special citizenship court to settle the claims by an act of December 5, 1877.

Other petitions from claimants of all classes in the Nation were brought before the agent S. W. Marston at Union Agency. Chief Thompson communicated to the National Council the information, adding that he was informed that the Indian Office had advised certain Negro claimants not to present their claims to the commission as the power of the commission was a question under advisement of that office. Chief Thompson viewed this action as an attack upon the sovereignty of the Cherokee Nation. However, it was now evident that the problem of intruders, first growing out of the refusal to grant citizenship to many freedmen, was now mushrooming as whites were entering the Nation in increasing numbers.

The question of citizenship for the freedmen remained a perplexing and an unsettled one throughout the seventies and most of the eighties. Dennis W. Bushyhead, who succeeded Chief Thompson in 1879, and the Indian Agent, John Q. Tufts, who succeeded Marston at Union Agency, were also unable to cope successfully with the problem. Tufts declared in 1882 that the main reason an agreement could not be reached that would give Negroes equal rights with the Cherokees was the fact that the question of citizenship of the freedmen was unpopular among the Cherokees and no Cherokee politician was willing to jeopardize his position by championing the measure. The unsettled situation was intensified in 1883 when a dispute arose over a payment of $300,000 to the Cherokee Nation for certain lands west of the ninety-sixth meridian.

In preparation for the receipt of the fund the National Council passed an act on May 18, 1883, over the veto of Chief Bushyhead, authorizing per capita payments to be made only to citizens of the Cherokee Nation of Cherokee blood according to the census rolls. The question of participation in the funds extended farther than the freedmen for it involved the Shawnees and Delawares who were incorporated into the Cherokee Nation at the close of the sixties. These Indians and the freedmen employed an attorney, J. Milton Turner, to prepare their claims against the Cherokee Nation upon the basis of the rights of Cherokee citizens and on February 6, 1886, Turner petitioned President Grover Cleveland to issue an executive order to compel restitution. The Indian Commissioner, J. D. C. Atkins, reported the proceedings to the Secretary of the Interior and recommended the course to pursue in order to require payment. A bill was passed and approved October 19, 1888, providing for an appropriation of $75,000 which should be used to make payment to all classes of freedmen and their descendants, and to the Delawares and the Shawnees, who were to share as each Cherokee by blood had shared. A further appropriation of $5,000 was approved March 2, 188, as the census roll indicated a larger increase than had been anticipated.

Although the Cherokee citizenship court functioned and passed upon claims to citizenship involving thousands of persons, the Office of Indian Affairs did not seem to regard the body as having any legal authority, for those not granted citizenship were seldom removed from the Nation. In fact the agents were usually instructed not to remove those unable to obtain Cherokee citizenship papers.

Social Agencies Reestablished

Life within the Cherokee Nation had been so completely disrupted by the war that the reestablishment of schools was delayed until about 1870, when a measure of political and economic stability had been accomplished. A national board and a superintendent were in charge of all schools with subordinate boards in local districts. This plan prevailed from the 1841 organization, though from time to time changes were made in procedures. The National Council in 1870 provided that the superintendent furnish plans and specifications for district schoolhouses and equipment, prescribe uniform texts, and assign, transfer and dismiss teachers. Instructors were paid according to attendance in their schools and no school was maintained with less than 16 pupils in average daily attendance. The superintendent received $700 annually.

Like most of the other Nations the Cherokees required the local community to build and equip the schoolhouse. The law of 1870 refused to provide a teacher and texts except where the national standards were met. Unlike any of the other Nations the Cherokees from the first had uniform texts and like other Nations supplied them free to all children who were citizens. The relatively few noncitizens paid tuition and furnished their own texts. By September 1871 almost every thickly populated locality had a school in operation. There were a total of fifty-nine, according to S. S. Stephens, the superintendent of public schools. Though the Cherokee Nation desired to bar the freedmen from citizenship they did not bar their children from sharing educational opportunities as had the Chickasaws. Three of the fifty-nine schools were devoted to educating Negroes and the number of their schools was considered by the Council to be in proportion to their population. The school funds of the Nation by 1871 were not sufficient for the establishment of institutions of higher learning.

The Nation's common schools decreased in 1872 to fifty-seven though the three for the freedmen were retained. The half-breeds who spoke English did well but the full bloods who spoke only Cherokee accomplished little. The children learned to read, spell and write the English language, but they did not understand the meaning of the words. They learned the forms and the sounds of letters and syllables without connecting them with ideas.

The Cherokee Female Seminary had been created by an act of the National Council in 1846 though it did not open until 1851. After the disruption of the Civil War the institution began its program again in the latter part of 1871 under the supervision of Mrs. Ellen E. Eblin, though its funds were extremely limited. By 1876 the enrollment was increased to ninety-four, and during the two years immediately following, the institution enrolled eighty-five and 147 students, respectively. Eighty-two of the 147 girls were unable to pay their fees and were boarded at the expense of the Nation. The curriculum for the girls was not quite as advanced as that of the boys in the Cherokee Male Seminary though the liberal arts, with the exception of music and logic, were represented. The sciences and homemaking were neglected.

The Cherokee Male Seminary likewise was established by an act of the National Council in 1846 and opened in 1851 but during the Civil War its building was used at various times by the armies and it had deteriorated badly as a result of abuse and neglect. In 1872 the building was used temporarily to house the newly created Cherokee Orphan Asylum, which continued there for two or three years. About 1875 the seminary resumed work as a high school, enrolling seventy-five boys. The next year's record listed 201 boys distributed through a primary department of two years, an intermediate department of three years and an academy of four years. After its reorganization this school resembled more the high schools of the other Nations in that it taught a large number below high school rank.

The academic department offered a varied curriculum. Included were Latin, geography, history, algebra, logic, elocution, physics, geometry, rhetoric, bookkeeping, English literature, trigonometry, philosophy, chemistry, astronomy, political economy and German. The enrollment grew and by 1880 there were nearly one hundred students in the academic department. The first graduating class since 1856 completed its work in 1882. The building burned on March 20, 1910, thus ending the history of Cherokee secondary education as a national enterprise. The Male Seminary was supported wholly from tribal funds except that money for board was supplied by the students. Unlike the Creeks, Chickasaws and Choctaws, the Cherokees never sent secondary or college students to the United States at national expense. From early days they cared for this problem at home as best they could.

In the autumn of 1873 the Council adopted new rules for the national school system, dividing the territory into three districts, to each of which a commissioner was appointed. These commissioners constituted a board of education whose duties were to assist the superintendent in supervising schools. Each one was held responsible for visiting and inspecting the schools in his district; for the adoption of uniform rules, regulations, and report forms; for studying local situations and providing proper education for all classes; for reporting fully and in detail to the Principal Chief; for discontinuing schools not making the required average daily attendance of thirteen; and for examining teachers and assigning them to their districts. Sixty common schools were in operation at this time. Of the sixty teachers, twelve were white and forty-eight were native Cherokees. There were 800 boys and 933 girls in attendance. The day schools numbered sixty-five in 1874, and the freedmen's schools had been increased to seven.

The school and orphan fund of the Nation was derived from fifty percent of the amount received from the government as interest on invested funds held in trust. In 1875, $72,297.97 was appropriated by the National Council for educational purposes, and it was proposed to use nearly $80,000 of surplus school funds in the enlargement and the equipping of the Nation's seminaries and orphanage in an effort to place them on a permanent basis. There was also in progress the erection of a building for an asylum of the deaf, dumb, blind and insane at an estimated cost of seven thousand dollars. Securing competent teachers was always one of the chief school problems of the Cherokees from the Civil War to 1899, when the elementary school system was placed under Federal supervision.

The Cherokee Nation made no effort to give its freedmen either high school or boarding school privileges prior to 1890 nor did there seem to be a demand for it. But in January 1890 the Cherokee board of education planned a boarding high school for Negroes to be supported out of national funds. After operating for two months with but two pupils, the school was ordered closed until an enrollment of twenty-five could be maintained. In the autumn it was reopened, but on November 12 it was again ordered closed. Twenty-five pupils were finally reported enrolled by 1897.

The Methodists resumed their activity among the Cherokee people in 1866 by reestablishing circuits in the Tahlequah, Fort Gibson, Sallisaw and Canadian vicinities. Several neighborhoods responded favorably to revivals and about three hundred individuals were added during the year. The Baptists had long been represented in the Cherokee Nation through the missionary work of Evan and John B. Jones, who had lived in the

Nation before the war. A large number of full bloods had been converted to this faith and after the war the number continued to increase. The Moravian denomination was also represented by 1869.

The Cherokees reestablished the *Cherokee Advocate* in 1870 as a weekly paper which was supported partly out of national funds. Some portions were in English and others were in Cherokee. During the Civil War the paper had not been published, and except for this suspension and once when the press and type burned in 1875, the paper was circulated until 1906. Liberal space was given to reports of the various schools with stories of closing exercises and special features of general school news and views. Its columns were an effective means of improving public opinion on education and heightening the general desire for more and better schools regardless of cost.

Summary

Although the war left the Cherokee Nation a devastated area improvements had been made by 1877. The Cherokees were emphatically an agricultural and stock-raising people and perhaps of all the Indian tribes they were considered to rank first in general intelligence, in the acquisition of wealth, in the knowledge of the useful arts and in social and moral development. They occupied an area in Indian Territory which comprised about five million acres. Of this at least two-thirds was unfit for cultivation and a large portion of the tillable area was of an inferior quality. Most of the untillable land was entirely worthless even for timber, as it consisted of stony ridges and valleys covered with a scrubby growth, mostly a kind of oak called blackjack. There were a few pine forests of very limited extent and some good timber on the streams and in the southern part of the Nation. The agent in 1871 declared that no country was ever less worthy of the high praise that it received than the eastern part of the Cherokee Nation. While the Cherokee country was poor and generally inferior to the rich states of the West it was well adapted to fruit raising and apples grew especially well.

Cherokee interest in agriculture manifested itself in formation of an agricultural society by 1871. The Cherokees also felt, inasmuch as other states in the Union were making rapid progress in all the branches of agriculture and the mechanic arts by means of their agricultural schools, that they could benefit from the establishment of an agricultural institution. They particularly wanted an experimental farm and garden established in connection with the school. Places of habitation were noticeably increasing and improving by 1871 and no longer were nearly all the houses mere log cabins. More than one thousand of them were comfortable houses built of hewn timbers with stone or brick chimneys. Many of them were weatherboarded so as to give the appearance of frame buildings. Many families had large double log cabins a story and a half high, with a center hall. By 1876 many Cherokee citizens occupied not only neat hewn double log cabins, but frame, brick or stone houses as well.

Political dissension was rampant in the Nation immediately following the Civil War. The southern faction or the Canadian Cherokees wanted a separate sovereign area, but while they were given the opportunity to live in an area away from the northern Cherokees the Nation was never split legally into two separate Nations as many of the southern Cherokees wanted. The factions lived and worked together though there was evidence of political strife even as late as 1875. Upon the death of John Ross in 1866 there was a realignment of parties. Though his nephew, W. P. Ross, was chosen to succeed him the younger Ross could not hold all of the old Ross following for he did not have the magnetism and political acumen of his uncle. Evan and John B. Jones and Lewis Downing, who had been followers of John Ross and leaders of the full blood faction, saw the possibility of uniting with certain leaders of the old Ridge or Treaty Party and the southern Cherokee generally. This combination of Downing, representing the full bloods who had heretofore followed John Ross, and the influential Joneses was the nucleus of a party that was long to rule the Cherokee Nation. The new organization became known as the Downing Party, and the opposition led by W. P. Ross was termed the National Party. This party formation began operating during the winter and spring of 1866–1867. When Downing was elected Principal Chief in 1867 he eliminated the two sets of delegates in Washington and appointed one delegation in the interest of unity for the Nation.

The National Council resumed its sessions, instituting a political structure much like that of the United States government, in the fall of 1866. The constitution was amended to be in line with the treaty of 1866. After this the National Council worked diligently to comply with the provisions of their treaty but some articles were more difficult for the Nation to initiate and complete than others. The question of citizenship for the freedmen was such a measure. Slavery was abolished voluntarily by the Cherokees in 1863. In Article IX of the 1866 treaty the freed slaves and the Negroes who had always been free were declared citizens; and they were entitled to vote, hold office and enjoy equal privileges in general by the amendment to the Cherokee constitution in December of 1866. Yet the issue was an unpopular one politically and the freedmen, Shawnee, and Delawares who had been adopted as full residents did not receive official sanction to share in tribal monies as each Cherokee by blood had shared until 1888. The six-month stipulation in Article IX concerning freedmen caused a great deal of difficulty also since it was almost impossible in that length of time for publicity to be given the provision whereby the widely scattered freedmen might return and become citizens of the Nation.

Articles XV–XX concerning land transactions and usage by the government were, with the exception of Article XX, initiated and completed without much difficulty. It was through Articles XV and XVI that the Delaware, Shawnee and Osage tribes were removed to the Cherokee country. Article XVII concerning the Neutral Land transaction was complied with in 1868. The Cherokees did not comply with Article XX concerning survey and allotment until joint action was taken by the Five Civilized Nations and the Federal government through the work of the Dawes Commission. The confiscation laws of the Cherokee Nation were repealed in Article III and payment for this property and the cost of permanent improvements were initiated in 1868. Lost property claims (Article XXX) and the reimbursement of those who had furnished provision and clothing to the group under Opothleyahola as stipulated in Article XXVIII were initiated by 1867. Claims for pension and bounties for Cherokee soldiers and their heirs were being paid by 1872.

Article XI, concerning the railroads, and Article XXVII, establishing a military post in the Cherokee Nation, provided numerous concomitant social as well as economic problems. The north-south railroad entered the Nation in 1870 and the east-west one in 1872. The story of railroad building throughout Indian Territory was generally the same: opposition on the part of the population; discrimination and land grabbing on the part of the railroads; and the influx of many undesirable individuals, furthering the increase of crime. The problem of the Federal Court being located in Fort Smith and the Federal government not removing intruders as the Nation desired was a vexing situation to the Cherokees. Since a military post was established in Fort Gibson during the war it had only to be maintained. A treaty provision specifically stated that no liquor of any kind was to be introduced except for medical purposes only, but the illegal flow of liquor continued and created boundless problems. Ninety percent of the crime was reported due to liquor and neither the United States government nor the National Council was able to cope adequately with this situation.

Trade for citizens of the Cherokee Nation flourished for Article X gave every Cherokee and freed person the right to sell any product of his farm, including livestock or manufactured products, and to ship or drive these to market without restraint or paying any tax which was then or might possibly be levied by the United States. Furthermore, Article VIII gave the Cherokees the right to issue no license to trade in their Nation unless it was approved by the National Council, except in the Canadian District. An outgrowth of Article X was the Tobacco Case involving Boudinot, Watie and the Federal government. The outcome of the case was significant in that it indicated that treaties were no longer binding as they had been and that the Federal government had changed its policy of dealing with the Indians as separate Nations by treaty.

Two important issues demanding attention from the Cherokees during the post war years were the removal and the settlement of the claims that the eastern Cherokees brought against the Cherokees who had removed to the West. As the western Cherokee sold land the eastern Cherokee wanted to share in the proceeds, and because of this desire they brought suit against the western Cherokees. Others wanted to remove to the West for various reasons after the Civil War. There was a removal of about one hundred and thirty persons in 1871 under the direction of J. D. Lang, and during the next four years about one hundred more removed. Even in 1881 removals were taking place, including the removal of the eastern Cherokee chief, a younger John Ross. The Court of Claims ruled in favor of the western Cherokees in 1886. During this time the Old Settlers group tried to get per capita funds due them from the Federal government by the 1835 and 1846 treaties and these claims were finally awarded in 1893.

The reestablishment of schools was delayed until around 1870. Schools and orphanages derived fifty percent of their funds from the Federal government as interest on invested money held in trust. The Cherokees seemed to have been the only one of the Five Civilized Nations to establish an institution for the deaf, dumb, blind and insane during the reconstruction period. Like most of the other Nations the Cherokees required the local community to build and equip schoolhouses. Unlike any of the other Nations the Cherokees had uniform texts, and like other Nations supplied them free to all children who were citizens of the Nation. The Cherokees never sent secondary or college students to the United States at national expense.

The Cherokees took an active part in the Okmulgee General Council as far as its use for the benefit of the Five Civilized Nations was concerned. They did not ratify the Okmulgee constitution for as a Nation they did not champion a consolidated government. The location of the Federal court in Fort Smith, Arkansas, the methods used by the marshals and court officials in making arrests and the manner of trials and punishment were as grievous to the Cherokees as they were to the other Civilized Nations. The controversial question between the Cherokees and the United States authorities of the jurisdiction over adopted whites intensified hostility during this period. A federal court was eventually established in Indian Territory in 1889.

The Cherokee people proved by their intelligence, their stoutheartedness, and their will to regain their position as one of the most powerful Indian Nations of the time that they were equal to the difficult task the Civil War willed to them.

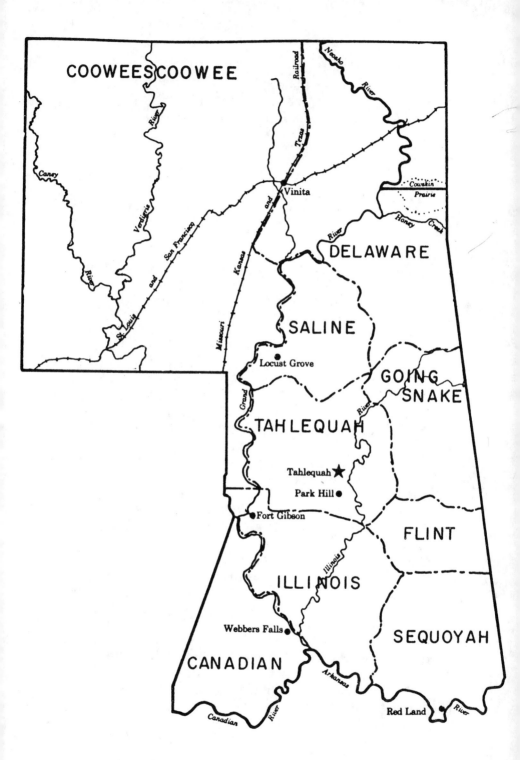

The Cherokee Nation

Chapter Eight

RECONSTRUCTION IN RETROSPECT

Following the Civil War the reconstruction period in Indian Territory provided a unique experience in United States history. Reconstruction of the lives of the Five Civilized Nations resulting from their forced removal from their homes east of the Mississippi River to Indian Territory had already been their tragic lot. The Civil War had interrupted the social adjustment and the economic and political advancement of these Indians. Now for the second time they faced the problems of reconstruction. Heavy hearts and bitterness were normal reactions for many but with courage, grim determination, hard work and capricious assistance from the Federal government and various religious organizations their houses and farms were rebuilt, though in some instances, upon a completely different domain. Self-sufficiency was obtained, crime and general lawlessness were curbed, and tribal governments, political harmony, schools, churches and economic prosperity were reestablished. Since the Five Civilized Nations had each allied with the Confederacy the problem of reestablishing a working relationship with the United States had to be encountered.

The initiation of the reconstruction process in Indian Territory was unlike the Presidential or Congressional method of reconstruction introduced in the states of the ex-Confederacy. The relations between the Five Civilized Nations and the United States were not based on the same constitutional structure as the relations between the states of the Union and the United States. Since the political relationship of the Five Civilized Nations with the United States government was basically international, the accepted method for working out political relations was through the negotiation of treaties. Therefore

192

treaties were consummated in order to reestablish political relations after the Civil War between the Five Civilized Nations and the United States.

The first major step was taken at a peace council that met at Fort Smith Arkansas, in September 1865. Though the Five Civilized Tribes had joined the Confederacy as Nations the Confederate sentiment was not unanimous. Large segments of the Creeks, Seminoles and Cherokees remained loyal to the Union in spite of the fact that the Union did not provide the assistance that had been promised. The majority of the Choctaws and Chickasaws shared the southern sentiment. When the peace council was called at Fort Smith, the loyal faction was promised some consideration because of the extreme suffering that it had endured, but the tenor of the proceedings was about the same for all. Any generosity or sympathy manifested by the United States commissioners was usually tendered to the faction that had openly demonstrated their Confederate sympathies rather than to those who had hung tenaciously to their faith in the Great White Father, only to be ignored or betrayed. The tribes were informed that they had forfeited all right to annuities, lands and protection by the United States. John Ross, the Chief of the Cherokees, who for so long tried to keep his Nation neutral was denied recognition as head of his Nation at the council by the United States commissioners although the Cherokee delegates reported by official documentation that John Ross was the choice of the majority of the Cherokees. The record also made it apparent that Ross remained neutral until surrounding Confederate strength gave him or the Nation no choice but to join the Confederacy.

At Fort Smith no satisfactory agreement could be reached between the commissioners and the representatives of the tribes, so a simple treaty of peace and amity was prepared by the United States commissioners and signed by all the delegates. This treaty contained no reconstruction measures and it left all questions growing out of the treaties with the Confederacy to be settled at a future time. The delegations were given copies of the proposed treaties containing the United States requirements for the reestablishment of relations and were invited to Washington in January 1866 for the purpose of concluding reconstruction treaties with the United States.

Double delegations representing the Federal and Confederate factions of each of the Five Civilized Nations appeared in

Washington. The negotiations were entered into on the part of the Federal government by Cooley, the Commissioner of Indian Affairs, Colonel Parker, and Superintendent Sells, all of whom served on the Fort Smith council commission.

The principal points that came up for settlement were: (1) the method of adjusting affairs between the loyal and the disloyal Indians, a problem applying especially to the Cherokees, among whom confiscation laws passed by the National Council had taken effect upon the property of those who were disloyal; (2) the status of the freedmen in the Nations; (3) compensation for losses of property occasioned by those who remained loyal to the Confederacy; (4) cession of lands by the several tribes to be used for the settlement of Indians from Kansas and elsewhere; and (5) the granting of right of way for railroads to enter Indian Territory from a north-south and an east-west direction.

The Seminoles signed first and then the Choctaw and Chickasaw Nations made a joint treaty. The United States Commission experienced some difficulty in negotiating with both the Creek and the Cherokee Nations and the Cherokees were the last to reach an agreement.

The Washington treaties of 1866 divided Indian Territory into two almost equal sections. The original area, the land that had been promised "in perpetuity" to each Nation, had been almost halved by the cessions of the Creeks, Seminoles, Choctaws, and Chickasaws and the Cherokee agreement to permit the government to settle other tribes in the Cherokee Outlet. Although these two sections were almost equal in land area the histories of the two areas were entirely different. The eastern section, that now became known as Indian Territory, resumed its development toward Anglo-Saxon–orientated civilization in peace and under orderly governments conducted basically by the Indians themselves until tribal dissolution began about 1898. In the western side that became known as Oklahoma Territory the Federal government settled tribes of eastern origin from Kansas and the nomadic tribes of the southern plains. The story of the process of their development was fraught with frequent war and disorder.

Reconstruction of the Five Civilized Nations in Indian Territory as viewed by the United States, seemed to offer the opportunity to extract from the Indians more of their land that had been given to them by the earlier treaties and to secure Indian concentration and a consolidated territorial government. These goals had been long sought. Too many tribes occupied land needed by western railroads or coveted by settlers to make acceptance of the status quo advisable in the eyes of the majority of the members of Congress. Congressional investigation revealed that but two areas remained as possible centers for Indian settlement, the public lands to the north of Nebraska and those to the south of Kansas. The administration of President Grant decided that all Indians must be gathered in these locations. This policy guiding the government's effort to confine Indian settlement within these areas was known as concentration. The popularity of the policy of concentration, the lack of knowledge of most Americans concerning Indian affairs and the apathy of the general public toward humanitarian movements during the period following the Civil War left but few to object to the postwar treaties made between the United States government and the Indians.

The Seminole Nation was the smallest of the Five Civilized Nations. This Nation experienced the unique situation of beginning their reconstruction period on an entirely different reservation than that which they owned when the war started. The fact that they ceded to the Federal government their old tribal land for fifteen cents per acre and then purchased their new land from the Creeks under Federal supervision for fifty cents per acre suggests that the Seminole delegates were not capable of coping with the sharp and even unethical practices of the Anglo-Saxon commissioners, who seemed intent on using the reconstruction process not to improve the condition of the Indians but rather to take advantage of them. In fact, the more trusting they were of the United States government the less favorable terms they received in their treaty.

Much dissatisfaction resulted from the fact that the land in the new Seminole reservation was not as fertile as had been represented, and problems developed between the Seminoles and the Creeks because their new reservation had been incorrectly surveyed. This boundary dispute was finally settled in February 1881. Disgruntlement was due to the fact that the new Seminole reservation was considered too small for themselves and the tribal members from Florida whom they hoped would join them in Indian Territory. But major reconstruction problems in the Seminole Nation were few. Article II of their treaty which abolished slavery and granted full civil rights to all persons whatever their race or color gave the Seminoles less concern than this same provision in the reconstruction treaties of the other Nations. Railroads during the reconstruction period did not ·bring problems to the Seminoles as in the other Indian Nations for the first railroad did not come to the Seminoles until 1895.

The general tribal atmosphere of the Seminoles was peaceful following the Civil War. Intertribal relations generally remained placid although at times the Indians of the plains gave them cause for complaint. The government of the Seminole Nation was not as complex as that of the other Nations of Indian Territory, as there was only one legislative body which in addition to its law making authority also sat in judgment upon all criminal cases. The laws were few but strictly enforced. The Seminoles had two principal chiefs until 1872, although the Seminole agent recognized the Chief of the northern faction as the one with whom he transacted all official business. The Chief of the northern faction during reconstruction was John Chupco and the Chief of the southern faction was John Jumper.

The Creeks made commendable process in the ways of Anglo-Saxon civilization during the postwar years. After the early years of reconstruction self-sufficiency was attained, but politics and the payment of claims created confusion and dissidence within the Creek Nation. The Creeks were divided before the war politically into groups designated as the Lower and the Upper Creeks. At the Fort Smith Council on September 18, 1865, friendly relations were established between these two factions. The Upper Creeks maintained their conservatism and the observance of old tribal ways, while the Lower Creeks were considered progressive in the culture of the Caucasian. Conflict over the manner of handling reconstruction problems was inevitable, although an agreement was brought about again in 1867, the same year that the Creeks ratified a new tribal constitution. But dissension between the two Creek factions continued throughout the tribal period. The Indians of the conservative element looked upon the adoption of the white man's institutions with disfavor. They seemed to wish for the primitive conditions of society and government which existed prior to the removal of the Creeks to Indian Territory and this element followed those who promised a government of that nature. The Creek chief recognized by the United States during the reconstruction period was Samuel Checote. Oktarharsars Harjo, known as Sands, led the opposing faction. Sands was elected chief in 1875 but was impeached and removed in 1876 and Ward Coachman completed his term.

All the treaties contained a stipulation concerning the establishment of a general council in Indian Territory. This requirement was complied with in 1870 with the calling of an intertribal council in Okmulgee, the capital of the Creek Nation. The Okmulgee constitution that came from this council was not generally adopted by the Nations nor did the council ever acquire the power of a lawmaking body. But the council was significant to the tribes for it aided in mediating peace between the United States and the plains Indians; it provided an avenue for issuing protests to the Federal government against their railroad policy and any attempt toward the formation of a consolidated territorial government; and it established a newspaper in the Creek Nation in May 1876, *The Indian Journal.* The Federal government ordered the council abolished in 1876 after it became apparent that it was not fostering the goals of the government but the tribes continued to meet annually at Okmulgee through 1878.

The Creeks as well as most of the other Indians of the Five Civilized Nations feared the railroads, for they considered them a menace to their tribal autonomy. Railroad construction usually brought problems for construction crews were lawless and disorderly, and they usually usurped their timber and other resources without bothering to provide the Nation with proper or adequate compensation. Criminals gathered at each temporary terminal and as the railroads advanced they left enterprising intruders within the Nation. The Creeks were particularly troubled at the increase of white traders along the railroads following construction of the first line in 1871–1872.

The abolition of slavery in the Creek Nation, the granting of citizenship rights and privileges to native citizens, including an equal interest in the soil and national funds to all persons lawfully residing in its boundaries, were evidently initiated at the ratification of the treaty. There seemed to be less prejudice toward the Negro than had been anticipated. This opinion was shared by General Sanborn who was sent to Indian Territory in early 1866 by Secretary of the Interior Harlan to regulate the relations between the freedmen and their former masters. Sanborn was convinced from a canvass of opinions that the Creek and Seminole Nations would not be as averse to incorporating the freedmen into the tribes as the other Nations. There was some effort made to eliminate the Negoes from the per capita payments but the loyal faction supported the freedmen and they began receiving remuneration in the summer of 1869.

A renewed interest in education was exhibited in the Creek Nation after the war though formal education was not started until about 1868. The freedmen were particularly anxious that their children be educated. Before the war the customs of the country prevented their sharing the benefits of schools but now that they were placed on a level of political equality with their former masters they seemed determined to profit by this situation. By 1876 all phases of life within the boundaries of the Creek Nation had made notable progress.

Although the Choctaws and the Chickasaws had been the most outspoken of the Five Civilized Nations in their sympathies for the Confederacy they received more favorable terms in their reconstruction treaty than the tribes that had suffered innumerable hardships for the Federal government. Neither the Choctaws nor the Chickasaws under the 1866 treaty had to adopt their freedmen as equals in soil or finances. These Nations had a leadership that better understood the machinations of the Anglo-Saxon and this enabled them more ably to cope with the issues at hand. The full-blooded factions of each Nation exhibited more faith in the integrity and justice of the United States government and they were therefore usually unprepared to contend with the particular strategem being presented.

The Choctaws and the Chickasaws cooperated to the extent of making a joint treaty although they did not agree on all issues. The Chickasaws as early as 1868 had endorsed sectionization of their land while the Choctaws opposed this issue strongly. Inasmuch as both Nations had to agree to the survey of their land for the purpose of allotment this feature of the treaty was not complied with until 1897 through the work of the Dawes Commission. On the other hand, the Choctaws finally decided to adopt their freedmen in 1885; though this date was about twenty years late they eventually complied with the provision. The Chickasaws never honored this stipulation at any time for the proportion of Negroes within their Nation was large in relation to the number of Chickasaws; and they evidently feared the political ascendency and dominance of Negroes as did many other states in the United States which had a similar population ratio.

The basic political structure of the Choctaw and Chickasaw Nation was disrupted no longer than the period of the war and their councils were activated in the fall of 1865. Their form of government was similar to that used in the various states of the Union. Each had a written constitution and each had civil and criminal laws. Their legislative bodies were of two houses similar to the United States Senate and House of Representatives. They each had their principal chief, although the progressive element usually referred to the executive as the governor. There was a judiciary regularly organized with inferior and superior courts. There were sometimes incidents between these Nations and the plains tribes but they were settled peacefully. The internal political strife and deep factionalism exhibited in Creek and Cherokee politics was not inherent within the politics of these people.

Schools for Indians were generally reestablished in the Choctaw country by 1871. Negroes were given an opportunity for education by 1874. The Chickasaw legislature provided for the reopening of the schools in 1867 and the Commissioner of Indian Affairs reported in 1868 that the common neighborhood schools had reopened. The Chickasaws provided no educational opportunities for their Negroes. Before the Choctaws adopted their freedmen and consequently provided schools for them the United States government and the missionaries assisted in the education of the freedmen. The fact that English was the usual language spoken by the teachers in the schools made it difficult for the Indians who spoke nothing but their native tongue to comprehend in a manner necessary for effective utilization of their conceptual tools. Consequently the mixed bloods were the great benefactors of the schools in the Choctaw and Chickasaw Nations and some continued academic training in the eastern states. The Nations paid large sums of money for the education of a few. There were the manual labor institutions which benefited the full bloods but these schools were inadequate in size and number and children had to be turned away. Obtaining competent teachers was also a problem. The Chickasaws spent more money per capita on education than any other tribe in Indian Territory but their system of education was ineffective for the masses. The fact that they handled their own money also kept outsiders from interfering with them either in a positive or in a negative manner.

Political dissension was rampant in the Cherokee Nation immediately following the Civil War. The southern faction wanted a separate sovereign area, but while they were given the opportunity to live in an area away from the northern Cherokees the Nation was never split legally into two separate divisions as many of the southern Cherokees wanted. Upon the death of John Ross in 1866 there was a realignment of parties. Though his nephew, W. P. Ross, was chosen to succeed him he could not hold all of the old Ross following as he did not have the magnetism and political acumen of his uncle. Evan and John B. Jones, and Lewis Downing, who had been followers of John Ross and leaders of the full-blooded faction, broke with W. P. Ross and saw the possibility of uniting with certain leaders of the old Ridge or Treaty Party and the southern Cherokees generally. This combination of Downing, representing the full bloods who had heretofore followed John Ross and the influential Joneses, was the nucleus of a party that was long to rule the Cherokee Nation. The new organization became known as the Downing Party; the opposition led by W. P. Ross became known as the National Party. This party formation began operation during the winter and spring of 1866–1867 and when Downing was elected Principal Chief in 1867 he eliminated the two sets of delegates in Washington and appointed one delegation.

The Cherokee National Council resumed its sessions, instituting a political structure much like that in Washington in the fall of 1866. Their constitution was amended to conform to the treaty of that year. After this they worked diligently to comply with the provisions of their treaty, but some articles were more difficult for the Nation to initiate and complete than others since they resulted in political problems. The question of citizenship for the freedmen was such an issue. Slavery was abolished voluntarily by the Cherokees in 1863 in accordance with President Lincoln's Emancipation Proclamation and Article IX of the treaty. The freed slaves and Negroes who had always been free were declared citizens and were entitled to vote and hold office by an amendment to the Cherokee constitution in December 1866. Yet the issue was unpopular politically and the freedmen, Shawnees and Delawares who had been adopted as full-fledged residents did not receive official sanction to share in tribal finance, as Cherokees by blood had shared, until 1888. The six month stipulation in Article IX concerning freedmen caused a great deal of difficulty also for it was almost impossible in that length of time for publicity to be given to the provision whereby the widely scattered freedmen might return and become citizens of the Nation.

Two important issues demanding attention from the Cherokees during the postwar years were the removal and the settlement of the claims that the North Carolina Cherokees brought against the Cherokees who had removed to the West, and the claims of the Old Settlers who were attempting to get per capita funds from the Federal goverment due them under the 1835 and 1846 treaties. These claims were finally adjudged in 1893 and the Old Settlers or their heirs received their money. The reestablishment of schools was delayed until about 1870. Schools and orphan funds derived fifty percent of their financial support from the government as interest on invested funds held in trust for them. The Cherokees seem to have been the only one of the Five Civilized Nations to establish an institution for the deaf, dumb, blind. and insane during the reconstruction period.

Reconstruction in Indian Territory for the Indian mixed-blood and the Negro freedmen was to a degree similar to that of the general reconstruction process for the conservative element and the freed Negro of the former Confederate states. Upon abolition of slavery the mixed bloods, like the former slave-holders in the states, expected but were denied compensation for their slaves by the Federal government. After the war the Choctaws and Chickasaws through their governments attempted to control the economic activity and status of the Negro. Regulations were drawn up similar to the contract, vagrancy and apprenticeship provisions in the postwar Black Codes in most of the states of the South. The mixed bloods throughout Indian Territory were generally as anxious to have modern economic innovations as the "New Departure Democrats" were to have industry and commerce become an integral part of the economy of the South. The turmoil exhibited over the problem of citizenship of the freedmen in the Cherokee, Choctaw and Chickasaw Nations was similar to the reaction of many conservatives of the South to the ratification of the fourteenth and fifteenth amendments to the Constitution of the United States.

Generally the Indian mixed bloods were favored over the full bloods by the Federal government though most of them had been openly sympathetic with the Confederacy.

Reconstruction in Indian Territory as viewed by the Indian full bloods and the mixed bloods involved different perspectives. The full bloods seemed to look forward to the end of the war and the period that followed as a time in which they could once again settle peacefully upon their land promised by the Washington government in their removal treaties. Here they could resume their life as it was before the war without being molested or concerned with the encroachments and problems of the white man. They expected to be assisted by the United States government until they could plant and harvest crops that would convert their status as total wards of the government to that of self-respecting and self-sufficient individuals.

As many of the Indian full bloods remained loyal to the Union, though confronted with measureless difficulties, they were bewildered, hurt and disappointed over the attitude and measures adopted by the Federal government during the post-war period. It was a fact that as Nations they had allied themselves with the Confederacy but they thought that the Washington government understood that they had not participated in the negotiation of the treaties with the Confederacy nor had they supported its cause. They felt that this fact would be kept in mind when instructions were sent from Washington conveying the requirements for the reestablishment of proper relations between the Civilized Nations and the United States government. They felt certain also that justice would be shown in the scope and size of compensation for the losses they sustained during the war. To their dismay none of these factors seemed to have appreciably affected the unfair treatment and exploitation that they experienced during the reconstruction period.

The reconstruction policies which the United States imposed upon the Five Civilized Nations indicated that the reconstruction treaties were not designed primarily to benefit the Indians. They were used instead as a means by which the Federal government could circumvent the old removal treaties and concentrate other tribes in the territory, thus releasing additional land for white settlement in other states as well as Indian Territory. Reconstruction in Indian Territory was a unique, as well as a complicated, disappointing, frustrating and tragic experience for the Indians. The reconstruction policies of the United States exploited the decision of the Five Civilized Nations to ally themselves with the Confederate States. The postwar treatment of loyal Indians in Indian Territory manifested little consideration of certain obvious facts such as the position of the Five Civilized Nations in relation to the border of the Confederate states; the southern sympathy indicated by Indian agents; the holding of investment bonds by southern states; and the abandonment of the area by the United States at the outbreak of the Civil War. The 1866 reconstruction treaties unquestionably provided the United States government with the vehicle by which land and desired political control of Indian Territory could be obtained. The blessings of the Anglo-Saxon laws and practices designed to foster tribal dissolution and ultimate statehood were instituted whether the residing inhabitants desired it or not, because it was "good for them" and for the progress of the western-oriented United States.

BIBLIOGRAPHY

Unpublished Material

Balyeat, Frank. "Education in Indian Territory." Doctor of Philosophy dissertation, Stanford University, Palo Alto, California, 1927.
    A comprehensive study of education in Indian Territory. A valuable source.
Benson, Bernice C. "The Creek Nation During the Reconstruction Period." Master of Arts thesis, Oklahoma State University, Stillwater, Oklahoma, 1937.
    An objective narrative containing the history of the Creek Nation during the years immediately following the Civil War. Clearly written with a helpful bibliography.
Buck, Carl R. "The Economic Development of the Chickasaw Indians: 1865-1907." Master of Arts thesis, Oklahoma State University, Stillwater, Oklahoma, 1940.
    A survey of the major economic developments for the Chickasaws from the years immediately following the Civil War until the dissolution of their tribal government. Not a comprehensive study, but serviceable in checking economic trends.
Byington, Cyrus. Papers. Library, Thomas Gilcrease Institute of American History and Art, Tulsa, Oklahoma.
    An extensive collection of the papers of an outstanding missionary. Not annotated, but classified by year.
Cherokee Collection. Library, Northeastern State College, Tahlequah, Oklahoma.
    Many of the original holdings of this library were divided and located in other research centers. But remaining letters of John Ross and early documents concerning the missionaries are of great value.
Cherokee Letters. Manuscripts Division, Library, University of Oklahoma, Norman, Oklahoma.
    A collection composed of letters of outstanding Cherokee personalities, miscellaneous letters, and Indian documents, including memorials and political platforms.
Cherokee Tribal Records. Indian Archives Division, Oklahoma Historical Society, Oklahoma City, Oklahoma.
Chickasaw Tribal Records. Indian Archives Division, Oklahoma Historical Society, Oklahoma City, Oklahoma.
Choctaw Tribal Records. Indian Archives Division, Oklahoma Historical Society, Oklahoma City, Oklahoma.

204

Creek Tribal Records. Indian Archives Division, Oklahoma Historical Society, Oklahoma City, Oklahoma.

These tribal records were transferred from Muskogee, Oklahoma. Well organized and in some cases indexed.

Department of the Interior. Records of the Bureau of Indian Affairs, Letters received by the Office of Indian Affairs, 1824–1880, Cherokee Agency. National Archives, Washington, D. C.

————. Records of the Bureau of Indian Affairs, Letters received by the Office of Indian Affairs, 1824–1870, Chickasaw Agency. National Archives, Washington, D. C.

————. Records of the Bureau of Indian Affairs, Letters received by the Office of Indian Affairs, 1824–1876, Choctaw Agency. National Archives, Washington, D. C.

————. Records of the Bureau of Indian Affairs, Letters received by the Office of Indian Affairs, 1824–1876, Creek Agency. National Archives, Washington, D. C.

————. Records of the Bureau of Indian Affairs, Letters received by the Office of Indian Affairs, 1824–1876, Seminole Agency. National Archives, Washington, D. C.

Letters, documents and other miscellaneous matter. Not indexed.

Dugan, E. J. "Education Among the Creek Indians." Master of Arts thesis, Oklahoma State University, Stillwater, Oklahoma, 1938.

An interesting account of educational developments in the Creek Nation.

Foster, Wade D. "The Federal Government and the Five Civilized Tribes During Reconstruction." Master of Arts thesis, Oklahoma State University, Stillwater, Oklahoma, 1957.

Covers the relations of the United States government and the Five Civilized Tribes during the period immediately following the Civil War. A concise and well-organized historical background for the period before the war.

Flowers, Marvin Paine. "Education Among the Creek Indians." Master of Arts thesis, Oklahoma State University, Stillwater, Oklahoma, 1931.

More comprehensive in scope than the thesis by Dugan. Deals with the total educational picture.

Kiker, Ernest. "Education Among the Seminoles." Master of Arts thesis, Oklahoma State University, Stillwater, Oklahoma, 1932.

A well-documented and useful study.

Pitchlynn, Peter Perkins. Papers. Library, Thomas Gilcrease Institute of American History and Art, Tulsa, Oklahoma.

Portrays, among other things, the extensive work of Pitchlynn as a delegate of the Choctaw Nation in Washington to secure the Net Proceeds Claim. Insight is evident in these papers on the political aspects of Choctaw life as well as the personal life of Pitchlynn.

Proceedings of the General Council of the Indian Territory for 1872, 1873 and 1875. Indian Archives Division, Oklahoma Historical Society, Oklahoma City, Oklahoma.

The 1870 proceedings can be found in the *Chronicles of Oklahoma*. Helpful in understanding the activities of the Five Civilized Tribes in intertribal council, they reflect the issues of the time and Indian reaction to them.

Robertson, Alice. Collection. Library, Oklahoma Historical Society, Oklahoma City, Oklahoma.

Contains a narrative account written by Alice Robertson on general conditions in Indian Territory, the reception of the Creek missionaries, and the political situation after the Civil War.

Ross, John. Letters. Library, Thomas Gilcrease Institute of American History and Art, Tulsa, Oklahoma.

Useful in providing information concerning Chief Ross's activity during the war and during the Cherokee negotiation of the Washington treaty in 1866.

Todd, Will R. "Federal Policy Relating to the Lands of the Five Civilized Tribes, 1865–1890." Master of Arts thesis, Oklahoma State University, Stillwater, Oklahoma, 1957.

A thorough study that supplies concise descriptions of the land areas of the Five Civilized Tribes before and after the Civil War.

Union Agency Files. Indian Archives Division, Oklahoma Historical Society, Oklahoma City, Oklahoma.

Useful records of the Five Civilized Tribes after they were consolidated into one agency located at Muskogee, Oklahoma.

Whittenberg, Mary E. "The History of the Union Agency and Federal Administration." Master of Arts thesis, Oklahoma State University, Stillwater, Oklahoma, 1949.

A well-organized thesis providing helpful general background on the administrative system of the United States for Indian Territory.

Government Documents

Cherokee Nation. *Constitution and Laws of the Cherokee Nation.* St. Louis: R. and T. A. Ennis, Printers, 1875.

————. *Constitution and Laws of the Cherokee Nation.* Parsons, Kansas: The Foley Railway Printing Company, 1893.

Choctaw Nation. *Constitution and Laws of the Choctaw Nation.* Dallas: John F. Worley Publishing Company, 1894.

Kappler, Charles, Jr., ed. *Indian Affairs: Laws and Treaties.* 6 vols., Washington: Government Printing Office, 1904.

Richardson, James D., comp. *A Compilation of the Messages and Papers of the President.* 11 vols., Washington: Bureau of National Literature, 1913.

United States. *Annals of Congress,* Eighth Congress, First Session. Washington: Gales and Seaton, 1852.

————. *Congressional Globe,* Thirty-seventh Congress, Second Session. Washington: Congressional Globe Office, 1862.

————. *Congressional Globe,* Thirty-eighth Congress, First Session. Washington: Congressional Globe Office, 1863.

————. *Congressional Globe,* Thirty-eighth Congress, Second Session. Washington: Congressional Globe Office, 1865.

————. *Congressional Record,* Forty-sixth Congress, Second Session. Washington: Congressional Record, 1880.

————. *Court of Claims Reports.* 169 vols., Washington: Government Printing Office, 1867–1965.

————. Department of the Interior. *Report of the Commissioner of Indian Affairs.* 60 vols., Washington: Government Printing Office, 1849–1909.

————. Department of War. *The War of the Rebellion. A Compilation of the Official Records of the Union and Confederate Armies.* 70 vols. (128 books in the United States Serial Set), Washington: Government Printing Office, 1880–1901.

————. *House Executive Document Number 1,* Thirty-seventh Congress, Third Session. Washington: Government Printing Office, 1862.

————. *House Executive Document Number 1,* Thirty-eighth Congress, First Session. Washington: Government Printing Office, 1864...

————. *House Executive Document Number 1,* Thirty-eighth Congress, Second Session. Washington: Government Printing Office, 1864.

————. *House Executive Document Number 1,* Thirty-ninth Congress, First Session. Washington: Government Printing Office, 1866.

————. *House Executive Document Number 204,* Fortieth Congress, Second Session. Washington: Government Printing Office, 1868.

————. *House Executive Document Number 1,* Fortieth Congress, Third Session. Washington: Government Printing Office, 1868.

————. *House Executive Document Number 287,* Forty-second Congress, Second Session. Washington: Government Printing Office, 1872.

————. *House Executive Document Number 1,* Forty-third Congress, Second Session. Washington: Government Printing Office, 1875.

————. *House Executive Document Number 47,* Forty-third Congress, Second Session. Washington: Government Printing Office, 1875.

————. *House Executive Document Number 96,* Forty-seventh Congress, First Session. Washington: Government Printing Office, 1882.

————. *House Miscellaneous Document Number 75,* Thirty-seventh Congress, Second Session. Washington: Government Printing Office, 1862.

————. *House Miscellaneous Document Number 46,* Forty-second Congress, Second Session. Washington: Government Printing Office, 1872.

————. *House Miscellaneous Document Number 94,* Forty-second Congress, Third Session. Washington: Government Printing Office, 1872.

————. *House Miscellaneous Document Number 40,* Forty-fourth Congress, First Session. Washington: Government Printing Office, 1876.

————. *House Report Number 52,* Forty-first Congress, Second Session. Washington: Government Printing Office, 1870.

————. *House Report Number 53,* Forty-first Congress, Second Session. Washington: Government Printing Office, 1870.

————. *House Report Number 30,* Forty-first Congress, Third Session. Washington: Government Printing Office, 1871.

————. *Official Opinions of the Attorneys-General.* 41 vols., Washington: Government Printing Office, 1851–1963.

————. *Senate Executive Document Number 1,* Thirty-seventh Congress, Second Session. Washington: Government Printing Office, 1861.

————. *Senate Executive Document Number 48,* Forty-first Congress, Second Session. Washington: Government Printing Office, 1870.

————. *Senate Executive Document Number 17,* Forty-seventh Congress, Second Session. Washington: Government Printing Office, 1883.

————. *Senate Executive Document Number 82,* Forty-ninth Congress, First Session. Washington: Government Printing Office, 1886.

————. *Senate Executive Document Number 1978,* Forty-ninth Congress, Second Session. Washington: Government Printing Office, 1887.

————. *Senate Executive Document Number 78,* Fifty-first Congress, First Session. Washington: Government Printing Office, 1890.

————. *Senate Executive Document Number 77,* Fifty-fourth Congress, First Session. Washington: Government Printing Office, 1895.

_____. *Senate Miscellaneous Document Number 106,* Forty-first Congress, Second Session. Washington: Government Printing Office, 1870.
_____. *Senate Miscellaneous Document Number 59,* Forty-fifth Congress, Second Session. Washington: Government Printing Office, 1878.
_____. *Senate Report Number 353,* Forty-seventh Congress, First Session. Washington: Government Printing Office, 1882.
_____. *Senate Report Number 1278,* Pts. 2 and 3, Forty-ninth Congress, First Session. Washington: Government Printing Office, 1886.
_____. *Senate Report Number 1680,* Forty-ninth Congress, Second Session. Washington: Government Printing Office, 1887.
_____. *Senate Report Number 552,* Fifty-second Congress, First Session. Washington: Government Printing Office, 1892.
_____. *Statutes at Large.* 78 vols., Washington: Government Printing Office, 1848–1965.
_____. *Supreme Court Reports.* 381 vols., Washington: Government Printing Office, 1926–1965.

Newspapers

Atoka Independent (Atoka, Choctaw Nation), October 26, 1877.
Cherokee Advocate (Tahlequah, Cherokee Nation), July 23, 1879.
Indian Citizen (Atoka, Choctaw Nation), October 7, 1895.
Vindicator (New Boggy, Atoka, Choctaw Nation), August 24, 1872.

Articles

Banks, Dean. "Civil War Refugees from Indian Territory in the North, 1861–1864," *Chronicles of Oklahoma,* XLI (Autumn, 1963), 286–298.
Bass, Althea. "William Schenck Robertson," *Chronicles of Oklahoma,* XXXVI (Spring, 1959), 28–34.
Benson, Henry. "Life Among the Choctaw Indians," *Chronicles of Oklahoma,* IV (June, 1926), 156–161.
Carr, Mrs. S. J. "Bloomfield Academy: Its Founder," *Chronicles of Oklahoma,* II (December, 1924), 365–379.
Davis, Caroline. "Education of the Chickasaws, 1856–1907," *Chronicles of Oklahoma,* XV (December, 1937), 427–428.
Debo, Angie. "Education in the Choctaw Country after the Civil War," *Chronicles of Oklahoma,* X (April, 1932), 255–266.
_____. "Southern Refugees of the Cherokee Nation," *Southwestern Historical Quarterly,* XXXV (April, 1932), 256–261.
Denison, Natalie Morrison. "Missions and Missionaries of the Presbyterian Church Among the Choctaws, 1866–1907," *Chronicles of Oklahoma,* XXIV (Winter, 1946), 426–448.
Foreman, Carolyn T. "Chickasaw Manual Labor Academy," *Chronicles of Oklahoma,* XXIII (December 1945), 338–357.
_____. "The Choctaw Academy," *Chronicles of Oklahoma,* VI (December, 1928), 453–480.
_____. "Organization of the Seminole Light-Horse," *Chronicles of Oklahoma,* XXXIV (Autumn, 1956), 340–344.

————, ed. "Journal of a Tour in the Indian Territory," *Chronicles of Oklahoma*, X (June, 1932), 219–256.

Foreman, Grant. "Early Post Offices in Oklahoma," *Chronicles of Oklahoma*, VI (March, 1928), 4–25.

Graebner, Norman. "Pioneer Agriculture in Oklahoma," *Chronicles of Oklahoma*, XXIII (Autumn, 1945), 232–248.

————. "Public Land Policy of the Five Civilized Tribes," *Chronicles of Oklahoma*, XXIII (Spring, 1945), 107–118.

————. "Provincial Indian Society in Eastern Oklahoma," *Chronicles of Oklahoma*, XXIII (Winter, 1945), 323–337.

Heimann, Robert K. "The Cherokee Tobacco Case," *Chronicles of Oklahoma*, XLI (Autumn, 1963), 299–322.

Holway, Hope. "Ann Eliza Worcester Robertson as a Linguist," *Chronicles of Oklahoma*, XXXXVI (Spring, 1959), 35–44.

"Journal of the Adjourned Session of First General Council of the Indian Territory," *Chronicles of Oklahoma*, III (June, 1925), 120–132.

"Journal of the General Council of the Indian Territory," *Chronicles of Oklahoma*, III (April, 1925), 33–44.

Meserve, John B. "Chief Checote," *Chronicles of Oklahoma*, XVI (December, 1938), 401–409.

————. "Chief Coleman Cole," *Chronicles of Oklahoma*, XIV (March, 1936), 9–21.

————. "Chief Lewis Downing and Chief Charles Thompson," *Chronicles of Oklahoma*, VI (September, 1938), 315–325.

————. "Chief Opothleyahola," *Chronicles of Oklahoma*, IX (December, 1931), 439–453.

————. "Chief Pleasant Porter," *Chronicles of Oklahoma*, IX (September, 1931), 318–334.

————. "Chief William Potter Ross," *Chronicles of Oklahoma*, XV (March, 1937), 21–29.

————. "Governor Benjamin Franklin Overton," *Chronicles of Oklahoma*, XVI (June, 1938), 221–233.

————. "Governor Cyrus Harris, Chickasaw," *Chronicles of Oklahoma*, XV (December, 1937), 373–386.

————. "Governor Dougherty Winchester Colbert," *Chronicles of Oklahoma*, XVIII (December, 1940), 348–356.

Morton, Ohland. "The Government of the Creek Indians," Part 1, *Chronicles of Oklahoma*, VIII (March, 1930), 42–64.

————. "The Government of the Creek Indians," Part 2, *Chronicles of Oklahoma*, VIII (June, 1930), 189–225.

————. "Reconstruction in the Creek Nation," *Chronicles of Oklahoma*, IX (June, 1931), 171–179.

"Okmulgee Constitution," *Chronicles of Oklahoma*, III (September, 1925), 216–228.

Royce, Charles C. "The Cherokee Nation of Indians," *Fifth Annual Report of Bureau of American Ethnology*, (1883–1884), 121–378.

Russell, Orpha. "Ek-Vn-Hv-Lwuce," *Chronicles of Oklahoma*, XXIX (December, 1951), 401–407.

Steen, Carol T. "The Home for the Insane, Deaf, Dumb and Blind of the Cherokee Nation," *Chronicles of Oklahoma*, XXI (December, 1943), 402–419.

Thoburn, Joseph, ed. "The Cherokee Question," *Chronicles of Oklahoma*, II (June, 1924), 141–242.

Wright, Muriel. "Early River Navigation," *Chronicles of Oklahoma*, VIII (March, 1930), 65–88.

_____. "The Removal of the Choctaws to Indian Territory, 1830–1833," *Chronicles of Oklahoma*, VI (June, 1928), 103–128.
_____. "The Seal of the Seminole Nation," *Chronicles of Oklahoma*, XXXIV (Autumn, 1956), 262–271.

Books

Abel, Annie H. *The American Indian as Slaveholder and Secessionist.* Cleveland: The Arthur H. Clark Company, 1915.
_____. *The American Indian as Participant in the Civil War.* Cleveland: The Arthur H. Clark Company, 1919.
_____. *The American Indian Under Reconstruction.* Cleveland: The Arthur H. Clark Company, 1925.
    The most detailed treatment of the Five Civilized Tribes for the period of the Civil War and Reconstruction to this time. Thoroughly researched, but highly opinionated.
Basler, Roy P., ed. *The Collected Works of Abraham Lincoln.* 9 vols., New Brunswick: Rutgers University Press, 1953–1955.
    Useful in following the contacts of Lincoln with Cherokee Chief John Ross during the Civil War years.
Beadle, John H. *The Undeveloped West.* Philadelphia: National Publishing Company, 1873.
    A very good account of the activities and early conditions of the West as seen by a traveler. Colorful and useful.
Benedict, John D. *History of Muskogee and Northeastern Oklahoma.* 3 vols. Chicago: The S. J. Clarke Publishing Company, 1922.
    Written by the man who was sent to Indian Territory by the United States government in the spring of 1899 to take Federal control of educational matters.
Cunningham, Frank. *General Stand Watie's Confederate Indians.* San Antonio: The Naylor Company, 1959.
    An interesting, but biased biography; it glorifies Watie and the Confederacy.
Crawford, Samuel Johnson. *Kansas in the Sixties.* Chicago: A. C. McClurg and Company, 1911.
    Helpful in understanding the problem of intruders in Kansas and the sale of the Cherokee Neutral Land in Kansas.
Dale, Edward E., and Litton, Gaston, eds. *Cherokee Cavaliers.* Norman: The University of Oklahoma Press, 1939.
    Contains material on slavery in Indian Territory, as well as much of the correspondence of the Ridge-Boudinot family of the Cherokee Nation. Provides useful information concerning leaders of the treaty faction who played important roles in Cherokee politics.
Dale, Edward, and Rader, Jesse, eds. *Readings in Oklahoma History.* New York: Row, Peterson and Company, 1930.
    A collection of some of the more important materials concerning Oklahoma history extracted from government documents, periodicals, newspapers, manuscripts and rare books. The Washington treaties of 1866 with the Five Civilized Tribes are listed in this volume.
Debo, Angie. *The Rise and Fall of the Choctaw Republic.* Norman: The University of Oklahoma Press, 1961.
    A well-organized and well-written history of the Choctaw Nation.

————. *The Road to Disappearance.* Norman: The University of Oklahoma Press, 1941.

A detailed history of the Creek Nation, and the best secondary source on the Creek Indians.

Eaton, Rachel. *John Ross and the Cherokee Indians.* Menasha, Wisconsin: George Banta Publishing Company, 1914.

Begins with the youth and early training of John Ross and continues to the reconstruction period. The section concerning the activities of Ross immediately before and during the Civil War is well delineated.

Farnham, Thomas J. *Travels in the Great Western Prairie.* Cleveland: The Arthur H. Clark Company, 1906.

Includes useful information concerning Indian Territory as observed and recorded by an early traveler through this area to Oregon.

Foreman, Grant. *Advancing the Frontier: 1830–1860.* Norman: The University of Oklahoma Press, 1933.

Supplies information concerning the adjustment of the newly removed Indians from the southeast to Indian Territory, and the establishment of peaceful relations with the plains Indians.

————. *Indian Removal: The Emigration of the Five Civilized Tribes.* Norman: The University of Oklahoma Press, 1953.

An excellent detailed account of the emigration of the Five Civilized Tribes from the southeastern United States to the area provided for them west of the Mississippi River.

————. *The Five Civilized Tribes.* Norman: The University of Oklahoma Press, 1934.

A detailed account of the rehabilitation and reconstruction of the Five Civilized Tribes in Indian Territory from 1830 to the beginning of the Civil War.

————. *A History of Oklahoma.* Norman: The University of Oklahoma Press, 1942.

One of the best one-volume histories of Oklahoma.

Gittinger, Roy. *The Formation of the State of Oklahoma.* Norman: The University of Oklahoma Press, 1939.

A thoroughly documented study with an excellent bibliography. Particularly useful in tracing the efforts or the United States to open this territory to white settlement.

Gregg, Josiah. *Commerce of the Prairies.* Cleveland: The Arthur H. Clark Company, 1905.

Contains much useful information concerning Indian Territory in the years before the Civil War.

Hill, Luther B. *A History of the State of Oklahoma.* 2 vols., Chicago: The Lewis Publishing Company, 1910.

A comprehensive pioneer work that describes the evolution of Oklahoma. The account of the Five Civilized Tribes before and during the Civil War is vividly portrayed.

Malone, James H. *The Chickasaw Nation.* Louisville: John P. Morton and Company, 1922.

Opinionated and of little historical value. Yet it is the only book-length study available on the Chickasaw Indians.

McReynolds, Edwin C. *Oklahoma: A History of the Sooner State.* Norman: The University of Oklahoma Press, 1954.

————. *The Seminoles.* Norman: The University of Oklahoma Press, 1957.

The best secondary source concerning the Seminole Indians.

Morris, John W., and McReynolds, Edwin C. *Historical Atlas of Oklahoma.* Norman: The University of Oklahoma Press, 1965.

A thoroughly researched and well-edited volume.

O'Beirne, Harry F., and Edward S. *The Indian Territory: Its Chiefs, Legislators, ánd Leading Men.* St. Louis: C. B. Woodward Company, 1892.

An interesting and excellent source of contemporary information concerning Indian Territory. Includes colorful information not usually found in the general histories of the tribes.

Priest, Loring B. *Uncle Sam's Stepchildren: The Reformation of United States Indian Policy, 1865–1887.* New Brunswick: Rutgers University Press, 1942.

A very good source for understanding and tracing the development of the administrative policies of the United States government with the Indian tribes. Well-written and thoroughly researched.

Ross, Mrs. W. P. *The Life and Times of Honorable William Potter Ross.* Fort Smith: Weldon and Williams Printer, 1893.

A comprehensive biography of William Potter Ross written by his wife. Includes the major addresses delivered by Ross during his lifetime.

Starkey, Marion L. *The Cherokee Nation.* New York: Alfred Knopf, 1946.

An excellent volume for obtaining background information on the Cherokees, particularly about the beginning of their missions and the work of their early missionaries.

Stewart, Dora A. *The Government and Development of Oklahoma Territory.* Oklahoma City: Harlow Publishing Company, 1933.

Provides background. Thoroughly documented.

Thoburn, Joseph B., and Wright, Muriel H. *Oklahoma: A History of the State and Its People.* 4 vols., New York: Lewis Historical Publishing Company, 1929.

Most useful for providing background material and information concerning the work of the vigilance committees in Indian Territory.

Wardell, Morris L. *A Political History of the Cherokee Nation.* Norman: The University of Oklahoma Press, 1938.

The best account of internal politics in the Cherokee Nation.

Woodward, Grace Steele. *The Cherokees.* Norman: The University of Oklahoma Press, 1969.

A well researched clearly written volume on the Cherokees.

Wright, Muriel. *A Guide to the Indian Tribes of Oklahoma.* Norman: The University of Oklahoma Press, 1951.

A superb and concise description of Indian life in the sixty-seven tribes of Oklahoma.

Index

Abbot, J.B., 59
Abolitionist activity, *see also* Slavery and Slaves
Abolitionist activity
  Keetoowah Society among Cherokees, 24
  law against, among Choctaws, 1836, 23
  missions' role in, 23-24
  opposition to in Indian Territory, 23
Adair, W.P., 78, 173, 174, 175
Agriculture
  among Creeks, 13
  among Seminoles, 83-85
Alberson, Isaac, 12
Alberty, Moses, 177
Aldrich, Cyrus, Representative from Minnesota, 67
American Bible Society
  publication of New Testament in Choctaw, 18
American Board of Commissioners for Foreign Missions (Presbyterian)
  and Choctaw education, 16
  withdraws mission support over slavery dispute, 23
American Emigrant Company, 162
Anderson, Charles, 94, 95
Anti-Christianity, *see under* Choctaws and Creeks
Apukshunnubbee, *see* Okla Falaya
Arbeka, 114
Arkansas Cherokees, 7
Arkansas-Verdigris River Settlement, 19-20
Armstrong Academy, 11, 17, 58, 146
  capital of Choctaw Nation, 141

Armstrong, William, 12
Army of the Frontier, 36
Asbury Mission School (Methodist), 20, 119-21
Atkins, J.D.C., 128, 182
Atlantic and Pacific Railroad (later St. Louis and San Francisco Railroad, or "Frisco"), 169-70
Atoka, 129, 146

Baldwin, T.A., 87
Baptist Board of Home Missions, 146, 149, 152
Baptist General Convention
  and Choctaw education, 16
Baptist Mission Board, *see* Baptist Board of Home Missions
Barnett, Ketch, 104
Barnett, Timothy, 117
Bemo, John D., 21
Benge, S.H., 77
Bethebara, 16
Bethel, 16
Bird Creek
  site of Creek-Confederate engagement, 33
Bloomfield Seminary, 19
Blunt, Brigadier General James G., 26, 35, 38-39, 134, 136
Board of Indian Commissioners, 163
Boarding Spring Council Ground, 19
Boggy Depot, 10, 152
Bogy, Lewis V., Commissioner of Indian Affairs, 173
Bok Tukle, 16
Boudinot, Elias, 24
  assassination of, 7, 8n
Boudinot, Elias C., 63-5, 78, 168-69, 172

Boudinot, W.P., 172-73
Bowlegs, Billy, Chief of Seminoles, 24
  death of, 37
Brain Town, 173
Breiner, Henry, 85
Bristow, Benjamin, Secretary of the
  Treasury, 135
Brown, E.J., 87
Brown, John, Chief of Cherokees, 7
Browning, O.H., Secretary of the In-
  terior, 68, 131, 162
Browning, Rev. Wesley, 19
Bryan, Joel M., 165
Bryant, William, Chief of Choctaws,
  132, 134
Bureau of Indian Affairs, see Indian
  Affairs
Burney Institute, 19
Bushyhead, Dennis W., Chief of
  Cherokees, 163-64, 165, 181-82
Bushyhead, Jesse, 173
Bussey, General Cyrus, 57
Byington, Rev. Cyrus, 16, 18

Cabell, Brigadier General William, 27
Camp Holmes, site of 1835 Intertribal
  Treaty, 10
Camp Napoleon, 55, 56
Camp Ross, Union Cherokee council
  at, 27
Campbell, Robert, 90
Carter, Colbert, 63, 71, 75, 90
Cattle-thieving
  in Choctaw-Chickasaw Nations, 44
  in Indian Territory, 40-41
Caving Banks, site of Creek-Confed-
  erate engagement, 33
Chahta Tamaha, see Armstrong Acad-
  emy
Checotah, 107
Checote, Samuel, Principal Chief of
  Creeks, 104, 107-08, 112, 114-16,
  118, 197
Cherokee Advocate, The, 8, 172
Cherokee Female Seminary, 183
Cherokee General Council, 7
Cherokee Male Seminary, 184
Cherokee Nation
  acreage and arability of, 186
  Act of Union, 1839, 7
  amnesty to Southern sympathizers,
    57
  citizenship granted North Carolina
    Cherokees, 165
  Constitution of 1839, 8
  convention at Tahlequah, 1839, 7

dissension between eastern and western leaders, 7
dissension between full bloods and
  other groups, 172, 174
divided delegation at treaty negotiations, 1866, 77
divided on secession, 24
Downing Party, 174, 176-77, 200
effect of war on education, 43
extends legal aid to Old Settlers, 166
formed by union of eastern and
  western branches, 7
General Amnesty of 1846, 9
Illinois Camp Ground convention
  1839, 7
inclusion of Delawares, 160-61
inclusion of Shawnees, 161
Intertribal Treaty 1835, see under
  Treaties
Kansas holdings ceded to U.S., 80
language problem in schools, 183
licensing of traders, 168
National Party, 174, 177-78, 200
Old Settlers, 7, 8, 189-90, 201
Old Settlers' claims granted by U.S.,
  165-67
other tribes permitted to reside in,
  80
payments restricted to those of
  Cherokee blood, 182
political dissensions in, 172-78, 187,
  200
printing press established, 18
problems in determining citizenship, 178-79
public schools established, 21-22
repudiate Confederate alliance, 27
returning Creeks in, 35
school system reestablished, 182-85
slave population, 1839, 22
Southern delegates recognized in
  Washington, 173
summary of Reconstruction Period,
  200-01
Treaty Council at Tahlonteskee,
  1839, 7
Treaty of 1828, see under Treaties
Treaty Party, 174
Treaty with U.S., 1866, see under
  Treaties
two factions of, 78
whiskey trade in, 170-71
Cherokee Orphan Asylum, 184
Cherokee Outlet, 7, 8, 194
Cherokees
  attitudes toward freedmen, 48

complaints against U.S. deputy marshals, 176-77
Confederate sympathizers, 42-43
difficulties of loyal refugees, 35-36
eastern, see North Carolina Cherokees
in Confederate Army, 26
losses sustained by Confederate sympathizers, 37-38
losses sustained by loyal faction, 43
loyal faction reimbursed for war losses, 168
loyal soldiers mustered out, 43
spoliation claims, 8
western, see Arkansas Cherokees
Cherokee Tobacco Case, 168-69
effect on interpretation of treaties, 169
Chesterton, Polly, 177
Chickasaw Academy, see also Chickasaw Manual Labor Academy
Chickasaw Academy, 19
Chickasaw Manual Labor Academy, name changed to Harley Institute, 149
Chickasaw Nation, see also Choctaw-Chickasaw Nations
Constitution of 1838, 11
Constitution of 1856, 13
education, 18-19
reaction to secession, 24
separation from Choctaws, 1855, 11
Treaty with U.S., 1852, see under Treaties
Chickasaw Orphans' Home, 149
Chickasaws
attitude toward freedmen, 48-49
loyal refugees, 37
use of Choctaw schools, 18
Choctaw and Chickasaw Central Railroad Company, 137
Choctaw and Chickasaw Thirty-fifth Parallel Railway, 137
Choctaw-Chickasaw Nations, see also Leased District, Negroes, and Okmulgee General Council
Choctaw-Chickasaw Nations, 11, 37
agreement to pay damages to loyal Indians, 130-31
agricultural recovery of, 126-27
cattle-thieving in, 44
claims against U.S., 155
Constitution of 1838, 11
controversy over lands held in common, 127-28
dispute over timber and coal royal-

ties, 127
education, 199-200
exempted from adopting freedmen as tribal members, 72
freedmen, status of, 131-32
land allotment controversy, 128
Net Proceeds claim, 133-36
occupied by Confederates, 44
reciprocal citizenship, problems of, 153
scandal over misuse of tribal money, 130
slaves in, 44
status of mixed bloods in, 11-12
summary of Reconstruction Period, 198-200
Treaty with U.S., 1866, see under Treaties
vigilance committees, 46-47
whites in, 45
Choctaw City, see Armstrong Academy
Choctaw General Council, educational appropriations, 17
Choctaw language
publications in, 17-18
use of, in Choctaw legislature, 141
Choctaw Nation
admission of whites to citizenship, 141-42
anti-abolitionist law, 23
anti-Christian Party, 18
Choctaw or Chickasaw descent required for Chiefs and legislators, 140
Constitution of 1834, 11
Constitution of 1838, 11
Constitution of 1857 (rejected), 11
Constitution of 1860 (compromise), 11, 139
divisions of, 10
education, 15-19
Intertribal Treaty, 1835, see under Treaties
language problems in schools, 144-45
law enforcement problems with U.S. citizens, 142-43
marriage law of 1875, 142
Mississippi Agreement, 10
Net Proceeds claim, 134-37
reaction to secession, 24
slave population, 1839, 22
suits against Missouri, Kansas and Texas Railroad, 138
Choctaws
attitude toward freedmen, 48
loyal refugees, 37

religious denominations among, 18
temperance societies among, 18
Chocte-harjo, 70
Christie, Smith, 77
Chuahla Female Seminary, 147
Chupco, John, Chief of Seminoles, 24, 70, 84, 88, 94, 196
Chustenahlah, loyal Creeks defeated at, 33
Claims, Cherokee spoliation, 8
Clark, Major S.N., 152
Clarkson, Colonel J.J., 26
Clear Creek, 16
Cleata Yamaha, 56
Clements, Courtland C., 165-66
Coachman, Ward, Chief of Creeks, 118, 197
Cochrane, John D., 130
Cochrane, John T., 134-35
Cochrane, Mrs. John T., 134
Coffin, William, 33, 35, 38
Colbert, 137
Colbert, Dougherty Winchester, Governor of Chickasaw Nation, 49, 57, 75
Colbert, Frank, 137
Colbert, Holmes, 71, 75
Colbert Institute, 19
Colbert, James, 137
Colbert, Pitman, 12, 22
Cole, Coleman, Chief of Choctaws, 127, 135, 139, 146
Coleman, Major ————, 49
Colman, Isaac, 37, 45, 59
Comanches sign Intertribal Treaty, 1835, 10
Confederate Alliance, repudiated by Union Cherokees, 27
Confederate Indian regiments, 26
Confederate War Department, 26
Confederates, depredations by, in Indian Territory, 43
   occupation of Choctaw-Chickasaw Nations, 44
Coody's Bluff, 175
Cook, George L., 58
Cooley, Colonel Dennis N., Commissioner of Indian Affairs, 40-41, 52, 58, 60-65, 68-70, 194
   intercedes on behalf of Confederate Cherokees, 42-43
Cooper, Brigadier General Douglas H., 27-28, 33, 56, 130
Cotochochee, Principal Chief of Creeks, 77, 113-14, 118
   death of, 115

Council of the Five Civilized Nations (or Tribes), see under Okmulgee General Council
Court of Claims, 164-65
Coweta, 20
Coweta Micco, 77, 109
Cowskin River engagement, 27
Cow Tom, 104
Cox, J.D., Secretary of the Interior, 91
Cox, John T., 162
Craig, John W., 171
Creek General Council, 14
Creek language
   written form developed, 19
   problem in education, 21
   publications in, 19-20
Creek Nation
   agriculture, 13, 99-101
   anti-government party (Sands faction), 109, 113-14, 117-18
   attempt to seize Creek government, 115-16
   attempts at unification, 108-18
   boundary disputes with Seminoles, 85-86, 101-102
   calls Council of all Indian Territory, 55
   commerce routes, 14
   Constitution of 1860, 112
   Constitution of 1867, 109-12
   development of written constitution, 14
   difficulties resulting from railroad development, 105-107
   divided on secession, 24
   education, 19-21
   factional contentions, 112-18
   Government Party (Checote's party), see also Creeks, Lower, 109, 113, 116-18
   Intertribal Treaty, 1835, see under Treaties
   law enforcement problems of, 107-108
   light-horsemen police force, 110-11, 114-17
   liquor prohibited, 14
   missionary expulsion and recall, 20
   printing press installed at Union Mission, 20
   public school system, 120-22
   secret movements outlawed, 116
   Seminoles in, 14
   slave population, 1839, 22
   stock raising, 99-100

summary of Reconstruction Period, 196-98
treaty with Seminoles, 1845, *see under* Treaties
treaty with U.S., 1856, *see under* Treaties
treaty with U.S., 1866, *see under* Treaties
·Upper and Lower, become Muskogee Nation, 109
Creeks
anti-Christian sentiment among, 20
attitude toward free Negroes, 23, 48
Confederate sympathizers, 35, 37
difficulties in exile, 33-34
educational advantages of mixed bloods, 21
in Confederate Army, 26
in Opothleyahola's band, 33
in Union Army, 26
kinship to Seminoles, 41-42
Lower (North of Arkansas River), 13, 109, 112, 196
attitude toward Upper Creeks, 14
loyal faction, remuneration for war losses, 103-104
McIntosh faction, 13
orphan fund controversy with U.S., 102-103
return to Indian Territory, 34-35
Upper (South of Arkansas River), 13, 109, 112, 196
attitude toward Lower Creeks, 14
Crosby, Colonel J. Schuyler, 46
Curtis Act (of 1898), 4, 172
Curtis, Charles, Representative from Kansas, 4
Curtis, Major General Samuel R., 38
Cushing, Caleb, Attorney General, 153
Cutler, George, 33

Davis, Jefferson, President of the Confederacy, 28
Davis, Rev. John, 19, 20
Davis, John Porum, 173
Dawes Commission, 198
proposes extinction of tribal land titles, 128-29
Debo, Angie, 109
Delano, Columbus, Secretary of the Interior, 128, 168
Delawares
in Cherokee Nation, question of per capita payments to, 182
inclusion in the Cherokee Nation, 160-61

Dell, V., Arkansas legislator, 151
Denison, 137
Dixon, Dr. J.B.G., 114, 116
Doaksville, 10, 139, 152
site of Watie's surrender, 28
Dole, William P., Commissioner of Indian Affairs, 38
plan for concentrating Indians, 61
Downing, Colonel ————, 48
Downing, Rev. Lewis, Acting Chief of Cherokees, 57, 59, 77, 107, 161, 170, 172, 174-75, 180, 200
Downing Party, *see under* Cherokee Nation
Dunn, J.W., 44, 59, 108, 112-13
Dwight Mission, 21

Eagletown, 10
Eblin, Mrs. Ellen E., 183
Edmunds, James M., Commissioner of General Land Offices, 58
Education, *see* Missions and various Nations
Edwards, Rev. Jonathan, 17
Elliot Mission, 16
Emahaka, Seminole girls' academy, 96
Emancipation Proclamation, 200
Eufala, 107

Fairfield Mission, 21
Farwell, John V., 90
"Father of the Choctaw Mission," 16
Field, F.A., 100, 114
Fields, Richard, 173-74
First Indian expedition, 26
Fleming, John, 19
Five Civilized Nations (or Tribes), General Council of, *see* Okmulgee General Council
Five Civilized Nations
as sovereign republics, 3
effect of Curtis Act on, 172
Intertribal Law of 1859, 10-11
land title extinction under Dawes Commission, 128-29
slavery among, 22-23
southern faction, relations with other tribes, 55
treaty delegations to Washington, 68
Folsom, David, 22
Folsom, Israel, 134
Folsom, Peter, 134
Foreman, Ellis, 177
Foreman, Major John, 36
Foreman, Rev. Stephen, 21
Fort Coffee, 17, 152

Fort Coffee Academy, 146
Fort Davis, 27
Fort Gibson, 8, 26, 28, 35-37, 43, 117,
   170, 176, 185
   return of refugees to, 36-39
   site of Creek-Cherokee land com-
      promise of 1833, 13
   site of negotiations for tribal har-
      mony, 57
Fort McCulloch, 26
Fort Roe, 34
Fort Scott, 27
Fort Smith, 142, 150, 176-77
   fall of, 28
Fort Smith Conference (or Council),
   38, 58-65, 123, 193-94, 196
   Cherokees reject loss of treaty rights,
      62
   consolidation of Indians, proposed
      by U.S., 61
   government position stated, 59-60
   Indian objections to treaty, 61-62
   Indians charged with forfeiture of
      treaty rights, 59
   loyal Indians assured of special
      treatment, 61
   removal of Kansas Indians proposed
      by U.S., 61
   treaty demanded by U.S., 60, 61
   treaty limitations, 62
   treaty signed, 62-64
   whites to be excluded from Indian
      Nations, 61
Fort Washita, 12
Fos-harjo, 70
Freedmen, see also Sanborn's Annual
      Report of 1866
Freedmen
   adoption by Choctaws, 152, 154
   agricultural   advantage   among
      Creeks, 99-100
   allowed to locate in part of Chero-
      kee Nation, 79
   attitudes toward, in Five Nations,
      48-49
   Cherokee refusal to accept non-citi-
      zens who marry into tribe, 180
   Choctaw refusal to accept non-citi-
      zens who marry into tribe, 152,
      153
   Choctaw attitude regarding adop-
      tion of, 144
   classified as intruders in Cherokee
      Nation, 180-82
   Congress   appropriates   Choctaw-
      Chickasaw money for schools of,

152
   declared Cherokee citizens, 173
   demands for full citizenship in Choc-
      taw Nation, 151
   desire for education in Creek Na-
      tion, 119
   difficulties due to scattered condi-
      tion of, 180
   employment regulations in Choc-
      taw-Chickasaw Nations, 150
   full civil rights granted by Chero-
      kees, 79
   full equality granted in Creek-U.S.
      treaty of 1866, 75-76
   given equal status in Seminole-U.S.
      treaty of 1866, 69
   high schools for, in Cherokee Na-
      tion, 185
   immigration into Indian Territory,
      45, 47
   Indian attitude toward removal of,
      to separate tracts, 51
   institute claims as Cherokee citi-
      zens, 182
   late returnees, attempts to grant
      Cherokee citizenship to, 180-81
   legal status in Cherokee Nation un-
      der 1866 treaty, 179
   never adopted by Chickasaws, 154
   own assessment of position in vari-
      ous tribes, 50
   petition for removal from Choctaw
      Nation, 151
   postwar difficulties in Indian Ter-
      ritory, 46-52
   proposal to locate separately in In-
      dian Territory, 47, 49-51
   receive share of U.S. payments to
      Creeks, 104
   relations with former masters, 46-52
   removal of, requested by Choctaws
      and Chickasaws, 131
   schools for, in Cherokee Nation, 183,
      185
   schools for, in Choctaw Nation, 147,
      152
   treatment stipulated in 1866 treaty
      with Choctaw-Chickasaw Nations,
      72, 73
   undefined status in Choctaw-Chicka-
      saw Nations, 132
   unpopularity of citizenship for,
      among Cherokees, 182
Freedmen's Bureau, 46-47, 147, 149,
   152
"Frisco," the, see Atlantic & Pacific R.R.

Garfield, James A., President of U.S., 164
Garland, Samuel, 134
Garrett, Colonel John A., 57
Garrett, John B., 58
Going Snake Court House, riot at, 177
Good Spring, see Tishomingo City
Goode, Rev. William H., 19
Goodland Academy, 147
Goodwater, 16-17
Gookins, Milo, 40
Graham, William, 116
Grand Council, of all tribes in Indian Territory, 55-56
Grant, Ulysses S., President of U.S., 91, 138, 163, 195
Greenfield, 16
Grierson, Colonel B.H., 117
Griffith, T.D., 135
Gritts, Budd, 172

Harlan Bill, for postwar organization of Indian Territory, 58, 61, 68
Harlan, James, Secretary of the Interior and Senator from Iowa, 39, 51, 67-68, 91, 162, 197
Harlan, Justin, 35, 41, 59
  petitions on behalf of loyal Cherokees, 43
Harley Institute, see Chickasaw Manual Labor Academy
Harley, Joshua, 149
Harney, Brigadier General W.S., 58, 63
Harris, Cyrus, first Governor of Chickasaw Nation, 13
Harrison, Benjamin, President of U.S., 133
Hawkins, Pink, Second Chief of Creeks, 112
Hayt, E.A., Commissioner of Indian Affairs, 132
Heald, Joseph G., 131
Herron, Major General Francis J., 57, 58
Hoag, Enoch, 89, 101, 116-17
Hoag-Williams Commission, 117
Hodge, David M., 108, 109
Honey Springs, battle of, 28
Hotchkin, Rev. Ebenezer, 16
Hunter, Major General David, 34

Indian affairs, administration of, 3-4, 66

Indian Home Guards, 26
Indian Intercourse Act of 1834, 14, 168, 170
Indian Journal, The, Creek newspaper, 197
Indian lands, suggestions for sale of, 41-42
Indian removal
  bills introduced in Congress, 1862, 67
  effect of gold rush on, 66
  President Jackson on, 5-6
  President Jefferson on, 5
  proposals to move Kansas Indians, 67-68
  to West, as a government solution, 66
Indian Removal Bill of 1830, 6
Indian self-government, President Jackson on, 6
Indian Territory, 194
  as source of food for Union and Confederacy, 28-29
  Cherokees arrive in, 7
  Chickasaws arrive in, 11
  Choctaws arrive in, 10
  Creeks arrive in, 13
  effect of 1866 treaties on, 81, 194
  end of Confederate resistance, 28
  inclusion of Cherokee lands in, 7
  organized as a Confederate military department, 26
Indian tribes, consolidation of, proposed, 68
Interior, Department of, 3-4, 66
Intertribal Peace Treaty of 1835, see under Treaties
Irwin, W.R., 58
Island, Harry, 104

Jackson, Andrew, President of the U.S., 5-6
James, G.D., 147
Jefferson, Thomas, President of the U.S., 5
Jessup, General Thomas, and Florida Negro problem, 15
Johnson, Andrew, President of the U.S., 58, 68
Johnson, Lewis, Chief of loyal Chickasaws, 49
Johnson, Colonel Richard Mentor, 16
Johnson, Robert W., Senator from Arkansas, 9
Jones, Rev. Evan, 24, 80, 174, 185, 200
Jones, Rev. John B., 24, 77, 169, 174,

177, 185, 200
  on Cherokee election day disturb-
    ances, 175-76
Jones, Robert M., 10, 22, 63, 71, 130
Journeycake, Jordan, 176
Joy, James F., 162
Jumper, John, Chief of Seminole
  Southern faction, 24-25, 93-94, 196

Kansas, legislature of, resolution on
  Indian removal, 67
"Katy," the, see Missouri, Kansas and
  Texas Railroad
Keetoowah Society, see also Abolition-
  ist activity
Keetoowah Society, 24
Ketzschmar, S.R., 168
Keys, Riley, 172, 173
Kingsbury, Rev. Cyrus, "Father of the
  Choctaw Mission," 16
Knights of the Golden Circle, secret
  pro-slavery society, 24
Koonsha Female Seminary, 146-47

Land, Joseph, 121
Lane, James, Senator from Kansas, 67
  introduces refugee removal bill, 38
Lang, John D., 90, 163
Lanniwa, Territory of, proposed, 67
Latrobe, H.B., 130
Leased District, 12, 71-72, 151
  negotiations concerning, between
    Chocktaw-Chickasaw Nations and
    U.S., 131-33
Lebanon Institute, 149
Lee, General Robert E., 28
LeFlore, Campbell, 75, 90, 153
LeFlore, Forbis, 144
Lehman and Company, 135
LeRoy, Kansas, 33
Lewis, Dixon W., 134
Lincoln, Abraham, President of the
  U.S., 32
Lincoln's Amnesty Proclamation, 28
Lilley, Mary M., 94
Lilly, Rev. John, 21
Locher Harjo, 116-18
Logan, James, 20
Logan, John A., 166
Loughridge, Rev. Robert, 20
Louisiana, divided into two territories,
  5
Love, Robert, 22, 75
Luce, John, 136
Lukfata, 16
Lyanubbee Female Seminary, 147

Lyon, F.S., 107, 114-17

McAlester, 139
McAlester, J.J., 138-39
McHenry, James, 109
McIntosh, Daniel N., 23-24, 77, 109
McKee, Henry, 134, 136
McKendree Manual Labor School, see
  Chickasaw Academy
Marriage Law, see Choctaw Nation
Marshall, Benjamin, 13
Marston, S.W., 138, 181
Matthews, Lieutenant Colonel Asa C.,
  57
Mekasukey, Seminole boys academy,
  96
Methodist Episcopal Church, division
  over slavery issue, 23-24
Methodist Episcopal Church South,
  Mission Board of, 19
Methodist Indian Mission Conference,
  19
Micco (Mikko) Hutke, 112, 115
  petitions for help against secession-
    ists, 33
Missionaries, concessions to and limi-
  tations on in Choctaw-Chickasaw
  treaty, 74
Missions
  Baptist, in Cherokee Nation, 185
  Baptist, in Chickasaw Nation, 149
  Baptist, among Choctaws, 16, 146-
    147
  Baptist, among Creeks, 19-20, 122
  Baptist, among Seminoles, 93, 95
  Methodist, in Cherokee Nation, 185
  Methodist, among Chickasaws, 19
  Methodist, among Choctaws, 146
  Methodist, among Creeks, 20, 119,
    121
  Methodist, among Seminoles, 95
  Moravian, in Cherokee Nation, 21,
    186
  Northern Baptist, among Cherokees,
    24
  Presbyterian, among Cherokees, 44
  Presbyterian, among Choctaws, 16,
    146
  Presbyterian, among Creeks, 19-20,
    119
  Presbyterian, among Seminoles, 93-
    95
  Southern Baptist, among Cherokees,
    24
  to Five Civilized Nations before Re-
    construction, 15-20

Missouri, Kansas, and Texas Railroad (the "Katy"), 105, 137-39, 169-70
Mitchell, E.S., 75
Mix, Charles E., 58, 59
Morris, D.M., 163
Morton, Ohland, 109
Moshulatubbee, 10, 18
Mountain Fork, 16
Murrow, Rev. Joseph S., 93, 146
Murrow Orphan Home, 146
Muskogee, 4, 107, 129, 137
Muskogee Female Institute, 122
Muskogee language, 95, 111
Muskogee Nation, see also Creeks, Upper and Lower, drafting of constitution for, 109-111

National Female Seminary, 22
National Male Seminary, 22
National Party, see under Cherokee Nation
Negroes
  academy established for, in Choctaw Nation, 147
  adoption problems among Choctaws and Chickasaws, 198-199
  among Seminoles, 14-15, 23
  as Indian interpreters, 69
  as lawless element in Choctaw-Chickasaw Nations, 45-46
  ban on fraternization among Choctaws and Chickasaws, 153
  bands from Texas in Choctaw-Chickasaw Nations, 150
  education in Chickasaw Nation, 149
  education in Choctaw-Chickasaw Nations, 149, 155, 199
  education in Creek Nation, 122
  education in Seminole Nation, 95
  educational privileges denied in Choctaw Nation, 147
  in Opothleyahola's band, 33
  incorporation into Cherokee Nation objected to, 63
  involvement in Creek politics, 114, 116
  limitations on citizenship in Choctaw Nation, 152-53
  on Seminole National Council, 88
  restrictions on, in Choctaw-Chickasaw Nations, 201
  treatment by Choctaw-Chickasaw vigilance committees, 46
  with Seminole refugees, 37
Neosho, 9, 35
Neutral Lands, 9, 165

disposal of by Cherokee-U.S. treaty, 162
New Echota, Treaty of, see under Treaties
New Hope, 17
New Hope Seminary, 145
Nocus Yahola, Judge, 117
North Carolina Cherokees, 162-66, 178, 201
  actions on claims, 164-65
  citizenship in Cherokee Nation recognized, 165
North Fork Town, 28
  site of Council of Five Civilized Nations, 1859, 10
Nuyaka, 116

Oak Ridge, 21
Okla Falaya (or Ápukshunnubbee), 10
Oklahoma, 6
Oklahoma Territory, 194
Okmulgee, 115, 117, 197
Okmulgee Constitution, 91-92, 197
Okmulgee General Council, 89-93, 123, 172, 197
  reasons for Choctaw and Chickasaw non-participation, 144
  resolution against railroad land policies, 92
  significance in history of Indian Territory, 92
Oktaha, 107
Oktarharsars Harjo, Chief of Creeks, opposition faction, see also Sands
Oktarharsars Harjo, 77, 104, 197
  death of, 116
  petitions for help against secessionists, 33
Old Settlers, see under Cherokee Nation
Opothleyahola, Chief of Creeks, 23-26, 76
  death of, 34
  leads loyal band to Kansas, 33
  letter to President Lincoln, 32
Osages
  Intertribal Treaty, 1835, see under Treaties
  treaty with Cherokees, 1865, see under Treaties
Our Monthly, Creek bilingual newspaper, 121
Owen, Robert L., 171

Page, John, 71, 75

Parker, Colonel Ely S., 58, 63-65, 68, 70, 194
Parker, Judge Isaac C., 142-43
Park Hill, Chief Ross arrested at, 26
Patton, Robert B., 60
Pea Ridge, battle of, 26
Peace conference, at Fort Smith, 1865, 38
Pegg, Thomas, 77
Perryman, Benjamin, 108
Perryman, James H., 19, 120-21
Perryman, S.M., 113
Perryman, Sanford W., 109
Perryville, 10, 28
Phillips, Colonel William A., 27-28, 36, 41, 162
Pickens, Edmund, Chief of Chickasaws, 12, 71, 75
Pike, Brigadier General Albert, 25-26, 27
Pine Ridge, 16-17
Pins, the, Creek secret society, 118
Pitchlynn, Peter P., Chief of Choctaws, 22, 71, 128, 133-36
Pleasant Grove, 18
Pomeroy, Samuel C., Senator from Kansas, 67
Prairie Grove, battle of, 27
Presbyterian Board of Foreign Missions, 21
Presbyterian Board of Home Missions, 93
Presbyterians, split on slavery issue, 23
Proctor, A.G., 35
Proctor, Ezekial, see also Going Snake Court House
Proctor, Ezekial, 177
Pushmataha, 10

"Radical Republicans," 47
Railroads
    and depletion of timber in Cherokee Nation, 170
    development in Creek Nation, 105-107
    involvement in Creek factional disorders, 114
    lobby for land grants in Indian Territory, 89
    rights of way, 136, 137
    rights of way in Cherokee treaty with U.S., 1866, 79
    rights of way in Choctaw-Chickasaw treaty with U.S., 73
    rights of way in Creek treaty with

U.S., 76
    rights of way controversy with Choctaws, 138
    rights of way, importance of in peace treaties, 69
    role in development of coal fields, 138
Ramsey, Rev. John Ross, 21, 93, 94
Reese, Colonel H. D., 62
Refugee removal bill
    introduced by Senator James Lane, 38
Refugees
    discords raised by return to Fort Gibson, 37
    in Kansas, 38
    return to Indian Territory, 38
Reverend Libeler, A., 130
Reynolds, George A., 40, 41, 84-85, 87, 95, 114
Reynolds, General J.J., 57
Ridge, John, assassination of, 7, 8n
Ridge, John Rollins, 78
Ridge, Major ————, assassination of, 7, 8n
Ridge-Boudinot murders, 1839, 7-9
Ridge party, Cherokee faction, see also Treaty Party
Ridge party, 78, 79, 200
Riley, James, 71, 75
Roberts, E.R., 117, 121
Robertson, Alice M., 118-19
Robertson, Ann Eliza Worcester (Mrs. William S.), 121
Robertson, William Schenck, 119-21
Robertson, Samuel, publisher of Our Monthly, 121
Robinson, Rev. John, 19
Robinson, L.A., 95n
Robinson, L.N., Commissioner of Indian Affairs, 86, 112
Ross, Daniel, 77
Ross, John, Chief of Cherokees, 7, 9, 22-26, 28, 57, 61-64, 172, 193, 200
Ross, John, Chief of North Carolina Cherokees, 164
Ross, Lewis, 23
Ross party, Cherokee faction, 78, 79
Ross, William Potter, Chief of Cherokees, 64, 172, 174-75, 178, 200
Rowe, David, Assistant Principal Chief of Cherokees, 178

Sac and Fox tribes, use of reservation by Creek exiles, 34
St. Louis and San Francisco Railroad

(the "Frisco"), *see* Atlantic and Pacific Railroad
Sallisaw, 185
Salomon, Col. Frederick, 26, 27
Sanborn, General John B., 47, 150-51, 197
Sanborn's *Annual Report* of 1866, 47-52
Sands, ————, 107, 108, 112-14, 118, *see also* Oktarharsars Harjo, Oktarsars-Harjo, Ok-ta-has Harjo
Sands faction, *see* Creeks: anti-government party
Sarcoxie, John, Delaware headman, 161
Scales, J.A., 173-75
Scraper, Arch, 177
Sells, Elijah, 40, 58, 64, 68, 70, 194
on sale of Indian lands, 41-42
Seminole Nation
annuity payment difficulties, 86, 87
arable land on new territory, 85
boundary dispute with Creeks, 85-86
disparities in land transfers with U.S., 70
division over secession, 24-25
education, 21, 93-96
final acreage of new territory, 86
financial grievances with U.S., 86-87
free Negroes in, 14-15, 23
inducements offered for secession, 25
Negro population, 1839, 22
Negroes on National Council of, 88
slaves in, 14-15, 23
strict law enforcement by, 88-89
summary of Reconstruction Period, 195-96
treaty with Creek Nation, 1845, *see under* Treaties
treaty with U.S., 1866, *see under* Treaties
tribal organization of, 88
Seminoles
attitude toward freedmen, 48
become self-supporting, 85
Confederate sympathizers, 24, 38
Federal payments for Civil War losses, 86
in Creek Nation, 14, 15
in Union Army, 26
in Opothleyahola's band, 33
kinship to Creeks, 41-42
poor farm management overcome, 83-85

refugees in Kansas, 36-37
return to Indian Territory, 37
Union sympathizers, 24
Shawnees, in Cherokee Nation, 161, 182
Shook, Mrs. H. C., 94
Skullyville, 10-11, 152
Slavery
abolished by Seminole-U.S. treaty, 1866, 69
abolished in Choctaw-Chickasaw Nations, 150
abolition among Indian tribes proposed, 60-61
among Five Civilized Nations, 22-23
economic factors, 22-23
Keetoowah Society, 24
Knights of the Golden Circle, 24
Methodist Episcopal Church split on, 23
Presbyterians split on, 23
Slaves, 10
among Seminoles, 14-15
and Creek veterans of the Florida war, 15
Cherokee slaves freed, 27
Choctaw-Chickasaw demand compensation for emancipation, 71
emancipated by Ross party of Cherokees, 78, *see also* Ross party
in Choctaw-Chickasaw Nations, 44
incorporation into tribes proposed by U.S., 60
owned by mixed-blood Chickasaws, 12
renumeration claimed by Choctaws, 135
runaway, intertribal law on, 10-11
treatment of in Indian Territory, 23
Smith, Caleb B., Secretary of the Interior, 68
Smith, Edward P., Commissioner of Indian Affairs, 128, 176
Smith, J.A., 137
Smith, James, 77
Smoot, Samuel, 131
Snow, Major George C., 37, 40, 59
Spencer Academy, 17, 145-46
Spokokogeeyahola, leader of disaffected loyal Creeks, 35
Spring Creek engagement, 27
Springplace, 21
Standley, J.S., 153
Stanton, Edwin M., Secretary of War, 38
Starr Boys, 8

Starr, James, 8n
Starr, Tom, 8n
Steel, Brigadier General William, 38
Stephens, Spencer S., 168, 183
Stidham, George, 113
Stockbridge, 17
Stonewall, 149
Supreme Court, U.S., 164

Tahlequah, 25, 28, 36, 57, 166, 171-72,
  178, 185
  Cherokee convention, 1839, 7
  designated Cherokee capital, 8
Talihina, 147
Tahlonteskee, 7
Taylor, Nathaniel G., Commissioner
  of Indian Affairs, 113, 175
Teller, Henry M., Secretary of the In-
  terior, 153
Temperance societies among Choc-
  staws, 18
Thlothlo Yahola, 113
Thomas, William T., 163
Thompson, Charles, Principal Chief
  of Cherokees, 163, 178, 181
Thompson, Nancy, 120
Tishomingo (City), capital of Chicka-
  saw Nation, 13, 143
Treaties, see also Fort Smith Confer-
  ence
  Cherokees with Confederacy, 1861,
    25, 62
  Cherokees with Osages, 1865, 161
  Cherokees with U.S., 1828, 7
  Cherokees with U.S., 1835, 189-90,
    201
  Cherokees with U.S., 1846, 9, 189-
    90, 201
  Cherokees with U.S., 1866, 77-80,
    160-63, 165, 167, 168, 169, 170,
    177-79, 187-89
  Cherokees with U.S., on Neutral
    Lands, 1868, 162
  Cherokees, Western, with U.S., 1828,
    7
  Chickasaws with U.S., 1852, 12, see
    also Treaties: Choctaw-Chicka-
    saw Nations
  Choctaw-Chickasaw Nations and
    McIntosh Creeks with Confed-
    eracy, 1861, 25
  Choctaw-Chickasaw Nations with
    U.S., 1866, 71-75, 126-27, 130-31,
    132, 138, 141-42, 149, 151-52, 154,
    198-99
  Choctaw-Chickasaw Nations with

  U.S., 1885, 133n
  Chocktaws with Chickasaws, 1855,
    12, 60, 136n, 141-42, 153
  Creeks with U.S., 1832, 102-103
  Creeks with U.S., 1855, 132
  Creeks with U.S., 1856, 15
  Creeks with U.S., 1866, 75-77, 99,
    108-109, 122-23, 127, 130-32
  Creeks with U.S., 1868, (proposed),
    113
  Creeks with Seminoles, 1845, 15
  Five Civilized Nations with U.S.,
    1866, 89, 144, 193-94, 203
    principal negotiating points, 68-
      69
  Intertribal Treaty, 1835, 10
  loyal Indians reassured on, 33
  Osages with Cherokees, 1865, 161
  Seminoles with Creeks, 1845, 15
  Seminoles with U.S., 1856, 69
  Seminoles with U.S., 1866, 69-71, 83,
    86
Treaty of Dancing Rabbit Creek, 133n
Treaty of New Echota, 1835, 6-8, 10,
  165, 167
Treaty party, see under Cherokee Na-
  tion
Treaty Party Council, 7
Tribal harmony, attempts at reestab-
  lishing, 57
Tufts, John Q., 181
Tullahassee, 121
Tullahassee Manual Labor School, 120
Tullahassee Mission, 119
Turner, J. Milton, 182
Tuskahoma, seat of Choctaw govern-
  ment, 141
Tuskalusa Colored Academy, 147

Union Agency, 4, 181
Union Indian regiments, 26
Union Pacific Railroad, 105, 137
U.S. Intercourse Act of 1834, 14
Usher, J. P., Secretary of the Interior,
  38

Van Dorn, General Earl, 26
Van Horn, R.T., Representative from
  Missouri, 89
Vann, David, Chief of Cherokees, 7
Vann, James, 174, 178
Vann, Joseph, 22
Veatch, Brigadier General James C.,
  46
Vinita, 170
Voorhees, Daniel W., Senator from In-

diana, 169

Wade, Alfred, 71, 75
Walker, F.A., Commissioner of Indian
    Affairs, 107, 116
Wapanucka Female Institute, 19
Wapanucka Male Academy, 149
War ,Department, 3, 66
Watie, Saladin, 78
Watie, Colonel Stand (later Brigadier
    General), 24, 27-28, 36, 56-57, 64,
    78, 168-69, 173
Weer, Colonel William, 26
Westville, 21
Wewoka, 116
Wheaton, Charles, 116
Wheelock, 16, 17
Wheelock Seminary, 146
Whiskey trade, in Cherokee Nation,
    170-71

White Catcher, 77
Whites
    admission to Choctaw citizenship,
        141-42
    in Choctaw-Chickasaw Nations, 45
    settlement in Leased District, 132-33
Wichitas, Intertribal Treaty, 1835, see
    under Treaties
Wilcox, Captain G., 57
Williams, Andrew, 117
Wilshire, W.W., 166
Wistar, Thomas, 58, 63-64
Worcester, Ann Eliza, 119, see also
    Robertson, Ann Eliza Worcester
Worcester, Leonard, 120
Wright, Rev. Alfred, 16, 18
Wright, Allen, Chief of Choctaws, 71,
    75, 130, 132, 139
Wright, John W., 86-87
Wright, Reuben, 131